DATE DUE

DEMCO 38-296

'TAMBO
LIFE IN AN ANDEAN VILLAGE

'Tambo

Life in an Andean Village

by
Julia Meyerson

University of Texas Press, Austin

First Edition, 1990

Requests for permission to reproduce material from this work
should be sent to Permissions, University of Texas Press, Box
7819, Austin, Texas 78713-7819.

♾ The paper used in this publication meets the minimum re-
quirements of American National Standard for Information
Sciences—Permanence of Paper for Printed Library Materials,
ANSI Z39.48-1984.

Library of Congress Cataloging-in-Publication Data

Meyerson, Julia, 1953–
  'Tambo : life in an Andean village / Julia Meyerson. —
1st ed.
    p.   cm.
    ISBN 0-292-78077-X (alk. paper). — ISBN
0-292-78078-8 (pbk. : alk. paper)
    1. Quechua Indians—Social life and customs. 2. Pac-
carictambo (Peru)—Social life and customs. I. Title.
F2230.2.K4M47   1990
985' .37—dc20   89-14812
                                                     CIP

For my parents,
who taught me a great love of travel
and a profound respect for other peoples and cultures;
for my husband, Gary;
and for Jason, our son.

Contents

Acknowledgments

I owe the existence of this book to many people and a couple of institutions. I must first of all thank the people of the village of 'Tambo for allowing my husband, Gary Urton, and me to live there and, among those people, especially Baltazar Quispe and Teresa Sullca, in whose house we lived and who stood by us in the difficult times and have become very dear friends: the story told in this book, itself, will make clear how much we owe them. And I wish to express my appreciation to the National Science Foundation and Colgate University for supporting Gary's research in Peru, which support afforded me, too, the opportunity to live in 'Tambo.

Many people have read the manuscript in its various stages toward becoming a book and offered critical comments, advice, and generous encouragement. Among these I wish to thank especially Gary, who has never failed to be cheerfully willing to read and re-read; Billie Jean Isbell and Tony Aveni, who have offered unceasing support and excellent advice; and also Robert Harberts, Harriet Gordon, Wendy Weeks and Robert Randall, Nancy Tucker, and Ellie Bolland. I want to thank Ellie and her husband, Nigel, too for years of moral support and encouragement as I worked on this book.

A couple of people played major roles at critical points in the production of the manuscript, and in this regard I would like to thank Pat Ryan and Jeannie Kellogg, both of Colgate University, for their invaluable services.

I dedicate a special note of acknowledgment and thanks to Peg Simon, also of Colgate University, for spending an afternoon teaching me how to spin.

I would also like to mention with gratitude two special friends of ours, Richard Bielefeldt and Jean-Jacques Decoster—Richard for many hours of inspired and inspiring conversation in Cusco in 1981 and 1982, Jean-Jacques for his warm and caring companionship and help, both in Cusco and in the field in 1987 and 1988, and for his reading and comments on the manuscript, and both of them for their support of my own endeavors in the field as well as Gary's.

Finally, this book would never have come into existence without the inspiration, gentle advice, and loving support of my friend Elizabeth Tallent, for whom, along with my husband, Gary, I really wrote my journal when we were in Peru. It was she to whom I wished most deeply to communicate the experiences of my life there, with whom I wished to share it in words. My letters to her—the language, the voice, the subjects—flowed into and out of my journal, and I have included a few fragments of those letters in this book. If it hadn't been for the imponderable distances of various sorts between 'Tambo and Eaton, Colorado, and the uncertainties of the international mail, this journal might instead have been one long letter.

Introduction

The photographs were wonderful. In one, an unpaved lane, narrow and steep, descended away from the camera, between adobe buildings roofed with fine, shaggy, gray-brown thatch and corrugated steel and red clay tiles, to end in—nothing, an emptiness bounded far off by mountains, hazy in the unfocused distance. In another, two dancers in long, fringed tunics, their faces and hair completely hidden by knitted masks, circled each other warily, with whips in their hands, in a small yard between adobe houses. In others, children: a couple of kids in a tree, taken close up; a trio of boys of graduated sizes sitting against a white-washed wall—all of whom, judging by impish grins, unabashedly enjoyed the exotic attention of having their pictures taken. These were my first glimpses of 'Tambo. My husband, Gary, an anthropologist, had spent a month in Peru, in this village, gleaning material on which to base a proposal to do fieldwork there. Armed with the notes he had taken in a slender, hardbound fieldbook, he wrote the proposal and submitted it to the National Science Foundation. In April of the next year, 1981, we were notified that the proposal would be funded. In May we left for Peru.

I am an artist, not an anthropologist, though after I had spent a month in Peru with Gary several years earlier while he was doing his doctoral research I was enough fascinated by Peru and by the idea of ethnographic fieldwork that I entered graduate school in anthropology. I abandoned the idea of a doctoral degree when I realized, after one semester of study, that I would have to give up my art for years in order to accomplish that goal. But now, in 1981, I would nevertheless have my chance to do fieldwork: in August, after a couple of months of travel on the coast of Peru, I found myself high in the Andes, in Cusco, preparing to live for a year in a Quechua village and finding it extraordinarily difficult to "prepare" for something of which I could scarcely conceive. (Since then, I have learned that you can seldom really prepare yourself for fieldwork anyway, no matter how intimately you know the place or the people, no matter how many times you have done it before.)

This, then, is the story of that year: our lives, the lives of the family who virtually adopted us, the life of the village. I set out to keep a journal, knowing that I would need some creative substitute for my art: my drawings are small and detailed, though abstract, and require a small amount of very clean space and a good deal of very good light, both of which I knew would be scarce in the village, as indeed they were; I completed only two drawings that year, working during brief intervals we spent in Cusco. The journal that I kept recorded a sort of descriptive narrative which ran almost constantly in my mind, by which I sought to capture the details, as if photographically, of everything I saw and which happened around me. That journal has become this book.

As a journal, written from day to day throughout the year that we lived there, it also reflected the workings of a subtle and gradual transformation which I underwent. When we arrived in 'Tambo, I knew virtually nothing useful to living a Quechua life in a Quechua village. I knew how the Quechua dress, the kind of houses they live in, the kind of food they eat. I knew a few dubious generalities of Quechua character. Of the language, I spoke only a few phrases, common ones necessary to being considered at least marginally polite, which I had learned when I had visited Gary: how to say hello and goodbye, some words of thanks, and the important words *manan intendinichu* ("I don't understand"). As we lived there, I gradually learned how to be a proper Quechua human being—learned the hard way, without benefit of a Quechua childhood. I learned to speak a little Quechua, a difficult language to learn without formal instruction, gauging my progress against that of the youngest grandchild of the family, Orlando, who was two and a half when we arrived in the village: at first, with my dictionary and grammar books, I had a slight and tenuous advantage over him; but by the time we left and he was three and a half, Orlando, with the natural facility and aptitude for language of a child of his age, had learned to talk circles around me and knew it. Nevertheless, I could, by the time we left 'Tambo, at least understand the general outlines and import of a conversation, even if I did not understand every word or speak well enough to participate in it. And I learned how to do the work that a young Quechua woman must do and how to behave correctly. And as I learned and our friendships grew deeper, I was drawn more deeply into the life we were living there and found myself making greater and greater intellectual and emotional investments in it. By the time we left, the perspective of an observer, from which I had begun to write my journal, had become, I felt, all but inaccessible to me.

Gary's chosen method of fieldwork is one normally called "participant observation," which means that we set out to learn Quechua life by living it ourselves alongside the people of the village. Life in a Quechua village is simple and hard, based on subsistence agriculture, so that the activities of every member of each family are determined throughout the year and indeed, for most, throughout their lives by the needs of the crops. We arrived in 'Tambo in August, as the agricultural cycle was just beginning, and found a place to live with a family in which we quickly assumed the roles of a son and daughter: every hand in a household is an invaluable source of labor, and so, because we wanted to work, these roles fell to us easily, naturally.

The agricultural year begins in 'Tambo in August and September, when the dry season—the Andean winter, a succession of warm cloudless days and stunningly clear and frigid nights—begins to draw to a close. The crops are planted in a more or less regular succession—depending on the climatic characteristics of the ecological zone in which they are planted and the length of time each crop requires to mature—during the months of late winter and early spring, in August, September, October, and November. 'Tambo lies in a middle zone of the vertical Andean ecological system and so has its corn fields below it on the mountainsides, legumes and some grains generally level with the village (at 11,500 feet in altitude) and slightly above it, most grains planted in fields above the level of the village, and potatoes in the high *puna* (about 13,500 feet), two or three hours' walk away. The crops are planted generally from low altitude to high altitude, beginning with the planting of corn in August and September and ending with the sowing of potatoes in October and November. The crops mature during the months of the Andean summer and early fall, watched over by tall crosses planted on hilltops to guard them against the hail and frosts of the transitional seasons.

Summer, the growing season, is the rainy season, when clouds hang close about the mountaintops, one seldom sees the sun, and it rains, in a good year, every day. The rough-cobbled streets of the village are slippery and treacherous, and unpaved paths are awash with torrents of rainwater and ankle-deep mud; roads through the countryside become difficult to travel and often impassable, closed by mud- and rockslides or washed away by seasonal rivers and streams. During these months, the fields are hoed and weeded, and the earth of fallowed fields is turned in preparation for the coming year's crops. In May, when the rains have ended, the potatoes are harvested. The grains and beans are cut and allowed to dry for threshing; the corn is harvested in June. After the grains are threshed, the final act of the agricultural cycle, people turn to the dry-season activities of weaving and building and repairing the damage done by the rains and to the wholehearted celebration of the numerous religious festivals that fall during those months.

And so, Gary spent most of his days during that year working with the men of our adoptive family in the fields, plowing or planting or weeding the crops, learning to use the traditional tools, the short, crook-handled hoes and the footplow, and his own back and legs and arms in unfamiliar ways. And he learned all of the other myriad tasks required by that life— cutting or gathering firewood or making adobes and building walls, constructing altars for festival celebrations or participating in those celebrations. I worked with the women of the family, doing women's work, mostly cooking and serving food but also tending the house, children, and animals. Our roles almost never ceased to fit us awkwardly, for although we were adults, the smallest details of the tasks we performed, from the efficient use of a footplow to the way to hold a knife when peeling potatoes, were achieved only with great and unendingly diligent and often erring effort, like that of a child. And yet, only we, in our desire not to embarrass or be embarrassed, seemed to feel that awkwardness, for our need to learn everything from the beginning, our clumsy inexperience, and our innocent not-knowing, which cast us as overgrown children in this world we were living in, afforded us our roles as son and daughter and allowed Baltazar and Teresa, the couple with whose family we lived, to become our "parents" and mentors, a relationship which was comfortable and natural in the context of the village and its traditional life and which proved to be warm and rewarding for all of us.

The family upon whose household we descended that August and with whom we lived for a little more than a year, don Baltazar Quispe Herrera and his wife, Teresa Sullca Llamaqchima, and their children Hugo, Daniel, and Leonarda, are truly remarkable and brave people, who accepted the long-term disruption of their lives which our presence in their home meant and also the challenge, monumental and trying, of teaching us how to be Quechua. Their understanding and their willingness and capacity to adapt were extraordinary, and they were, with few lapses, exceedingly patient and kind. Without their reliable friendship and care, our experience in 'Tambo, both intellectually and emotionally, would have been far less rich. We are deeply grateful to them and hope to repay them, if it is possible, with a generosity as abundant as theirs for sharing their home and their lives with us. We are indebted too to their married daughter Juana and her husband, Ricardo Achawi Palomino; to the community of 'Tambo and its officials—especially the governor of the district, don Carlos Araujo; the district judge, David Araujo; the president of the village, Julio Wallpa; and the mayor, Nicasio Sullca—for the tolerance which became genuine acceptance and which allowed us to live there, and to many other individuals who honored us as guests in their homes and as friends. They will always be remembered.

'TAMBO
LIFE IN AN ANDEAN VILLAGE

1. The beginning

Dear Elizabeth, I am reading Hemingway, *A Moveable Feast*, which is very nice to read here because the Paris that he writes about seems in character very much like Cusco is now, except that Cusco doesn't have the money that Paris had and therefore can't support artists and writers. Instead, there are anthropologists and archaeologists drinking the good coffee in the cafés and having good cheap dinners in little restaurants and peñas and quintas and drinking the wines from Ocucaje and Tacama. Like this: when there is no more sun on the patio, I take my book and walk down Calle Sapphi, where we have rented a room, to the Plaza de Armas, huge Spanish churches on two sides, and sit on a bench in the sun to read; and now I write at a table in an empty café where the music is sometimes classical, sometimes Spanish criolla, and they have an Italian espresso machine and very good coffee and beautiful pastries. It's also nice to read Hemingway after reading someone like García Márquez (much as I love García Márquez—I've just finished *One Hundred Years of Solitude* for the third time) because Hemingway is so spare and straightforward and clean—García Márquez' crazy world is all around me, here, and what I need from a book now is plain North American English. This is one of the books I brought along with me to keep me sane: no matter how much you like a language and enjoy hearing it spoken, after a while you think you'll go crazy if you hear one more person babbling something that isn't simply *comfortable*, isn't English, and then it's good to lose yourself in a good English novel. (This is something Hemingway also writes about: trying to find books to read in Paris.) I know I didn't bring enough books—it's impossible of course—and I don't even know if I brought the right ones. How do you know what you should read for more than a year? You ask if you can send books. Well, I don't know: I would love it if you did, anything you like or think I might like; I'll need them! Maybe you could try it once and we'll see if it works. One thing that you learn quickly here is not so much that nothing works efficiently, as it appears at first, but that everything, everything is arbitrary, and that's all it is, even though things sometimes seem more to be deliberately *con*trary. Your letter reached Cusco in four days, including a Sunday; Gary got one from New York last week in three days. The first ones we got here took about ten days, and mail has been known to take three to six weeks. Sometimes packages get through, sometimes even a thick envelope won't make it. Our luck seems to be pretty good right now (although over the weekend, some group of protestors exploded a bomb in front of the post office, breaking all of the windows, and it's hard to know how this will affect the service . . .). So we might try.

I do feel at home here, somehow, and the things I miss about home are much less habits and things and places than simply people. But Cusco is such a beautiful city—sometimes I look up and am still surprised to see the mountains: snow-capped Ausangate far off beyond the southern end of the valley, the afternoon light changing the shape of the near mountains around the city, in every view of them the bell towers of some church, Belén or the cathedral or San Cristóbal. We have been out into the *campo* (the country) twice now, once to 'Tambo where we will be working, once to Misminay where Gary lived before, and the better I know Cusco and each time we return from the villages where people still live as they always have for hundreds and hundreds of years, in thatched adobe huts and farming precarious fields on the mountainsides with simple wooden plows, the more I understand the grandeur and majesty that must have been Cusco when it was the Inca's city. It is wonderful to turn a corner and find yourself in a narrow street walled with Inca masonry: the stones are odd shapes and cut like pillows so the surface is convex and the joins depressed; there is no mortar, and the stones have hardly shifted in the chaos of earthquakes that have toppled the Spanish churches. And one day I was standing on a corner when a man drove a herd of llamas out of a steep side street into Calle Sapphi and across it; the llamas had burdens tied on their backs and held their heads high, bright pink and red tassels in their ears—instead of branding them, people here pierce the animals' ears and thread yarn tassels through them.

I asked Gary about mailing books, and he said that they seldom
arrive here: they are stolen somewhere along the way in Peru (these
people obviously don't realize the importance of books: if they were
smart, they would simply hold them for ransom). If there is something
I need or want or something you would like to send, T. is coming
to Peru in January, and you can send it to him in Hamilton and he
can bring it. I will send you his address. That certainly complicates
the lovely simplicity of sending a friend a good book, but it might be
safer . . .

Cusco! We arrived, after weeks of travel on the coast—and having
spent most of the night in the Jorge Chávez International Airport
waiting for the early flight—quite exhausted and a little disoriented on a
Sunday morning two weeks ago. The contrast between Lima and Cusco is
stark: Lima big and brisk and cosmopolitan, very sophisticated, and
Cusco ancient, traditional except for its accommodations to the growing
tourist trade, and unhurried. It's something like the difference between
New York City and Boulder, Colorado, or Sante Fe. Señora Reinaga gave
us a small, cold, dark room—the only one available—at the Hostal Familiar, Gary's old place on Calle Sapphi, and we slept for hours. In the
afternoon, we could hear the explosions of fireworks, and when we went
out—to the Café Ayllu for coffee and the pastries for which it is famous
among frequent travelers to Cusco and those who read the best-selling
guide books—we could see the bursts of flame and little clouds of smoke
drifting over the church of San Cristóbal on the hillside below the Inca
ruins of Sacsahuaman and walked up to see what the celebration was. It
proved to be the day of San Cristóbal himself, and in the courtyard of the
church, flanked along the mountainside by an Inca wall with trapezoidal
niches (the place was called Qolkampata in the Incas' time), we found a
crowd of people, few of them *gringos,* standing around the vendors'
stalls, eating criolla food, and drinking beer and *chicha.* We had missed
the formal part of the celebration, the procession of the image of the saint
through the courtyard, but the scaffolds which had supported the fireworks still stood, and a couple of bands were playing, and a few Cusqueños still danced. We bought *chicha.* The music, the taste of the *chicha,*
and the heft of the enormous glass it was served in; the feel of the thin,
crystalline air cooling in the late afternoon of a winter day in the Andes;
the vista of Cusco below us, narrow streets and red-tiled roofs slowly engulfed by the shadows of the mountains, began to establish some bear-
ings for us, striking familiar chords in our memories: Cusco.

We spent a couple of days hunting for a room to keep in Cusco for the
year—the rent is an investment in sanity: a place to keep books and

papers and clean clothes while we're in the field and to come back to without the agonizing search for a hotel room when we're tired, in need of a hot shower, clean clothes, a meal eaten at a table, a real bed. We ended up back at the Hostal Familiar with a room for fifty thousand *soles* a month, a little more than a hundred dollars at the present exchange— a lovely room at the very back against the hillside, reached through a series of courtyards and passages and stairways, with a view of the red-tiled roofs descending to Calle Sapphi and the ruined outer walls of Sacsahuaman on the hilltop across the narrowing valley. One large room with a partitioned bathroom (hot water in the mornings they tell us, and sometimes at night), with walls of rough stone and whitewashed adobe, a wooden floor, a high sloping ceiling of white stucco supported by dark eucalyptus beams with a small skylight between them; outside, there is a low-walled patio lined with potted plants—cacti and succulents and geraniums which grow as big as small trees here. One bed, table, and chair for each of us (Peruvians don't seem to believe in double beds, at least not in the *hostales* we usually end up staying in). We bought a few things to make it a little less an *hostal* room, more our home for a year, if only occasionally: a small table for my things since Gary would have the big table for his books and papers and notebooks, another lamp, a small kerosene stove, and a kettle and cups and saucers and spoons for coffee. And from Alicia's shop on the Plaza Regocijo, a couple of fine Bolivian textiles—a small old Taquile piece, traditional green and red and white, and one from Potolo, a rich black with a thin red and orange border and a double band of fantastic birds woven in deep red down the center. I spent a couple of days in bed with a stubborn case of *gripe* (the Peruvian-Spanish generic term which encompasses, at least in its folk definition, the same vague set of indistinct respiratory ailments of varying severity which we call a cold), which we attributed to exhaustion and change of climate. And we spent hours studying Quechua from a collection of grammar books which we found in little shops on the plaza. And any otherwise unoccupied time and all of our literary energies were devoted to an intensive effort to communicate our address in Cusco to everyone at home who wanted it or might possibly write us a letter.

Finally we felt firmly enough established in Cusco and began to prepare ourselves to go out to 'Tambo. We went down one day to the market and bought lots of bread—though Gary tells me they have built ovens for baking bread in 'Tambo—and coffee and sugar, carrots and garlic and coca, and tins of fish, most of these provisions to be gifts. We got up at four the next morning, put on layers of clothing against the winter night, and set out. At the Plaza, unable to face the long, cold, dark walk to the lower market, we woke the driver of one of the cabs waiting for an early morning or late night fare—there were still men drinking in the bars along Calle Sapphi—and had him take us to the neighborhood of Belén, called Belempampa, where the trucks which go to 'Tambo and Paruro and other villages in that direction leave from. There are "truck stops" like this one in almost every one of the outlying neighborhoods of Cusco, where trucks arrive from and leave for villages beyond that edge of the city; many, if not most, of the inhabitants of these neighborhoods have come to live in Cusco from those villages and now run small businesses— shops and restaurants and boarding houses—catering to their former fellow villagers.

Two of the trucks waiting for passengers in Calle 21 de Mayo were bound for 'Tambo: the one we chose not to get on left first, but ours pulled away from the *paradero* soon after dawn. The trucks are big, heavy, flatbed trucks, with wooden floors and sides and a gate at the back, which lumber, engines grinding, over the mountain roads. They are the only means of transportation for most of the inhabitants of the Andes outside the cities. Most have a name painted in ornate letters across the front of the compartment above the cab, the name of a saint or a local shrine to which the owner has devoted his fate or something flashy and modern, like Superman. This one was called San Martín.

We had arrived early, and I had inspected the uninviting interior of the truck and decided that the most comfortable place to sit would be on the spare tire which lay on the floor of the big wooden box; Gary sat on one of two boards which spanned the back of the truck a little more than waist high just behind the cab. My seat on the tire proved distinctly *un*-comfortable: it bounced, and I had to hang on tightly to it not to be thrown off; I had a recurring vision of cowboys riding bulls in rodeos. By the time the truck left Belempampa, it was so crowded that I had no choice but to hang on; there was not even room for me to stand. The back of the truck was filled mostly with women surrounded by big, cloth-wrapped bundles and baskets and with children and a few small animals, chickens and a dog and a kitten. The men sat on the boards just behind the cab, where Gary had chosen to sit, or stood in the front near the others. There was little conversation; whether it was because of our presence or because of the cold and the hour, I don't know. We observed each other dispassionately, as though we were simply fellow travelers enduring the discomforts of the journey side by side, like riders on New York subway trains, though they must have been as intensely curious about us as Gary and I were about them.

Though I couldn't see the route, I knew by the temperature that we climbed to a high pass then descended into a valley. We stopped in the valley at a town called Yaurisque, and some people got out to eat plates of hot stews and rice. When we continued, we climbed again to a lower pass and then came down gently toward the river valley of the Apurimac. The

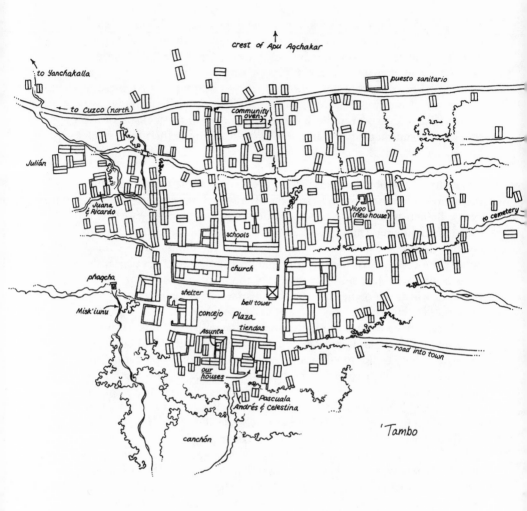

crest of Apu Aqchakar

to Yanchakalla

← to Cuzco (north)

puesto sanitario

community oven

Julián

schools

Juana & Ricardo

Hugo (new house)

to cemetery

phaqcha

church

Misk'iunu

shelter

bell tower

concejo   Plaza

Asunta   tiendas

road into town

our houses

Pascuala

Andrés & Celestina

canchón

'Tambo

sun was high by then, and people seemed to have warmed up, both literally and figuratively, and talked among themselves, all in Quechua. I made my way, the difficulty of the endeavor causing some amusement and some annoyance, to the front of the truck to stand beside Gary so I could see.

You come into 'Tambo, which is high above the Apurimac, from above, the road making broad switchbacks across the mountainside long before the village comes into view. From the road above, the village is impressive, bigger than any I had seen before, a dense complex of adobe buildings, many of two stories, with mostly thatched or tiled roofs, close as a small city around its broad plaza and church. The land all around the village, after several months of dry season, was dull and brown, but above the village is a thick eucalyptus wood, and there were deep green eucalyptus in clumps all around the perimeter of the village. We passed through the very top of the village, where there are a few walled compounds above the road and others immediately below into which we could see: pigs, chickens, dogs, a few children, and sometimes an adult who glanced up briefly as the truck passed, too quickly perhaps for the sight of two pale *gringo* faces among the others to truly register in their minds. There was the unmistakable smell of a village, a rich combination of eucalyptus smoke from the cooking fires, the smell of wet earth, the barnyard smell of the animals. The road took us around the mountainside into the dry fields, out of sight of the village again, and when we came back around, we came right into the village, into the plaza, where there are a few little shops in a row along one side. At the end of the plaza is the *concejo* (town hall), a large and impressive building of two stories with glass-paned windows and a red-tiled roof, painted, like most provincial government buildings, a bright turquoise, faded by the fierce Andean sun. And above the plaza on the eastern side, across from the row of shops, stands an enormous, old, rambling adobe church, secure within the adobe walls, pierced by arched windows, of the churchyard.

It was midmorning. There were a lot of people in the plaza, some waiting for passengers or cargo or the return trip to Cusco but most of them apparently just hanging around to see who or what would get off the truck that day. I felt painfully self-conscious; two *gringos* in blue jeans with big backpacks, we couldn't have been more conspicuous if we had worn bells or waved banners. I was glad we had someplace to go. We headed for the shop which belonged to the daughter of Baltazar Quispe, the man with whose family Gary had stayed when he came last year to explore the possibility of working here. This is where Gary had met Baltazar, in Juana's shop: he had arrived on a morning in August very much like this one and, when he had found someone to introduce himself to and had explained that he wanted to stay for a month, had become the responsibility of the highest-ranking town official who could be found at the moment. That was Baltazar, who was the village treasurer and had happened to be right here in his daughter's shop, for better or for worse. Now we intended to go to him and ask if we could stay for a little while, while we looked for a place to stay for the year. But when we reached it, the door of Juana's shop was closed, and an elaborate antique sort of lock hung from the hasp. So we skirted a large boulder near the door of the shop and turned into a lane that led down at a fairly steep pitch from the plaza; a white-washed board nailed to the wall of the storehouse across from Juana's shop read Calle San Juan—San Juan Street. The lane had been roughly paved at some time the way Inca roads were paved, with cobbles the size of small melons, designed for animals and people on foot, not for wheels. There were high adobe walls on each side, broken on the left by a couple of imposing wooden gates, on the right by a third one, farther down. Beyond that, the walls continued for a short distance and then gave way to shrub and *kantu* bushes hung with flowers like bright magenta trumpets.

We turned into a narrow passage between two buildings just across from the last gate. It led us to a small clearing with Baltazar's house— actually a series of one-room buildings built against the high wall of the compound just above, closely enclosed on one end by a wall and on the other by a sort of fence made of a tangle of branches—on the uphill side. Three small, separate houses stood below Baltazar's. We went into the yard of Baltazar's house and found that no one was there either, all of the buildings closed and locked, so we put our things down and sat on an earthen bench along the wall of the kitchen to wait in the sun. Opposite us, at the street end of the yard, was a two-story storehouse, with a railed balcony outside the upper story door that ran the width of the building. An earthen stairway and, where that ended, a short wooden ladder led to the balcony. Between the storehouse and the kitchen was a second two-story building, with one small window high in the wall. Another room had been added to this building, just outside the kitchen door—Gary had helped to dig the foundation for it when he was here last year. Baltazar had called it the *comedor* (the "dining room"). It had been finished much more finely than the other buildings, which were plain rough adobe with thatched roofs: the *comedor* had a tiled roof and two large arched windows, and the outer wall had been white-washed. At the end of the kitchen was a small walled enclosure which housed a faucet standing on a bare pipe wired to the kitchen wall above a concrete basin. Outside the yard at the end of the clearing was an *horno* (a Spanish-style adobe oven, shaped like a beehive) encircled by the beginnings of the foundation of a shelter apparently to be built around it.

After a while, a man came with a bundle, went into the *comedor,* and then came out and stayed to talk to us. He was from Espinar and had come to trade *bayeta* (a loose hand-woven wool cloth) for corn; the *maíz* of 'Tambo is known to be especially good, and people come from highlands all around to trade for it. A little later, another man came, a dealer of aniline dyes from Paruro. Then Juana arrived with another young woman named Felícitas. Juana is spectacular; she is about twenty-five and looks, somehow, in spite of the layers of heavy *bayeta* skirts, all faded and stained, the several cheap, machine-made sweaters which have also seen better days, the battered and shapeless fedora, and the black rubber sandals, like some exotic beauty from the cover of *Vogue* magazine, with high cheekbones and a stunning smile—and all of her very even, very white teeth—a finely chiseled nose and dark, dark brown eyes which are slightly oblique. Gary introduced me to her, and though she spoke only Quechua and I understood virtually nothing of what she said, I knew she was warm and bright and friendly and as unmindful of our foreignness as it was probably possible for her to be. In her presence I felt much less a stranger than I had just moments before.

Juana and the young woman with her had both been spinning when they came into the yard—in fact, every woman we had seen in 'Tambo had been spinning—so Gary announced to them that I wanted to learn how to spin. This, as I had feared it would, made me immediately the center of attention; had it been left to me, I would have approached someone about learning to spin at a much more private moment, when I was much more sure of myself. But it gave us all something to focus on besides the questions and tales of the other two outsiders, the traders. The two women sat down promptly, as glad for the distraction as we were, and demonstrated the procedure, and Juana put her spindle and a ball of doubled fine purple thread, which she was spinning into a fine yarn, into my hands. And I spun—thank God for the lessons I'd had before we left the States!—clumsily at first and then much better, though I had trouble with the technique of rolling the shaft of the spindle between the palms of my hands and letting it drop, still spinning, to the ground. Juana went with the dye dealer to get a bottle of *trago*, or cane liquor, from her shop (a *negocio*—a "business deal"—he said, winking at us) and returned with another spindle and ball of purple thread. Gary and the men proceeded to drink an uncounted number of bottles of *trago*, and though Juana didn't, I and the other young woman and an old woman who came from next door, who was spinning raw wool, drank some; the women giggled in Quechua about getting drunk, and the dye dealer gradually became morose and talked sadly about the wonders of highland women and love: unmarried, he had spent a couple of years in Lima and probably knew too much of the world to be happy in the highlands even if he had not been happy in Lima. He had also, obviously, already been drinking.

In the early afternoon, Daniel, a son of Baltazar and his wife Teresa, came home. He was wearing his school uniform—gray pants and V-necked sweater and a white shirt, many times washed and wearing thin, and *ojota*s and no hat; in the villages, where everyone always wears a hat, children are forbidden to wear their hats to school. He greeted Gary and Gary introduced us, and he sat with us for a while, just listening to the conversation. He must be about fourteen and is a handsome boy, though his features are stronger and not as fine as Juana's. Juana sent him to fetch her weaving—by now it had also been revealed that I wanted to learn to weave—a brightly colored piece in reds and greens and white on a backstrap loom: the warp of a piece of weaving can be rolled up around the wooden supports of the loom and carried easily. She set this up at the other end of the enclosure, and the women all moved with their spinning to where she worked, leaving the men and their *trago*. I watched and spun and watched. The dye dealer had said she was a good weaver: she was quick and deft, and the patterns were not simple ones—at least they didn't look simple to me. Once she stopped and pointed to one band of pattern and pronounced a word in Quechua, which I assumed to be a name; I repeated it, and she named all of the patterns as I repeated each name. I realized suddenly—a moment of enlightenment—that this was what we had come here for: this is what anthropologists go to the field for, to learn such things as the names of patterns of weaving. I also realized that I'd never remember them or know what they meant unless I wrote them down, and I went to borrow Gary's little notebook and pen from him. I asked her, through Daniel, who speaks Spanish, to repeat them for me, tried to sound the words out and spell them in Quechua, and, under Daniel's guidance, drew hurried diagrams—explaining in Spanish that it was so I could remember them. I am fairly comfortable in Spanish with the Quechua people, mostly men, who speak it: it is a second language for both of us. A little while later she named the parts of the loom for me, and I wrote them down: I am still trying to discover something that resembles the words I wrote down—as I understood them—in the Quechua dictionary. Understanding Quechua, I discover, requires training oneself to hear subtle differences in sounds to which we are not accustomed: there are six separate sounds closely akin to our single, simple "k" sound, three or four variations of "t" and of "p"—their pronunciation and recognition, of course, critical to expression and the understanding of a speaker's meaning. It is a training I have just begun.

Toward late afternoon, we decided to take a walk, mainly to escape the *trago*: the drinking clearly could, and would, have gone on to a point at which we would all have been sorry. Daniel first showed us to the second story, the *marka*, of his father's storehouse, where we could sleep, and we left our backpacks there and walked down out of 'Tambo and out onto the mountainside. It is a beautiful place, with jagged peaks across the river and in the distance and smoother hills all around the village. During the afternoon, I had looked up from the yard once in a while and had been struck powerfully by the fact that we were sitting on the side of a mountain; from the yard, you look out into open space to the face of another mountain in the distance. 'Tambo's fields and pasture lands are all around the village, both above and below it on the mountain, and there are many little villages, its annexes, on nearby hills. We returned to 'Tambo—a little reluctantly, not sure what awaited us at the house—and found Juana, now weaving at the other end of the enclosure near the kitchen where the men had been, and the dye dealer, still drinking and in sorry condition. The *bayeta* trader drifted back from somewhere, and the other young woman and an old man who was chopping wood in the neighboring yard came over. Gary bought another bottle of *trago* to offer them. They drank it and Juana refused the dye dealer another, saying, "No hay: se terminó" ("There isn't any, it's gone"), so gradually everyone drifted away again, including the dye dealer and the man who had been chopping wood, who said that he would come and get us in the morning to eat breakfast with him. (He didn't, but it was one of those requisite social gestures, a promise made for the sake of good manners which may or may not be kept, no hard feelings.) We gave Juana some bread and a can of tuna, she gave us some boiled potatoes, and we retired to the storehouse for sandwiches of tinned fish, mandarin oranges, and chocolate bars. A little later, Juana and Daniel, trailing a couple of little boys, came and brought us some cloths to lie on and another ball of purple thread: my assignment. Though it was only eight, we were exhausted, having risen at three-thirty in the morning, and slept almost immediately, a full twelve hours.

We took a long walk the next morning, out onto a hilltop above the Apurimac, to see the river. The hill is carpeted with potsherds, some Inca, many more recent, and some much older; it is the highest point on this side of the Apurimac, above where a tributary flows into the river: we speculated that people may, for hundreds of years, have brought jars of *chicha* to this summit as some kind of offering or tribute, perhaps to the river, whose name means, more or less, talking god. We sat on the hillside for a long while, gazing across the fields and villages on this side, across the river to the mountains of the Otra Banda, watching birds soar through the bright air. We decided to leave the next day instead of on Saturday as we'd planned, feeling that the situation was a little awkward: earlier on the day we had arrived, Baltazar and Teresa had gone to Cusco to sell barley and would not be back until Saturday. Juana had her own husband and three children to care for and anyway no longer lives in her parents' house where we were staying. This left poor Daniel, just a kid himself, to look after us, and a couple of *gringos* are unwieldy guests in a village under any circumstances. We would leave Daniel the photographs Gary had taken of them the year before, tell him and Juana when we would be back, and go. We walked back to the village along the old trail, lined with maguey and cacti and *kantu* bushes and buzzing with big black bees, instead of by the road.

On the way back into town, we stopped to see the president of the village, a young man named Julio Wallpa. Gary introduced us, explained that he had been there a year ago and what we wanted to do—to live there for a year—and showed him the letter of introduction from the university where he teaches, which had been translated into Spanish. The *presidente* took a long time with the brief letter and looked a little blank but assured us that we'd be able to find a house to live in. We spent the rest of the afternoon walking and sitting on the hillsides watching the changing light, and I kept Juana's spindle with me and spun while Gary wrote his notes. We hadn't seen Juana since early in the morning, when she had come to give us bread and *café con leche* for breakfast, which she prepared in her mother's kitchen; by the end of the day we had seen Daniel only twice, once on the path out to the fields to the west when he was going to bring the cows in and once after dark, when he came to the storeroom where we were getting ready for bed to get some grain for the animals and to offer us one of his schoolbooks to read—he remembered that Gary was always reading or writing.

The next morning he came to fetch the photographs, and we gave him the rest of our oranges; in return, he gave Gary some *llipta* he had made. *Llipta* is a dried paste with which coca is chewed, made from the ashes of wheat or barley mixed with a little *trago* and sugar. At her shop we gave Juana the carrots and garlic we had brought and her spindle and then sat in front of the shop to wait for the truck, watching the people in the busy plaza: women carrying water jugs on their backs, men driving burros and horses with burdens of grain in huge sacks to be taken to Cusco on the truck, men with long wooden plows and sometimes a pair of bulls, children going to school—the schoolteacher had crossed the plaza at one end, blowing a whistle—and a little girl carrying on her back wrapped in a *lliqlla* (a carrying cloth tied around her shoulders) a baby, hardly smaller than she was, and knitting as she walked.

The truck came and when the passengers from Cusco had disembarked, we got on. There were good comfortable places to sit on the sacks of grain, but I wanted to see this time, so I stood. The land between 'Tambo and Cusco is high and quite rough and very beautiful—that keen, uncompromising beauty of harsh environments. The road crosses *puna* land at the highest points, cold and desolate, forbidding, where

woman carrying
a baby in
a lliqlla
(marina and yong)

nothing much seems to grow except rocks. The town of Yaurisque proved to be a fairly large and busy place, with hot springs to which people come from Cusco to bathe, some cars and the buses to Paruro and other traffic, and electricity and a telephone. In the high land nearer to Cusco, flocks of llamas grazed, with tassels of bright-colored yarn in their pierced ears, and there were fascinating villages with houses built of stone instead of adobe and small fields and pastures ringed by fences of stacked stone, each one causing us an ache of curiosity. We arrived in Cusco with a vague sense of letdown after the exhilaration of the trip and our days in 'Tambo, and before we'd gotten to our room on Calle Sapphi, we'd made plans for our next visit.

2. Natividad

On Friday, the fourth of September, we got up at four in the morning to catch the truck for 'Tambo which would leave about five-thirty from the *paradero* in Belempampa. It was raining, hard, and we should have taken this for an evil omen if only we had recognized it. The truck and the street and sidewalk around it were crowded with people: the festival of Natividad, 'Tambo's major festival of the year, was to begin on Tuesday, the eighth, and many people were going to visit or were returning to 'Tambo from Cusco with supplies for the celebration. We struggled onto the truck with our two big backpacks and Gary's small one, too much to keep a close watch over all at once, and in the midst of the crush of people and all of the jostling and shoving for space to stand, someone, clearly a professional thief, quickly and deftly opened Gary's pack and removed our camera and the telephoto lens and the folder which held our passports, though it must have been assumed to contain money, and was off the truck and gone before we discovered the theft.

Gary turned his back to me for a moment, and I said to him calmly, naïvely, "Did you know your pack was open?" I started to close it, but as I interpreted his reaction, my heart sank. He asked me if the camera was there, on top where he had packed it so it wouldn't be crushed, and I said no and searched the pack for the lens. We didn't find out about our passports until we had gotten off the truck, out of the crowd. We stood in the street, wet and discouraged, while two patrol cars of the Guardia Civil cruised the nearby streets pretending to look for the thief, whom we knew as well as they that they wouldn't find: he was probably long gone, and anyone who steals cameras in Peru can sell them through the black market for twice their cost in the States and can easily afford to bribe the Guardia enough not to look very hard. We spent most of the morning in shops and the bank and various offices, buying and filling in forms and filing useless police reports and getting a letter from the U.S. consul in Cusco to serve as identification; the acting consul until October, when the usual consul returns from his vacation, happens to be one of the friends we have made, Leo, who is from Florida and runs a café and bar farther down Calle Sapphi toward the plaza. It was a difficult and bitter day; dealing with bureaucracy in Latin America is seldom satisfying. At least, sitting with Leo in his café that morning over gloomy cups of coffee, we learned of a camera we might buy when its owner returns to the States.

And we started, with little enthusiasm, again the next morning, feeling cynical and pessimistic. But the sky was clear, the stars sharp, and the dawn beginning to show in the east, far down the valley, when we reached the truck stop. It was a beautiful morning, and I was allowed to ride in the warm cab of the truck, safely out of the crowd of passengers which I was reluctant to join again, and so shared the driver's view of the whole route. The trip was blessedly uneventful, and we arrived in 'Tambo in much better spirits than we had begun in. The plaza was full of frenetic activity and lots of people, but I felt less self-conscious than I had the last time because we were expected. On the way to Juana's shop, we were stopped by a man whom Gary had met last year who greeted us enthusiastically, seemed to approve heartily that Gary had brought a woman with him this time, and invited us to come to his house to visit him during the festival. Juana's shop was open—a windowless cubicle in large part filled by a table which served as a counter and with shelves along the back wall and the side wall by the door and a bench along the front wall just inside. The truck driver sat on the bench drinking an Inca Cola from a bottle. Juana, a bit more reserved now, encountering us in public, said she thought Baltazar and Teresa were home, so we went back down Calle San Juan to their house. It was deserted. We remembered that we had told Daniel we would be back the day before, so it was no wonder there was no one there. We sat down to wait, and waited alone for most of the day, shifting from the sun to the shade and back again when one and then the other became unbearable: during the winter months in the Andes, the difference in temperature between the sun and the shade can be thirty, even forty degrees—eighty in the sun against a wall, forty-something in the shade on the other side of the street—both extremes felt with an uncommon intensity, perhaps because of the sparsity of the atmosphere. A little nervous now about actually meeting Baltazar and Teresa, I had a much soberer sense of what we were proposing to do, and I had hours to spin, this time, a find thread of apprehension which tied itself into complicated knots in my stomach. I came to know the other end of the yard, the end near the street, well: the long wooden plow that hung above the ground floor entrance to the storehouse just under the balcony; the sort of bin beside the door, built of poles and withes held together with coarse rope, full of hay; the short section of wall, weeds growing through its thatch, which enclosed the yard on that end. And at our end of the yard, the crude fence with shards of broken pots and old rubber sandals tucked in along its base and the small, thatch-roofed houses on the lower side of the clearing and above their roofs the jagged, sawtooth line of the western horizon, very near, drawn by a couple of formidable ridges. The only sound was the unfamiliar music of the wind in the eucalyptus trees. I felt a profound sense of distance and exposure, a sense which certainly had something to do with being a stranger in a very foreign place and having no idea what might happen next, not just in the next moment but for the next year of our lives, a state of vital suspense; but it also had something to do with the vast expanse of empty blue over our heads, with the impossible silence except for the wind, with the very scale and extremity of the landscape.

Finally, late in the afternoon, Teresa appeared, a small woman, about my size, and slender under the layers of clothing she wore: the calves of her legs and her ankles below the fraying scalloped hems of her skirts were thin, and her hand when I took it slight and bony. She seemed a little shy at being so formally introduced. Her face is kind and gentle, long rather than broad, and rather care-worn. I would guess her to be in her forties, but she may be older than that—it is difficult to guess with any real confidence because many of the cues we rely on to judge a person's age are skewed here: our hair may begin to gray when we are only in our thirties, but theirs doesn't seem to until they are truly elderly, in their seventies or eighties; and here, too, a person may lose many or even all of his or her teeth very early in life, while we lose many fewer and lose them later, and the loss is carefully camouflaged. She wears her hair in the traditional way, in two long braids that fall to her waist behind her, held together by a length of dark yarn, its ends twined into her braids so they won't swing. In the States, usually only a little girl would wear her hair that way. Teresa's hair was deep black beneath the brim of her hat, and she had most of her teeth, and it was only the gentle lines in her face, the prominent veins in the backs of her hands, the faint stoop in her posture from years of carrying burdens, that made her look a middle-aged woman. Gary spoke to her in Quechua—most of the women in the village, Gary says, speak only Quechua, though most of the men are bilingual—inquiring after Baltazar. She said he would be home soon. Then she slipped into her kitchen and emerged a few minutes later bearing two enormous milkshake-sized glasses of *chicha* for us, like the glasses they serve *chicha* in in the city. We thanked her profusely, as is customary in Quechua, and the thanks were mostly sincere since we had had nothing to drink except a single, dreadfully sweet soft drink Gary had gotten from Juana's store soon after we arrived, though the quantity of *chicha* in those glasses was daunting. *Chicha* is extremely filling and is not normally sipped and savored but is drunk down in great draughts. As we sat contemplating the task of finishing our *chicha*, Teresa closed up her kitchen again and picked up her spindle and left, saying that she would be right back.

We took our time drinking the *chicha*, which was very good, thin and clean and faintly sweet. Soon after we had finished it and set the glasses on the bench against the wall of the kitchen, Teresa returned with Baltazar, about whom I had heard so much from Gary. He was in a jovial mood—in fact, he was rather drunk—and exclaimed when he saw Gary, "Ah, Señor Gavino, ¡aquí está! ¿Cómo está, *Papa*? ¿*Allinllanchu*?" gripping his hand as if they were lifelong friends, and then turned to me, "Señora Julia, ¡mucho gusto! ¿*Allinllanchu*?" and asked Gary, "Does she also speak Quechua?" He is a small man, no taller than, if even as tall as, I am, and he is crippled. He told Gary last year that six or seven years ago—eight now, I guess—a horse he was riding stumbled, throwing him to the ground beneath its hooves, and then fell on him, breaking his leg. The leg had healed firmly but had healed shorter than the other one, so that he walks now with a severe limp, with his left arm cocked at a sharp angle to his body for balance. Something about his manner, the simple force of his presence even in his somewhat disheveled state, made it clear that this hadn't, somehow, been a terrible handicap for him. He is clearly a self-confident, well-respected, and perhaps powerful man: he was the village treasurer last year and is now, he told us, the *segunda* (head man) of his *ayllu*, which (according to Baltazar) is the largest and most important *ayllu*, or social group, of the village; they are both elected positions. His face is roundish, broad and flat across the cheekbones and the bridge of his nose, and his skin a coppery brown, darker than Teresa's, from the sun; it's an expressive face, with lines sharply drawn in a fan at the corners of his eyes and from his nose to the corners of his mouth. Gary says he is a good storyteller, and I can easily imagine it. His clothes were all machine-made—except for the tire-rubber sandals—bought in the market and worn in patched layers: a couple of pairs of pants, one over the other; an old, olive drab, aviator-style jacket of quilted nylon over an old V-necked sweater over an old, faded shirt; and the usual old, tired, sweat-stained fedora.

He took us into the central room with the high window to talk. We sat just inside the door, at the end across from the storehouse, on a spare bedframe covered with thin matted sheepskins. He sat on a long wooden

CHATO WITH TIN CUP

bench along the wall across the doorway from us, his left leg extended stiffly in front of him into the dusty, fading, late-afternoon light falling into the room through the open door. Teresa came in with a clay pitcher full of *chicha* and a couple of chipped, enameled tin cups. She sat just beyond the wedge of light, squatting on her heels on the floor the way women do—only men sit on benches or chairs—with her skirts tucked neatly under her buttocks. Gary offered to buy a bottle of *trago* as a gesture of goodwill, a sort of house gift, and Teresa went to get it. Then while Gary and Baltazar talked, Teresa served us *chicha* and Baltazar *trago*, and it gradually grew dark and Baltazar lit a small, homemade kerosene lamp which cast a smoky, yellow light into the room. The five-hour truck ride and the long wait and the anticipation and the sun finally had their effect, and I only half listened to the conversation, turning to lean back against the headboard of the bed. There was a second bedframe at the back of the room, with a mound of heavy blankets heaped on it, and a small simple wooden table. The room was filled with large baskets and bundles and various tools, and some smaller baskets and plastic bags and other objects hung from the beams and poles of the ceiling. Behind us where we sat on the bed, a long pole had been suspended, parallel to the ceiling and to the wall at our backs, which served as a sort of closet; it was draped with sweaters and shirts and skirts and pants and a few pieces that stood out among the more ordinary clothes—something of rough, dark *bayeta* with rows of colored fringe, a fine gray poncho, and a fancy, lace-trimmed, pink satin blouse with a peplum, which I knew because Gary had taken a picture of Teresa in it last year. Gary explained to Baltazar that we wanted to stay for a year, that we needed a place to live, and that we could either stay with a family, as Gary did during his first fieldwork, or maybe find an abandoned house to live in. We knew that Baltazar would offer to put us up, not only for that night but for the whole year, and at the moment, tired as we were, that possibility appealed to us as if it meant clean sheets and a feather bed. What Baltazar offered us was the room we were sitting in, obviously the room they sleep in, which would mean that they would have to move into one of their storerooms or the kitchen to give us the most comfortable room in the compound, or at least the biggest one, and which didn't make any sense. We agreed to postpone the discussion until the day after the festival, when he would have had time to think about it and we would all be more clear-headed. They installed us for the next several nights in the storeroom below the one we had slept in before, which was mostly occupied by a large bin constructed of poles and straw, full of seed potatoes, and a stand of upturned storage jars as high as my waist. Among them we just had room to lay our sleeping bags out on a few layers of sheepskins and tattered old ponchos and one heavy, handwoven blanket of thickly spun wool which they offered us to break the damp cold from the earthen floor. I must have lay there for all of thirty seconds before I fell soundly asleep.

When we woke the next morning, the day was already well under way. Baltazar was busy making bread in his big, new oven, for people who bore some aspect of ritual responsibility for the celebration of the festival. The Quechua year is calibrated by the dates of these festivals of Catholic saints, dates of the Spanish calendar. Each village celebrates certain different saints' days and other signal dates in the religious calendar such as Christmas and Easter, observing them with ceremonies and festivity of varying elaboration. The responsibility of organizing and carrying out these celebrations is called a *cargo,* and here in 'Tambo, each festival *cargo* belongs to a specific *ayllu.* Within the *ayllu,* the burden of responsibility for the celebration of the festival falls to an individual member of the *ayllu;* some festivals are traditionally the obligation of the *segunda* of the *ayllu,* but most are assumed more or less voluntarily by one *ayllu* member or another: the fulfillment of a *cargo* can be a formidable task, requiring the construction of great altars in the plaza, the hiring of bands to provide music, the recruitment and costuming of dancers—the traditional requirements vary from festival to festival—and the provision of food and *chicha* and *trago* for all of the performers and men and women who help the *carguyuq* (the bearer of the *cargo*) and his wife. But though the cost in time and resources and labor—and emotional tension—is tremendous, the fulfillment of these responsibilities, along with other civic and religious duties, brings the reward of increased prestige in the community, and to enjoy in his old age esteem as a respected elder of the community, a man must perform a number of these *cargos* in his lifetime. And so the travail of fulfillment of festival *cargo*s is, usually, sought after, though not without some careful consideration.

It was these people, the *carguyuq*s, who came that day to have Baltazar make bread for them. There were no introductions, but our presence seemed somehow to be accepted quite easily; I had expected to be constantly an object of curiosity, but everyone had more pressing concerns, and we were simply appreciated for the two extra pairs of hands we could lend to the work. The *carguyuq* himself was sometimes present, but more often it was his wife and his children who came, and we all worked together. The women brought big bags of flour, a lump of lard, a handful of salt tied in a cloth, a pitcher of thick, sweet *chicha* called *qonchu* (the dregs of the jar) to leaven the bread, and *chicha* and some coca and sometimes *trago* for Baltazar.

Working in the *comedor,* Baltazar dumped the flour into a big metal tub and packed it against one side. Teresa brought hot water from the fire and poured this and cold water into the tub to make the lukewarm water that was needed, and the *qonchu* and salt were added. Baltazar laboriously kneaded the great mass of thick dough, then covered the tub with a cloth to allow the dough to rest. He also rested, chewing coca and drinking the *chicha* the woman served him in generous quantity, and then built a fire of eucalyptus wood in the oven. When the dough had risen, Daniel took sections of it, kneaded it, and on a table made of boards supported by eucalyptus stumps, rolled it into thick logs, pieces of which he broke off and tossed to the women kneeling on cloths spread on the floor. We rolled the pieces between our palms into balls and squeezed the balls almost in two between the firm edges of our hands, twisted the narrow rope between the almost-two balls and pressed them together, flattening the bread with the heels of our hands. With the last of the dough, Daniel shaped *wawitas* and *caballitos* (babies and little horses) and llamas and coca leaves. Sometimes a little of the last of the dough was sweetened with eggs and sugar. The little breads were carried out of the *comedor* on boards in complicated relays and thrust into the oven at just the right moment; and then we waited, the air rich with the mingled scents of baking bread and eucalyptus smoke, sometimes offered a cup of *chicha* by the woman whose bread was baking. And finally the bread was done and the prop that held a piece of sheet metal against the door of the oven removed, and with a crooked branch, the bread was scooped out, brown now and hollow-sounding, into waiting cloths to be carried home. The woman always gave Baltazar some—the big breads shaped like coca leaves were made especially for him—and one to each of the children who gathered around and usually one or two to each of us, and everybody ate hot, fragrant bread right out of the oven. We repeated this process all day long, making batch after batch, from ten in the morning until almost midnight, and went to bed weary, Gary and I, and slightly ill from eating too much bread before it cooled from the oven.

By the time we reached the plaza the next morning, the men of the *ayllus* were already working, building the *cancha* (the enclosure for the bullfight) and already the scaffolds for the two great altars had been raised on the side of the plaza below the churchyard. We watched for a while, Gary standing with the group of men with whom Baltazar was working, I sitting at the edge of the plaza with other women and girls. The trucks that arrived from Cusco in midmorning bore essentials for the festival which ranged from the most secular to the most ecclesiastic: loads of beer and bottled soft drinks, musicians and instruments—in the open compartment above the cab of Paisano 2 was balanced an upended Andean harp—and finally the priest who would celebrate mass during the eight days of the festival.

The memory of that week is a vast confusion of images, like a painting of all I remember of it smeared by a careless sleeve before the paint was dry. Besides the difficulty of realizing that these were the first days of a *year* I am to spend in this place where I understand almost nothing and no one was the chaos of the festival, and the sleeve that smeared the picture was the great quantities of *chicha* and *trago* that flowed through the village during those days.

Chicha and *trago* are staples of celebration in Quechua life, and of many other activities as well. *Chicha* is a very mild beer, made from corn which has sprouted; boiling and fermentation purify the water from which it is made: although a rudimentary water system has been installed in 'Tambo, the local result of a government program to provide potable water to villages, people still seldom, if ever, drink plain water—the habit of centuries of deriving water from contaminable streams and springs. They sometimes drink infusions, such as teas made from wild herbs and plants or, rarely, coffee. But to quench thirst, people drink *chicha*, wherever in the Andes corn can be grown or obtained in sufficient quantities to make it. In those places—which is everywhere except in villages at the highest altitudes—*chicha* is also a staple nutritional element of the diet: germination tremendously increases the amount of available protein in the corn.

Germination is induced, at least in 'Tambo, by spreading a quantity of dried corn on a cloth or a sheet of plastic, dampening it, and covering it with another cloth or sheet of plastic weighted by rocks. When it has sprouted, the corn is laid on a cloth in the sun day after day to dry, and then it is ground using the grinding stones found among the accouterments of every woman's household. The corn mush that results is added to great pots of water and boiled, and then this liquid is strained through straw-lined baskets into large storage jars. Though it may be drunk immediately, it is usually allowed to rest for a couple of days, and the process of fermentation begins. It is a time-consuming task, and a woman usually prepares a fairly large quantity each time she makes *chicha*. The *chicha* drunk daily is normally very mild, though naturally it grows stronger as fermentation continues until the supply in the jars is gone, and *chicha* made for festivals is sometimes deliberately allowed to ferment to a somewhat greater potency. Children are given half-cupfuls or sips of *chicha* from an adult's cup. It is rather an acquired taste: *chicha* is thick, of an unappetizing color—a sort of sickly yellow—and an untrustworthy texture, and extremely filling; I remember describing it to someone after my first experience of it as a corn milkshake made with beer instead of milk.

But *chicha* is distinctly more than just a beverage that one drinks when one is thirsty. To guests in a Quechua household or at a public ceremony, *chicha* demonstrates hospitality and the security of the household: that the man of the house provides well for his family—so there is plenty of corn—and that the woman, the backbone of the Quechua household, is capable and attentive to the basic needs of her family and their guests. A Quechua woman would be mortified to find guests in her house and have no *chicha* to serve them. Even among the members of a family, *chicha* is served and drunk with a measure of formality: words of offering and of gratitude are always spoken each time *chicha* is proffered, accepted, and drunk, and the cup or glass returned to the woman who served it. *Chicha* carries a good deal of symbolic significance: it is a necessary offering of thanks, along with the meals that are served them, to the men who help another man in his fields—a gesture mirrored by the man's wife, who serves *chicha* to the women who help her cook for the men. Because all agricultural tasks are performed using footplows and hand tools like hoes—advanced technology is represented here by the wooden scratch plow drawn by a pair of bulls—each man enlists the help of other men to complete each task, in a single day if possible, with the understanding that he will work for each of those men for an equal amount of time. In the fields, then, *chicha* signifies reliability, an assurance that the debt of labor is recognized and will be repaid. In the fulfillment of ceremonial obligations too, *chicha* is essential: in this context, it again demonstrates the security of the household of the *carguyuq*, his ability and his wife's, and their generosity; and because the fulfillment of those responsibilities entails a tremendous amount of labor and support, *chicha*, and the quantity in which it is served, reveals the extent and solidarity of the network of kin and spiritual kin upon which the family can call for aid. The greater the formality of the setting in which *chicha* is served, the greater its symbolic significance becomes, and the more elaborate the rituals of serving and accepting, the more profuse the thanks.

Trago is another thing. *Trago,* in Spanish, means a swallow or gulp, and is the name of the clear, bitter, and very strong alcohol which the Quechua drink. The Spanish introduced the process of distillation to Peru at the time of the Conquest, and liquor was distilled, as in most of tropical America, from sugar cane. Cane liquor was adopted at some point into the ritual life of the Quechua as a sort of amplified form of *chicha,* but the cost of rum and its cheaper version, *caña,* must eventually have become prohibitive; the stuff that is substituted for it today is most often raw grain alcohol, which is bought in Cusco and transported to villages in large aluminum tins and subsequently diluted to some lesser strength, though often not enough, and sold for a few *soles* a bottle—a bottle of *trago* here costs the equivalent of about seventy cents. *Trago* is potent and vile and as essential, or more so, as *chicha* in the ceremonial and ritual life of the Quechua. Unlike *chicha,* people do not drink *trago* every day; it is reserved for special occasions, though these may sometimes be invented. *Trago,* and the rituals of its use, comprise an even more symbolic currency: *trago* asks favors, pays homage, and binds agreements and contracts; it blesses, gives thanks, and honors people and sacred beings. Its inavailability at the time of certain occasions can undermine to the point of futility the purpose of a ceremony. The acts of serving, accepting, and drinking *trago* are formal, stylized—a ritual language which expresses, always, the relationships inherent in the circumstances of the immediate context of the people sharing it, and between them and the world they live in, the earth, the mountains.

We walked down from the village to the field of the young *presidente* Julio Wallpa that afternoon to help plant corn, at his invitation; they were plowing with two long, wooden scratch plows, like the one that hung above the door of the storeroom at Baltazar's, each drawn by a pair of bulls. As they finished, Julio's wife and another woman brought food and *trago;* men poured *chicha* into cow's horns from big skin bags. The *chicha* was good, but the *trago* so strong that even the men couldn't drink it without grimacing. The effect of *trago,* always drunk in shots from a tiny cup called a *copita,* like a shot glass, filled again and again and served to each guest in unceasing succession until the bottle is gone (and often succeeded by another until funds too are depleted), seems not so much to be to make one very drunk very fast, as to simply remove one from his immediate environment and the normal passage of time, place him at a slight distance, and abandon him there. It was in this somewhat dazed and bemused state that we wandered back toward 'Tambo, overtaken and passed by the workers eager to get home, and seemed to spend much of the following days.

During the day, the bull ring and altars had been completed, the altars' thirty- to forty-foot scaffolds decorated with red and white painted panels and banners and shallow mirrored boxes containing the images of saints. A different *ayllu* had the responsibility for each altar and for sections of the bullring. At night, a bonfire was built in front of each altar and, later, one between them; and at one a record player blared, while at the other a band played. In front of both, men danced (I think they were all men and that all of the women sat just at the edge of the firelight—my powers of observation and memory were not their most acute, somewhat impaired by the *trago*, and I stayed only until I could escape, after a horn full of *chicha* and two *copitas* of *trago* in succession and a dance with a very lively old man, and left Gary to fend for himself.) On Tuesday, we heard music early in the morning and the bells of the church tower. There was a procession of the images of saints which had been brought to 'Tambo from surrounding villages and as far away as Yaurisque: twelve in all, including those of 'Tambo—two I think; they were carried on litters, men bearing the large images, boys the small ones, led by the priest and two or three other men in white tunics edged with lace over their dull *campo* clothes. One of these carried a censer, another a covered silver plate. A table covered with a white cloth was placed before the first altar, the one nearest the descent from the churchyard, and the procession stopped there, and while the censer was swung over the table, the crowd of people who, barefooted, had followed the procession through the plaza knelt and sang a hymn, their hats in their hands and many of the women with their shawls drawn over their heads. The table was moved as the procession went to the second altar, the same procedure repeated there. Then the procession turned and passed in front of the town hall and then along the row of shops and finally climbed the steep street at the end of the churchyard, accompanied by its two bands, playing different songs at the same time on trumpets and bugles and drums and a couple of flutes. We climbed up to the edge of the churchyard and watched the procession retreat into the church, the images entering through the door backward to face the followers, the bands remaining outside.

We found a place among the crowd of village people on the slope above the plaza just below the wall of the churchyard to watch the bullfight and soccer games: teams from a number of villages were to play something like a tournament. The teams may have come from the annexes of 'Tambo or from the villages from which the saints had been brought—I don't know how the mechanics of the tournament related to the religious elements of the festival. The plaza was full of people. Vendors of fruits and vegetables and candy and small manufactured things—combs and barrettes, plastic toys, needles and thread and safety pins and shawl pins— had come from Cusco, and others had set up concessions of food and soft drinks and beer. The soccer field was laid out in white chalk, with wooden goalposts set up at each end of the plaza. The first game was interrupted by the beginning of the bullfight or, rather, by several horsemen who rode up impressively, followed by a band, which seemed to us to portend something. The horsemen rode diagonally across the plaza—across the soccer field—and out, up the steep street at the end of the churchyard, and the game continued until the *toreros* appeared, entering the plaza from the street from which the horsemen had ridden. Three of them were dressed in a costume—black pants and white shirt with a scarlet sash— the elegance and dignity of which were spoiled only by their tennis shoes, and a couple wore more ordinary clothes. The bulls and *toreros* were from Yaurisque. With them when they came into the plaza came people carrying between them cords hung with small banners of rose and gold and white cloth and a couple of white T-shirts with decorations of the same colors; these were hung across the front of the town hall which formed one wall of the ring. One by one, the banners and shirts were attached by some means to the bulls, to their tails or to the rise of their backs, perhaps with something sharp to hurt and enrage them. The bulls, however, were rather unpredictable; some performed with the fury expected of them, but some looked merely confused, and from some of them there seemed almost no reaction at all to the red and pink capes swirling before them. And some of the *toreros,* though hardly professional, were good, like dancers with their capes, leading the bulls into partnership in the classical choreography, though few, unfortunately, by the standards of the traditional bullfight, were actually challenged by a difficult animal. But one, one of the men dressed in black and dazzling white and scarlet, had the back of his shirt slashed open by the horn of a bull, for which he received long and enthusiastic applause; the gash was fastened together and he returned to the bulls something of a hero. There was also a young man in ordinary clothes who was nearly trampled by a bull; he lay for long—interminable—moments on the ground under the angry, flying hooves before the bull was drawn away and he, perhaps not supposed to have been there to begin with, was chased from the ring by the governor. And there was a young boy, perhaps the most lovely to watch, dressed in black and white, skillful, graceful with the pink cape as he faced the enormous animals.

After the bullfight, when each of the bits of cloth had been won by a *torero,* the soccer game continued and we wandered away. We sat in the evening drinking *chicha* and *trago* with Baltazar and Teresa and some other men and women in a storehouse, partially filled with cases of beer for the festival, which belongs to Baltazar, on the plaza across Calle San Juan from Juana's shop.

On Wednesday morning, the early stillness was embroidered by the sounds of music somewhere in the village and the voices of the church bells. There was a procession of the sacrament, carried in what looked like an elaborate medieval monstrance, with a fringed canopy borne over it on poles, led again by the priest and men in white tunics. The followers again were barefooted, and people standing near the route of the procession were scolded by a church official with a *vara* (a long wooden staff bound with silver) for having shoes or a hat on and moved away or took them off.

Later on, Gary and I walked out of the village to a hillside, the slope of one of the *apu*s, Apu Aphitu, where Baltazar and Teresa had gone earlier. From the plaza we had seen the people gathered there, arranged in two groups facing each other in lines, one above and a little to the east of the other, and could see people carrying *qero*s full of *chicha* between the groups as they served each other. Gary recognized this ritual from a description in one of the chronicles of life in the Inca Empire that were written just after the Conquest. The idea that it might be a vestige of an ancient Incaic tradition lent this affair a romantic and somehow noble aspect, a decorum which it failed to maintain when we had actually arrived there. Some people had begun to leave by the time we got there, though they'd been there all day and all of the previous day and, for all we knew, all night. The two lines had broken up, though the women still sat in a group to one side with their *chicha* jars, and some people still danced to the music of a straggly, dissipating band. Everyone was very drunk and set out immediately to help us achieve a similar state, forcing *trago* on us with irresistable determination. I was surrounded by leering men: it seemed that the rules of sexual discretion had been suspended by simple drunkenness or by some tradition of the festival. The men talked about my blond hair and joked with Gary about trading me to them for their wives. Some of the men were in costume; one was dressed as a woman. A man in an olive-drab army uniform dragged me away to dance with him; holding me tightly, painfully, by the wrist, he put a scarf in my hands and bade the band play. As we danced—I was afraid not to, for fear of giving offense and uncertain of the mood—he caught me around the neck with his own scarf, drawing me much closer to him than I wanted to be, and released me to catch me again. Once he tried to flip the hem of my skirt up with his scarf. Nobody apparently wanted to see this performance end, so the band played the song twice and was beginning it again before Teresa, to whom I gave fervent silent thanks, led me away to where the women sat. I was given two *qero*s of *chicha* by eager women, and Teresa tied a cloth with a jar of *chicha* wrapped in it around my shoulders, so, obviously we hoped, I couldn't dance any more, and we prepared to leave with her and Baltazar. Even with the two of them speaking on our behalf, it proved difficult to convince the celebrants to let us go.

That afternoon, we christened Baltazar's oven, which had been completed just before the preparations for the festival had begun, with a bottle of Coca-Cola: it was a major ceremony. We bought, because we were to be the oven's sponsors, seven bottles of beer and two of *trago*, and Baltazar provided two more of *trago* and Teresa *chicha*. After the days of having nothing except our morning coffee to drink that wasn't at least mildly alcoholic, and being simply *thirsty*, I could see Gary almost trembling with the bottle of Coca-Cola in his hand, real Coca-Cola, which may at that moment have been the only one in 'Tambo, at the prospect of shattering it unopened on the bricks in front of the oven. The man, Teófilo Villacorta Arula, who had built the oven had come from Nayhua, where he lives, for the ceremony, and Baltazar's sister and her husband and their children had come, and the old people from next door, don Andrés Llamaqchima and his wife Celestina Champi, who are Teresa's aunt and uncle; Andrés and Celestina were the old woman and the man chopping wood we had encountered the first day. And we became, officially, the godparents of an oven named Gregoria Munaypata— it was the day of Saint Gregory, and Teófilo insisted on a proper name in the feminine form, Gregoria, because the oven is female, and Munaypata, which means pretty place, is the name of the little *pampa* where Baltazar and Teresa's house stands—amid much drinking and dancing to the music of a battery-operated record player. We probably spent that evening drinking too, but I don't remember.

The next day we escaped. We took a long walk to the caves of Tambo T'oqo, which in traditional Quechua mythology is the place from which the original four Inca brothers came. Baltazar wanted us to drink *chicha* with him and his guests that afternoon and made us assure him that we wouldn't be gone long, saying that it should only take us three hours to walk there and back, and tried to give us "one for the road"—the phrase translates literally from Spanish into English. But we slipped away and dawdled all the way to Tambo T'oqo, though it was cloudy and a cold wind blew, exploring other caves along the way. When we got there, the sun had come out, so after inspecting the caves—which, in a flippant mood attributable maybe to the sense of freedom of having successfully dodged the day's drinking and, a more serious concern, to the trial of being strangers in a foreign place in the midst of an important religious occasion, we judged not too impressive, considering that these three shal-

low caves full of bird droppings were the origin place of the Incas—we sat
for hours warming ourselves in the sun on the hill below the caves, eating
bread and oranges and talking. We didn't return to 'Tambo until the children were bringing the animals home, found no one at the house, and
went to bed sober that night, remarkably thankful for such a simple
blessing.

We decided, abruptly, a little desperately perhaps, to go back to Cusco
the next morning. We had been waiting for an opportunity to talk to
Baltazar about renting a room from him for the year, but it was apparent
that, as the festival is celebrated for eight days, he wasn't going to have
time, nor probably be sober enough, to discuss it for several days more,
and besides, Gary was out of cigarettes—he'd given a lot of his supply
away: good cigarettes are a luxury to be shared. We threw our things together and saw the last procession of the festival and part of the *despedida* (the farewell) for the saints, when people gathered in the schoolyard at the top of the hill to see them off, from the back of the truck
named San Martín. Our room in Cusco greeted us with a tranquillity and
a gratifying sense of familiarity which at the moment we badly needed.

3. Corn planting

Dear Elizabeth, Your letter was here when we returned from our second visit to 'Tambo; we had gone out for the festival of Natividad, the village's major festival, celebrated during the week of the eighth, and, we hoped, to find a permanent place to stay there, which we couldn't arrange because everyone was occupied by the celebration. The truck leaves 'Tambo in midmorning, making the two long climbs and descents up into the *puna* and down into the Yaurisque valley and then up and down into the Cusco Valley. It stops down below the lower market, past the railroad tracks, in mid- to late afternoon, and a little weary—it's not a difficult trip, just a long one to make riding in the crowded back of a truck: often in this season as many as fifty people make the trip—we walk up Avenida Grau toward the post office carrying our big backpacks. The post office is not on the way home, and it's a steeper walk home from there than from the lower market, but already we know that we will always go there before we go home. Three letters, and we stop in a café halfway up Avenida Sol to the plaza for a cup of coffee and to read them, though I save yours until I get home. At home, we slide the packs off our shoulders to stand on the floor against the bed: there is another weariness, not physical but intellectual—the disorientation of returning to Cusco from the *campo*. However odd and backward Cusco may seem to us, the crowds, the traffic, the pace are overwhelming. Gary goes out for a sandwich, and I sit on the bed with your letter and begin to unbraid my hair—it is long enough now that I can wear it in two braids the way the *campesina* women do, though my braids are as short as a little girl's. Here, where I read your letter, the sun falls across the opposite hillside and through the blade-like leaves of the eucalyptus which shade the patio in the afternoon; a cat who lives mostly in the red-tiled world of the rooftops above the courtyards and street, a gray-and-white tom whose fights we can hear at night, sits in the sun in the curve of a tile across from our window.

We stayed a week in 'Tambo this time, the longest I have been in the *campo* ever, though our stay was much briefer than we had planned: our supplies ran out because we gave a lot away, as one is supposed to—people are extravagantly generous here. When I write it—*a week*—it doesn't seem much of an accomplishment. It is hard to say why and how it is so difficult, though there are aspects of the difficulty—mainly that of being one who is so essentially *different* whose purpose is to learn to be as *like* as it is possible to be—which are easily understood. I wear a skirt in the village, a full denim skirt with a ruffle at the hem, not at all like the skirts they wear, but at least recognizable as a woman's clothing. And yesterday in the market I bought a heavy woolen shawl like the ones they wear, thick as blankets in red or green or blue with black patterns—mine is blue; while we were there, women were always sending their daughters home to bring a shawl for me, obviously not warm enough in a down vest which leaves my arms uncovered except for my shirt sleeves. Next time I will leave the vest in Cusco. During the festival, there were processions of statues of saints, brought from all of the surrounding villages, led by the *cura*, or priest, who came from Cusco on the truck one morning: crazy parades of priest and images carried on litters, twelve of them, and a crowd of people and at least two bands of trumpets and drums and sometimes flutes playing different songs at the same time. One afternoon there was an amateur bullfight and each day there were soccer games between the teams of the different villages. In between, when the women of the house were working, I helped, in the house peeling raw potatoes with a knife—so much more slowly than they, who peel the whole skin from a potato in one long spiral—or cooked ones with my fingers as they showed me or in the yard in the sun sorting grain spread on a cloth. And I learned a few words of Quechua, the kind you learn when you only know a few words of a language: how to say, What? and, I don't understand, and, What is this called? But once when I spoke one of these barely communicative phrases and it was understood, I realized that I was speaking the language that the Inca themselves spoke. And there is so much to understand simply by knowing the language. You know, this is all very exciting for me, though I have already felt

confused and frustrated and hopeless at times and know I will feel that
way often. I hope I can be less confused in the telling: I can see as I
read over what I have written what a jumble it is. But then it was a
chaotic week in the life of the village, and there will be months ahead
of cooking food and planting crops and the quiet days of the rainy
season when it rains every day and when the work in the fields is done
everyone sits comfortably inside. I cherish the experience of every moment, and so I want to give this to you somehow, if I can . . .

We returned to 'Tambo on the Tuesday following the festival, the
fifteenth, a beautiful clear morning, and again there was room,
barely, for me to ride in the cab of the truck, with the schoolteacher and
her little daughter and another man besides the driver—a little crowded,
but warm. We slept on the floor of the storeroom that night, where we
had slept before, and the next morning talked to Baltazar and Teresa
about arrangements for renting a room from them; they seem truly to
want us to stay here. We settled on the storeroom we were sleeping in—
without the potatoes which are stored there and with one of the beds
from their room and the little table (this was Baltazar's idea)—and two
meals each day for seven thousand *soles* a month. This is a ridiculously
small amount to us, a little more than five dollars, but a small fortune
every month in 'Tambo and a regular income, so that while it seemed to
us the least we would owe them for allowing us to live there, we worry
about its effect on their lives, their relations with other people in the village. We paid them for half of September and also bought from Juana a
lliqlla she'd woven. I will need one. We worked for several hours after
lunch clearing the storeroom, taking down the tools—the short-handled
hoes called *lampa*s and *kuti*s and the footplows, or *chakitaqlla*s—filling
huge woven bags full of seed potatoes, carrying out the *raki*s (the large
chicha jars) Teresa kept there, and storing all of these things in the room
Baltazar and Teresa sleep in and the storeroom above it. I swept the floor
with a bundle of slender branches, and we brought in the bed from their
room—a simple wooden frame with no cushioning—and the table,
which they apparently don't use, and made a sort of stool out of two
adobes stood on end and tied together with a rope to support each other.
We blessed the house by each of us sprinkling a few drops of *trago* from a
cup onto the floor at either side of the door and a few in the center of the
room: home. It's a proper house, with our two metal cups hanging from a
gnarled stick suspended from a beam, the little kerosene Primus stove in
the corner, a blue plastic basin for washing, the *lliqlla* we bought from
Juana to sit on on the low earthen bench along one wall, our clothes
draped over a bar hanging across one side just below the ceiling, and lit at

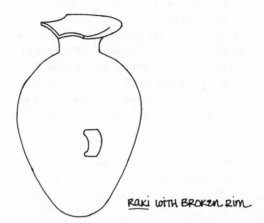

RaKi with BROKEN RiM

night by candles and a small kerosene lamp made from a little bottle, a bottle cap, and a bit of string. A few days later, with Baltazar's help, we broke an adobe out of the side wall for a window.

The next few days were quiet. Our presence here seems to be accepted with remarkable ease—maybe a function of a natural kind of disbelief: I'm sure that they, like we, don't realize the full implication of our proposal—which we announce so easily—to live here for a year, that if we stay here as we have arranged to do, they will have to deal with us every day. How can this be comprehensible, really? We are terribly foreign and our arrival unexpected, unforeseen; we don't in any way fit into their lives as they know them, as they have always lived them—for Baltazar and Teresa the experience of fifty-some years. And a year is a long time. For now, they seem to see us as a couple of unusual, possibly interesting, guests and surely recognize certain advantages offered by our presence, like, undeniably, the income our room and board will represent. And we have demonstrated to them that we are willing, indeed want and expect, to work, though it must be clear to them already that there is no recognizable form in which they can return this favor as they would for other people in the village—by working for them in turn. And, faced now with the very concrete reality of something which has been for so long only an idea, a bit of elaborate imagining, Gary and I seem to grope for some foundation on which to base expectations of our immediate future, even of tomorrow: as it is, we have none—no history, no relationships of family or friendship to delineate the boundaries of our lives here, no instinct based on even the brief but daily experience a small Quechua child would have—only untested intuition derived from our knowledge of Quechua life in general. Except for a few phrases, I don't even speak the language enough to understand what's going on. So we seem to grasp for something that will anchor us, to accept unquestioningly these newly formed alliances though they have no precedent in any of our lives and their actual nature, I expect, will be revealed to us only by time, to assume friendships so that we can know, from moment to moment, how to behave with each other.

On Thursday, Gary helped Baltazar build up the adobe walls around the oven, preparing to roof the little shelter. I spent the day with Teresa, spinning and helping her cook, grinding dried sprouted corn for *chicha* in an old food mill fixed to a stump and peeling potatoes, a task which seems to be traditionally delegated to children if they are available, a category into which I fit easily because I don't know anything. Baltazar had to attend a *faena* (a community work project) the next day to clear an irrigation ditch near Qoipa, the master *acequia* of his *ayllu*, Ayllu Nayhua. He invited us to walk halfway with him and managed somehow that neither he nor Daniel would actually be seen walking with us. He sent Daniel ahead of him in the morning with a horse loaded with a big skin bag full of *chicha* across its back and then sent us ahead of him saying that he would catch up with us. About halfway, Daniel had slowed enough that we almost caught up with him, and Baltazar came cantering around the bend behind us on his horse—because he is crippled, Baltazar always rides a horse if he must travel any distance. We stood in the road and he pointed out the villages we could see from there, telling us their names, and the *apus*—the greatest of the encircling hills, sacred to the community—and an old hacienda; and then Gary gave him some cigarettes and coca for him to offer to the men he worked with, and he and Daniel went on. We sat in the sun on a hillside overlooking the fields down toward the Apurimac for the rest of the morning and then walked back to 'Tambo. Baltazar came home about sundown, very drunk as Teresa had predicted: such important work is always accompanied by plenty of *chicha* and probably *trago* as well. The next morning he returned to the *faena*, and I sat to spin with Teresa. Another woman came, and Teresa began serving us *chicha* in earnest, saying something about getting drunk in the morning, apparently determined that if men can get drunk while they're working, women can too. Gary went to visit Angélico, the son of the governor, as he was clearly not included in the party: Teresa did not serve him even once, though he was sitting near us—an unthinkable breach of Quechua etiquette—having apparently elected Gary to represent all men. Soon after he left, though, the other woman left too, and Teresa got up to do something else. I felt the effects of the *chicha*, strong *chicha* left from the festival, for hours.

On Sunday, Baltazar, Teresa, and Daniel packed food and filled big,

several-gallon plastic jugs with *chicha* to go up to Baltazar's sister's house
for the night: she lives in a small settlement, Wayninpampa, about an
hour above 'Tambo on the road toward Cusco, and they keep Baltazar
and Teresa's sheep there; their daughters pasture them in the broad
pampa around the community, and Baltazar and Teresa go once in a
while to check on them. Teresa served us breakfast and an early lunch
before they left; from then on, eleven-year-old Leonarda was in charge.
We were admonished by Baltazar and Teresa as they left to put the six
young chickens back in their pen for the night and the ladder across the
gate, and then they set out, Baltazar on his horse. As soon as they were
gone, Leonarda and Jaime and Eloy, Juana's two older boys, perhaps four
and six or so, got into the *chicha*. Children are allowed to drink *chicha*,
but though it is very mild, they are usually only given half cupfuls or a
little from an adult's cup, and they must develop a great curiosity about
the elaborate rituals of drinking *chicha* and what happens to people when
they drink a lot of cups full. With Leonarda as hostess, they were soon
giggling in the kitchen, though perhaps it was only the thrill of the forbidden that made them giggle. She brought the jug outside and served us
some, with a child's studied formality, evidently having decided to do
everything her mother usually does. We went out visiting, and she spent
the afternoon cooking, though without Teresa's incomparable nutritional
wisdom and expertise: when we returned, she served us toasted corn and
beans and both boiled and fried potatoes—all favorite foods of children—looking after us as a woman looks after her guests. And then we
caught the chickens, Jaime helping in his mischievous fashion, and we
helped her feed the cows, which Daniel and Leonarda's older brother
Hugo had driven home from the pasture. (Unfortunately, after Teresa's
two good meals in the morning, the potatoes we'd been offered at the
house we visited, and Leonarda's well-meant generosity, Celestina brought
over a big bowl of ground *tarwi*, a kind of nutty-flavored bean which we
love, with potatoes and *mot'e*, and then the widow Pascuala, who lives
next door and whose corn field Gary was to help plant the next day, a
bowl of hot soup. Everyone seemed to have been advised that we needed
to be fed, which we appreciated, but we ended up having to transfer a lot
of this unexpected bounty to our own bowls and feed it to Sandor, the
dog, after dark and were almost caught at it by Leonarda. You can't refuse such care and generosity and wouldn't want to, but you could easily
eat yourself sick.)

Leonarda is the youngest of Baltazar and Teresa's children. Although I
don't understand what she says to Teresa when we are working together
or what Teresa says to her, I learn a lot about Leonarda from the tone of
their voices and the tenor of the exchanges between them: Leonarda is

blithe and willful and insolent and seldom does what Teresa asks her to. Teresa often scolds her, though the scolding seems to make little impression on her. Leonarda takes after Baltazar in the cast of her features and seems to have inherited his renegade spirit as well; or maybe she's just going through some normal phase of pre-adolescent behavior. Between Juana, the eldest of the children, and Leonarda are three boys, though the first son, Jesús, went to Lima to find work some years ago and has not been back since then. Then there is Hugo, who must be about seventeen or eighteen. We have gotten to know him only slightly; he is shy and aloof. He had returned from Puerto Maldonado, down in the jungle to the east where he had been working for three months in the logging camps or the gold mines, just before we first arrived here. He seems to spend most of his time now with other young men of the village; we see them in the plaza sometimes playing soccer. He and Daniel look very much alike except that Hugo is taller and more slender, his features more sharply defined: they have the same smooth dark skin and very dark eyes and lovely smile, like Juana's, and the same shock of thick, straight, black hair. Of the whole family, Daniel is the most open and unselfconscious with us. He often comes to visit us in the evenings and would sit and ask questions and talk to us for hours if we didn't finally tell him we were tired and had to go to bed. He seems to feel an irresistible curiosity about us and our habits and indulges it unabashedly. We give him cups of instant bouillon or hot chocolate which Gary brings from Cusco.

We have finally sorted out Juana's family as well: all of the little boys we have seen around the house—of whom, now that we've learned to recognize them and call them by name, there turn out to be only three—belong to Juana. Jaime is her oldest child and spends a lot of time here with his grandparents, helping them with small chores and pasturing the animals with Leonarda, and often sleeps here. Jaime is a distinct and indomitable personality, irrepressible and mischievous, and a little clown, always making faces and playing tricks. His little brother Eloy looks almost exactly like him, so much so that we still often cannot tell them apart, except for Eloy's constantly runny nose and the fact that Eloy is Jaime's opposite in personality, very quiet and shy, almost unnoticeable, as if he were Jaime's shadow. The smallest is Orlando, who is only two and a half and still round with baby fat but with a lovely, pudgy little face which promises his mother's beauty. He is intrepid and often tags along with Jaime while Eloy stays close to his mother. Their father is a young man named Ricardo, who came to 'Tambo from Paruro. We have met him only once, when he came on Sunday to talk to Baltazar about some business. Jaime gets his devilish imp's face from his father and, I suspect from that brief encounter with Ricardo, much of his manner as well.

Monday was dull and gray, and I was glad of the prospect of sitting in Pascuala's kitchen, cooking for the men who would plant her field, instead of alone in our house while Gary worked. She gave us breakfast early in the morning—two bowls of soup each and *mot'e; mot'e* is dried corn which is broken off the cob and then boiled; there is always a pot of it in every house, and it is served with almost every meal. So began another day of eating too much. Gary fetched a *lampa* (a short crooked hoe with a spade-like blade) from Baltazar's *comedor* and was collected to go to another house for another breakfast and *chicha* and back to Pascuala's for more fortifying *chicha* before finally starting down the path with don Andrés to the field. I went home to finish my chores—washing our coffee cups and sweeping the dirt floor—then picked up my spindle and returned to sit with Celestina in Pascuala's kitchen, squatting on the floor near the door, something my bones and muscles have yet to grow accustomed to.

The point of such cooking is to demonstrate gratitude for the help provided, without which no agricultural task could be completed, so meals served in the fields are bountiful and a little bit special, the only times, usually, except for festival meals, when meat is served. After Pascuala served us yet another bowl of soup, we set about catching two of Pascuala's *qowi*s.

Before the introduction of the domesticated animals of the Old World, *qowi*s (guinea pigs), along with the llama, were the main source of meat for the people of the Andes. They are still the most commonly eaten meat—pigs and chickens and sheep and goats are too costly to acquire and keep to eat except on extraordinary occasions—and a "flock" of a dozen or so guinea pigs inhabits the kitchen of every household. Though they live in a sort of symbiotic relationship with the family, they remain an essentially feral population adapted to the particular environment of the Quechua kitchen, making daring forays from dark corners behind *chicha* jars and stacks of firewood to snatch vegetable peelings from the working and eating area and roaming the kitchen freely only when the house is empty and at night. Sometimes the children bring green plants from the pastures for them, but other than this they are never deliberately fed, and they are not named or treated as pets in any other way. I can see why.

Pascuala's kitchen is divided toward one end by a waist-high wall in which at floor level are two square openings of maybe a foot. Pascuala crouched by one of these and began fishing around behind the wall with a stick. After a moment, a *qowi* ran out and darted along the wall and into the other opening, like a carved figure on an old clock. Pascuala beckoned Celestina to sit in front of the other hole, covering it with her skirt, and fished around until more *qowi*s emerged and, finding their route of escape blocked, scurried under the woodpile or behind the stacked pots in the darkness of the corner. Then Celestina and I each sat in front of an opening while she poked her stick into the woodpile or her hand among the pots until she and Celestina had captured the two she wanted: big ones and as plump as any *qowi*s I'd seen. I watched the rest of the process as I peeled pots of potatoes, grateful—more so than they might ever have suspected—for their assumption of my lack of knowledge and skill as a cook. Pascuala killed the *qowi*s by wringing their necks, turning the heads completely backward then straightening them, and laid them on their backs on the floor before the fireplace. She gave me a small clay pitcher of *chicha* and said something about a *t'inkasqa* and showed me that I should sprinkle *chicha* with my fingertips over each *qowi*, then pour a little into their mouths and on their bellies—it was either their bellies or their sexual parts: she was not very precise in her demonstration, but they both giggled. She gave Celestina a cup, and Celestina did the same and we both drank. The *qowi*s were scalded by dunking them into a pot of boiling water, and most of the silky hair was pulled off; what was left was mostly shaved off with a knife, though the hair never seems

Qoncha

to get completely removed and wasn't this time. Then a crosswise slit was made in the belly of each, and the entrails removed by pulling them out through it. Pascuala put all of the entrails into a bowl, setting aside the livers in a separate bowl: these, the livers, were cooked in the coals of the fire and given to us later to eat. The entrails were cleaned, intestines and all, meticulously and rinsed with clean water. Blood was caught and saved in a bowl. Several potatoes were diced into very small pieces, soaked in the blood, then stuffed into the cleaned stomachs of the two *qowi*s. Pascuala put the stomachs into the coals at the mouth of the fireplace to cook, and we also ate these before we went down to the field. She cut the jaws of the *qowi*s open with a knife and then worked with her back to me for a while. When she turned, she had put each animal on a skewer, lengthwise, and tied their hind feet to the sticks, the top ends of the sticks braced against the upper jaws of the animals. Into the cavities of their bodies she stuffed leaves which proved to be wild mint, the potatoes left from stuffing the stomachs, and some of the cleaned entrails, and the *qowi*s were propped in front of the fire to cook. She went out and returned with a lean ham hock, cut off a chunk of it, and occasionally rubbed the *qowi*s with it to baste them with the meager fat while they cooked. When they were nearly done, Pascuala made cuts to test the progress of the cooking between the bodies and both forelegs of each.

Everything was ready: *tarwi* ground on a stone and cooked with diced potatoes, a combination of rice and macaroni, cooked after first toasting it brown in a dry pot over the fire, *mot'e,* and the *qowi*s. The animals, their skins brown now, were taken from the fire and, still on the skewers, rudely hacked into pieces: the heads cut off, and the legs, and the rest into apparently random pieces. Celestina and I were each given a large plate filled with some of everything we had prepared, including the choicest parts, the legs, of the *qowi*s and the delicacies: the livers and stomachs. We ate and then packed the food into pots and plates and small plastic pails and wrapped those in cloths to keep the food warm. Pascuala got a bottle of *trago* from one of the shops and then wrapped everything in *lliqlla*s which we tied around our shoulders—only Pascuala and I were going to the field, so our loads were large and heavy—except for two plastic jugs full of *chicha*. I took the bigger one. I found the trail difficult and slow with the weight of the *lliqlla* on my back and the heavy jug in my hand upsetting my equilibrium. I also felt slightly ill: besides the meals and all of the *chicha,* which is very filling, I had also been offered three large potatoes, ones too nice I suppose to chop up and cook into mush and so given to honor the guest, though I managed to sneak two of them back into the pot when no one was looking; and Celestina had not been able to finish the meal Pascuala had served her, and so gave it to me as well. It would have been unforgivably rude to refuse it. There must be some polite way of coping with this problem.

It was much farther to the field than we had been led to believe—the Quechua, perhaps expressing an optimism required by the exigencies of their environment, will invariably tell you that the route you must follow is perfectly flat (*pura pampa*), virtually an impossibility in the Andes, and that the place to which you are going is very close by ("¡cerquita no más!"). It was down at the bottom of the broad slope of the mountainside below 'Tambo, almost to where the land drops off to the river. I fell farther and farther behind Pascuala until she stopped finally to let me catch up and then stayed with me to hurry me along. When we arrived, there was another woman sitting by the field, and the men were nearly finished with their work. Four men: Gary and old don Andrés and two young men, Lorenzo and Fortunato, who is Pascuala's nephew. Lorenzo drove the team of bulls—a striking team, one mostly black and white, the other blond—and don Andrés, walking behind the long scratch plow, dropped the seed into the furrow with an easy rhythm. Gary and Fortunato, side by side all day, were breaking clods with their short hoes to cover the seed and by now, in the companionship of hard work and *chicha*, were calling each other *compadre*. We put down our burdens, and the woman who had been waiting there gave me a horn full of *chicha*, which was unfortunately difficult to drink but more difficult to refuse without hurting her feelings; and then I wandered away, ostensibly to find a private place, and simply never came all the way back to where the women sat waiting for the men to finish. I sat on a bank a little distance away, out of range of the *chicha*, to watch the motion of the planting. In the field beyond Pascuala's another group planted, an odd group, only two men with a short plow and a hoe and a thin woman in dark clothes and a dirty white market woman's hat who was planting the seed, although normally only men plant corn. The scene had an eerily forlorn feel about it, the three figures isolated on the mountainside under a gray and threatening sky, in sharp contrast to the warm camaraderie of shared work I had felt all morning in the kitchen and which was apparent among the men in Pascuala's field.

When the men had plowed and planted the last furrows of Pascuala's field, they sat near the women and I rejoined the group, and the food and *chicha* and *trago* were served. It turned out that the woman who was there when we arrived—I never learned who she was—had also brought food, though Pascuala apparently had not known that she would, and had already fed everyone, so no one really wanted anything to eat. I knew how they felt, precisely, and when Fortunato generously gave me his plate, I turned my face away to the dark mountains of the Otra Banda with tears, which I couldn't let them see, of simple, childlike misery in my eyes: I knew I would die if I had to eat that much more. I didn't: I gave it back to Pascuala—which may have been gauche, even rude, but I could feign a *gringa*'s ignorance of good manners. And the *trago* actually made me feel better somehow.

The sky had grown darker and more evil-looking all afternoon, and finally it began to hail. If the weather is good, men will often sit for some time after a day of work, enjoying the rest and the refreshment of food and drink, and for a few minutes, the men seemed determined to enjoy even the hail; but soon we hurriedly packed everything up and started the long, wet climb up the hill. When we reached the houses, Baltazar and Teresa had returned from Wayninpampa and welcomed us, Baltazar also a bit drunk, and we all crowded into Pascuala's small kitchen. Baltazar sent Leonarda to get the record player, and we managed somehow to dance in the tiny space between the fireplace and the earthen benches along the walls, the grinding stone and the *chicha* jars. At some point, I realized that Pascuala was crying. The combination of *chicha* and *trago* has a tendency to bring tears to anyone who has any reason at all to cry, and I felt very bad for her. I never understood why she was crying; maybe in combination with the *chicha* and *trago* and the relief of the day's trying effort being over, the inherent sadness of her situation—being without a husband, having to depend upon the good will and charity of relatives and friends—overcame her. And Baltazar had been gently teasing us, Gary and me, urging us as he often does to call each other *yanachay*, a term of endearment (it means "little dark one") which couples use to call each other, and I thought that maybe that, on top of everything else, had only emphasized to her her aloneness. Really, I couldn't interpret her tears at all, but I reached over to her behind Teresa, put my hand on her arm and squeezed it, not even sure that that gesture would be understood, hoping that its simplicity and sincerity would translate into Quechua. Small comfort from a near stranger.

The next morning, Baltazar and Teresa seemed gratifyingly pleased at the work we had done, independently of them, as if we had begun to prove ourselves, doing voluntarily the work that is expected of an adult man and woman. I felt that we had, in a small way, if only to ourselves.

4. San Miguel and the anniversary of the district

We went back to Cusco for a few days toward the end of the month, mainly to take showers—it is going to take a while to become accustomed to not bathing: it's something people seldom do at an altitude of eleven thousand five hundred feet in ice-cold mountain water—and stayed in Cusco a couple of days longer than we intended to. It seems to be our fate that we never get to 'Tambo on the day we plan to, not because we don't try, but because something always happens. We got to the truck stop a little after five, earlier than usual, and there was not a single truck waiting there. Not one. We were told that one had already left, the fast one—a small, white truck with no name painted above the cab, whose young driver is always looking at his watch and periodically crosses himself. We waited, and some other trucks came but not bound for 'Tambo, and finally all of the villagers who had been waiting for a ride to 'Tambo left the truck stop. We'd waited for more than an hour, and it was well after dawn. We had to assume that if *they* gave up there was no hope, and we lifted our packs onto our backs, picked up the new split-reed mattress we had bought for the bed and the jug of kerosene, caught a cab and went home. It was just as well: I spent the rest of the day in bed, with a fever, a sore throat, and a cough that made me long for home, wondering melodramatically—maybe it was the fever—if I would ever see my parents and my sister again. I stayed in bed most of Saturday as well, and we left finally on Sunday without even having unpacked. There had apparently been a sudden increase in the price of gasoline and at the same time a shortage—vendors hold back supplies in anticipation of the new, higher price—and these circumstances had prevented a lot of the usual truck traffic.

We helped Baltazar make bread on Monday, a huge amount, for just one family. Gary went to bed in the middle of the afternoon, not feeling well, a condition diagnosed as *gripe*, which apparently I had had and Teresa as well just before we returned, and I helped Baltazar at the oven, stoking the fire. After the family had packed up all of the bread and gone home, Baltazar gave me one of the *wawitas*, the bread babies, which they had given him.

The twenty-ninth of September was the beginning of the festival of San Miguel. It was also Teresa's birthday, and relatives and friends began to gather at breakfast time for soup and a sweet milk punch Teresa had made spiked with *trago*. The birthday completely overshadowed the festival for the family for two days, which they spent drinking *chicha* and *trago*, the *trago* sometimes mixed with the achingly sweet soft drinks sold in the shops, a concoction which tastes like cough syrup but at least doesn't smell like *trago*. I represented us at the party while Gary rested, still recovering from his illness. The drinking and dancing went on all day, though Teresa herself was absent some of the time, at the house of her *ahijado* (godson), who had a *cargo* for San Miguel, and on through the night until about four in the morning, though I went to bed about nine. They began again the next morning, but we—Gary feeling somewhat better but wary of the effects of the *chicha* and *trago* on his still-fragile health—took a long walk, out to the saddle of Qeruru, where we sat for hours above the steep *quebrada* of a little tributary of the Apurimac, talking and watching the light on the mountains of the Otra Banda.

Today, as we sat quietly in our house reading and writing, Baltazar came over to talk, possessed of that extreme solemnity of which only the very drunk are capable, about the reaction to us in the town, about how people were wondering aloud why he was apparently running a hotel for *gringo* tourists. When he is drunk, he has a strong tendency to repeat himself, so we were impressed by at least the possibility that there was overwhelming public criticism of Baltazar because of us, though after a while we began to suspect that he may simply have been voicing his own fears, emphasized by *chicha* and *trago*, and once everybody sobered up, everything would be all right. We listened attentively, saying little because it was hard to know what to say: if it is true, it is no real surprise to us. It is the kind of reaction that might be expected and something that we know we will simply have to weather. Our immediate future depends on whether Baltazar and Teresa are willing to ride it out with us, but that was obviously not the moment to discuss it with Baltazar, no matter how urgent it seems to us that we talk about it. Maybe tomorrow.

But the celebration continued on Thursday, and on Friday they completely disappeared—they were gone by the time we woke and returned only after dark, having spent that day drinking too, at the house just above theirs, with the family of a friend of Hugo's who had just returned from Puerto Maldonado.

Late that night, long after we had closed the door, Baltazar came in to talk, very frankly, he said—said it over and over again, in fact—about how important it was that Gary show his papers to the local authorities: the president, the mayor, the governor of the district, the director of the schools. Gary had given Baltazar a copy of his letter of introduction from the university, and Baltazar now seemed to believe that this document and any others Gary could produce would dispel any suspicion regarding our motive for being here and Baltazar's for putting us up. It seemed best, of course, to do it right away, immediately, so they planned to go together first thing the next morning, before Baltazar returned to the work on the irrigation canal, to visit the village officials. Gary also suggested that he address the next town meeting—a general community assembly during which the village's business is discussed and decisions are made—whenever it was called, to explain personally to the gathered townspeople who we are and what our purpose is in coming to 'Tambo. Baltazar agreed enthusiastically that this was a good idea and that Gary should do so at the very next meeting. He left with the promise that he would wake us early the next morning so he and Gary could call on the village authorities. We went to bed with some sense of relief. We had begun to feel helpless, not knowing for certain exactly what the reaction to us was in the village but fearing the worst, having to rely on Baltazar's drunken interpretation, and not really being able to talk to him about it because of the endless concurrent celebrations of birthday and festival. At last we could do something positive to influence our own fate.

Saturday morning, however, we woke later than usual, without a knock on the door, and we found Baltazar gone: Teresa said he had gone to a town meeting—they are often called unexpectedly—and in spite of their fervent agreement that it was important that Gary meet with this gathering at the first opportunity, he had not even wakened us. Gary considered going to the meeting anyway but hesitated to intrude unannounced and possibly put Baltazar in an awkward position, so we sat and waited for him to come home. When he returned, he left almost immediately for the *faena*, and he seemed pointedly to avoid us as he saddled his horse and collected his things. Had he forgotten? Or had he deliberately left Gary behind? We complained to each other of the frustration of never apparently getting a straight story or the whole story from anyone about what is going on, how people are feeling, what their intentions really are: we have these conversations, especially with Baltazar, which do not subsequently seem to bear any relation to any reality which is apparent to us. Maybe this is a cultural difference, and the simple honesty that we assume about such things is not so important to these people; or maybe they only treat *us* this way, so foreign that the rules do not apply to us. But it is profoundly disorienting.

After Baltazar had gone, Hugo and Daniel and Jaime came to collect Gary to go with them to a field just above the village to break up the earth in preparation for planting. The earth had been turned with footplows and lay in huge slabs which had been baked hard by the dry-season sun. Each of them carried a short-handled hoe; Jaime had a miniature one. I helped Teresa cook a meal and in the early afternoon went with her to bring it to Gary and the boys in the field. We returned to the village as soon as they had eaten, but they didn't come home until the brief tropical twilight after the sun had set. Baltazar's day was even longer though: we had hoped that the morning's confusion would be dispelled before the day ended, but Baltazar had not returned by the time we blew out the candles and went to sleep.

Baltazar and Teresa were gone again the next morning by the time we awoke. Daniel and Hugo reported that they had gone to a house-roofing—the owners of a house to be roofed gather together as many people as possible to help finish the work in one day, rewarding them with plenty of food and drink and a hearty celebration when the work is done. Baltazar and Teresa would probably not be back until very late, and we were on our own again. Gary decided to take matters into his own hands. We had already spoken to the president of the village, and Gary had met the governor, so he determined to go to visit the mayor. He asked Hugo and Daniel if he would be at home. Hugo said yes, but Daniel quickly corrected him, saying no, he wasn't at home. We withdrew to our house to recoup and try to think of some constructive way to spend another long day with nothing to do. We decided to walk down to Nayhua, 'Tambo's largest annex, far below 'Tambo in the river valley, on the bank of the Apurimac. We would want to go there eventually anyway. Daniel tried to talk us out of this expedition as well, but we were not to be dissuaded, and he finally gave us the name of one of his father's *compadres* there. We collected a few things and our sleeping bags to take along and set out feeling absurdly smug just to be doing something other than sitting around the house waiting for something to happen. The descent and the climb back the next day were physically involving and felt good, and we saw the village, which is lovely and tropical, nearly a mile below 'Tambo in altitude, and sat by the Apurimac, the headwaters of the distant Amazon, with our feet in its icy water, and we made friends with people who will be contacts for us in Nayhua should we ever need them. We began the climb to 'Tambo with a small and newly unaccustomed sense of accomplishment and satisfaction.

Nayhua was a respite. As we climbed toward 'Tambo, we also returned to the state of mounting tension that we had briefly left behind, and as we approached the village, a vague oppression made the small burdens we carried subtly heavier, the mountainside steeper. By the time we reached 'Tambo, we had conceived the idea of going back to Cusco for a few days to collect ourselves and perhaps to gain a clearer perspective on the situation we were in. The yard was quiet when we got there, only Teresa at home. We made ourselves some coffee and then offered her some, which she accepted with a charming combination of childlike delight—coffee is a luxury, like anything that must be bought, and they seldom have it— veiled by her dignified grace. We spent a good part of the afternoon sitting with her in the yard while she worked at small chores, and she and Gary talked occasionally in Quechua.

Baltazar had begun talking weeks before, soon after we had christened the oven, about making an expedition to Cusco to buy tiles for the roof of the little shelter over the oven. Gary, as the oven's godfather, was to go along, not only, I suspected, because it was spiritually appropriate, but also because as the ritual sponsor of the oven he could probably be obligated to contribute substantially to the cost of purchasing and transporting the tiles. But that was all right; if the trip went the way Baltazar was planning it, it would be an opportunity for Gary to confirm and fortify his relationship with Baltazar, which seemed at the moment to be flagging. Baltazar had said they would travel together to Cusco on the truck and stay with his sister who lives in the city. They would buy the tiles there and contract with one of the truck drivers to transport them to 'Tambo. Baltazar went on and on about what a good time they would have and Gary, responding to his enthusiasm, promised to take him out to lunch in a nice restaurant. Baltazar had originally planned to make the trip on the fifteenth of October, then decided to go on the tenth, today, which was then only five days away. If he did mean to go, we didn't want our escape to Cusco to interfere with the project, so Gary asked Teresa if Baltazar was going to Cusco to buy the tiles on the tenth. She said no, and something about the way she said it implied that it had seemed to her an absurd question, as if she had said, Whatever gave you that idea? We decided to go to Cusco the next day.

A little later in that afternoon's fitful conversation, Teresa told Gary about the house-roofing they had been to, and we learned whose house it had been. It was the mayor's house—the mayor, whom Daniel had told us would not be home that day.

We sat outside Tuesday morning, talking with the family, and after we had noted all of the things they wanted us to bring for them from Cusco, Baltazar offered us new plans for today, Saturday, his trip to Cusco to buy tiles apparently forgotten: we would prepare the seed potatoes on Friday when Gary and I returned, and on Saturday we would plant. Baltazar rhapsodized: the men—Baltazar, Gary, Hugo, and Daniel—would go to the field, bringing *chicha* and coca. Leonarda and I would follow with *mot'e* and potatoes for eating and perhaps *trago,* and we would build a *wathiya* (an oven of earth and stones) and bake potatoes, and maybe Gary and I would bring some canned tuna from Cusco and we would all eat this feast and drink *chicha* . . . We began to look forward to it immediately: it would be the first time we would all work together, we and the family. We assured him that we would be back on Friday—if we waited to return until Saturday, it would be too late when we arrived to plant that day.

The days in Cusco were hectic and hardly restful: we had barely enough time to get done the things we wanted to accomplish—all of the correspondence, getting our clothes washed, restocking our supplies, and buying the things Baltazar and Teresa wanted. We left, nevertheless, yesterday, Friday morning, feeling as if we had hardly been there. Baltazar was at the *faena,* and we spent a peaceful day helping Teresa around the house and helping Daniel prepare the seed potatoes, breaking off the sprouts which had begun to grow as the potatoes lay in the moist darkness of the storeroom, a process which he called simply *akllay* (to select or choose), though most of the selection of potatoes for seed had apparently been done at the time of harvest and storage. Baltazar returned home after sunset with Hugo from the *faena,* with a story on his lips which, a little drunk, he had apparently been repeating to Hugo himself all the way home—about how Hugo had heard some men say that if Baltazar Quispe was not there the next day, they wouldn't be able to work, as if someone had said, "Boy, I just don't know what we'd do without don Baltazar . . ." He told the story a few more times for our benefit, while Gary asked Hugo about the *faena.* We asked him if this meant that we weren't going to plant today, and Baltazar explained that Gary would go with Hugo and Daniel to the field to plant the potatoes. We were disappointed and, finally, angry. Gary told him then that what he wanted was to work with Baltazar, not just to work, and that if Baltazar wasn't going to plant this time, he didn't intend to either, pointing out to Baltazar that he had told us something that we had counted on, arranged our own plans around, apparently, now, for no purpose. He understood, in the end, that we were upset, and I think he understood why, and we parted formally and courteously. He came over to our house a few minutes later to say that we would postpone the planting until Monday when they could all work together. As if to appease us, he started to talk about our plans to make bread tomorrow, for ourselves for the first time since we've been here, about the pleasure of working together, the women shaping the bread, the men tending the fire, and everyone eating fresh bread hot out of the oven with butter Gary and I had brought for the occasion. We had bought real yeast and shortening and a whole arroba—twenty-five pounds—of fine white flour, which had not been easy to get out here. We wanted it to be special for them. But a little while ago, Daniel mentioned as we were looking at the instructions printed on the package of yeast that they would get up at three in the morning to heat the oven. This seemed ominous to us: Baltazar never to our knowledge, even for festivals when he knows he will be busy all day, starts making bread at three in the morning, and it was unlikely that anyone was going to get up at three in the morning to do it just for the fun of it. When we asked Daniel why, he explained that his father was going to work on another community project, to build a house for an old woman, tomorrow. We felt almost wicked, resenting involuntarily Baltazar's commitment to help to build a house for an *abuelita,* as Daniel put it (a "little grandmother"). But we won't bake bread tomorrow either. We didn't press Daniel; we will talk to Baltazar later.

Maybe we expect Baltazar to make a commitment to us which he isn't able to make or, more likely, which he simply doesn't understand. But Gary has begun to feel that he is being used, that he simply does Baltazar's everyday work while Baltazar is out gaining status by performing community services and valiantly commanding his *ayllu*'s efforts—and receives nothing in return. In more than a month, Gary has not once worked with Baltazar in the fields, though he has worked with other men once or twice and with Daniel and Hugo. He enjoys of course working with Daniel and Hugo, but he didn't come here just to learn how to break clods. When he works with Baltazar as he has when he is baking bread, he learns things the boys can't tell him about traditions and history and the reasons for things. He could learn as much from other men perhaps, but he hasn't had much chance to work with others because most of his time has been monopolized by Baltazar, if with nothing more than grandiose propositions. Why will they so elaborate our humble mutual plans if they know that, in the normal course of events in their lives, they so often don't end up doing what they've planned? I realize that part of the problem is our own need, in our position of relative insecurity here, for inclusion, for reassurance, our need to discover some element of this life on which we can depend, assume, and take for granted. And part of the problem is that each party to this odd relationship between Baltazar and Teresa and us probably understands that relationship differently, and it has not been made clear that what Gary wants in exchange for his labor is knowledge, a lot of which he will gain simply by being in Baltazar's presence as he does what he normally does. But right now all we really want is to know what is going on, not to be kept in the dark, and I begin to feel somehow humiliated, used, that our good faith is being abused, and resentful. I try to suppress those feelings: I know they are harmful, if only to our work here, and that probably, living here within their society, I haven't even a right to feel them—they have their own lives to live and we are intruders. So, unless we can resolve this with Baltazar somehow, either we must get used to it—or find somewhere else to live, start all over again. In the meantime: we determine to make our own plans based on our needs, wants, and convenience, regardless of Baltazar's proposals.

Even the aspects that have become most familiar and simple, almost mundane, about such a deeply foreign experience seem unfamiliar and confusing when one pauses to really think about them. So one is left finally with only oneself as a core of familiar reality, almost only habits and a few cherished possessions which could not be left behind more than with oneself, because environment affects self and with few sort of recognizable situations to respond to, even your own behavior, the inflection of your own voice, your own gestures seem almost like someone else's. I am glad for odd little things—and sometimes foolishly moved by them—like the rings I wear, my great-aunt Celia's engagement ring which my grandmother gave me and the garnet Gary bought for our wedding, the scent of my perfume when we go back to Cusco, my tall gray cowboy boots standing by the bed there. Reassurances, tangible ones, that I am still me, however I am altered by this experience.

The difficulty, whatever it really was, with Baltazar eases gradually as we get to know each other better and since Gary and I resolved not to expect anything to proceed as planned. So: maybe we have learned a lesson.

Teresa seems to be the most stable element in the family, patient and kind. She and I have grown fairly fond of each other, and she comes now to our house to visit with us sometimes as she spins. I work with her during the day, grinding *wiñapu* (the dried sprouted corn) for *chicha*, peeling and cutting potatoes, cutting the leaves of some wild greens called *yuyu*, which grow in the corn fields, for a dish called *yuyu hawcha*. And she talks to me, as she might talk to a child though without a trace of condescension, repeating words and phrases as if talking to herself so I will finally repeat them, suddenly recognizing their meanings, and learn the words gradually. And so we communicate, she in Quechua, I with a few words of Spanish, which she seems to understand a little, and fewer of Quechua and many gestures and demonstrations; and a companionship with which I feel increasingly comfortable begins to develop. Juana came over one morning with some little bits of weaving, the narrow warps for the tiny woven straps called *watu*s which are used to tie skirts, and gave me one to work on, showing me how to weave the pattern. I struggled with it almost continuously for a couple of days. Teresa never learned to weave *pallay* (the patterns), extraordinary in a Quechua village where almost all women weave—Juana had learned from other girls when she was young—and one morning when I sat outside bent over my little tangle of yarn, Teresa came and sat down close beside me and took it out of my hands to try it. It was touching to see her struggling with as much difficulty as I had, she who spins so finely—putting in a few rows, saying, No, that's no good, taking them out again saying, I don't know, I don't know how to do it; both of us studying it, shaking our heads in puzzlement, laughing at ourselves. I wanted to hug her.

Gary went with Daniel to Qeruru one day to gather firewood. Hunting through the brush for dry branches, Gary found in the bushes a condor feather—enormous, more than a foot long, as thick as my little finger at the shaft, black as a moonless night, clean and unbroken. Daniel coveted it, and Baltazar said it was good luck: its presence was so powerful that we felt it almost had to be an omen of some sort. We marveled at the thought of the creature that had borne it.

Tuesday was a busy day: Thursday the twenty-second of October is the anniversary of the district—it was officially designated a district by President Belaúnde himself in 1964, and one of Baltazar's favorite stories is of Belaúnde, the president of Peru, landing in the plaza of 'Tambo in a helicopter to preside over the ceremony. Though not a traditional holiday, it is celebrated with many elements of traditional festivals—bands, dancers, and of course lots of *chicha* and *trago*—and Baltazar has a *cargo* for it. I have learned something about *cargo*s: it is the wife who does all the work. Baltazar put up the money for a band of local musicians, made the arrangements, contracted the musicians and dancers, and gathered costumes for the boys who were to dance, borrowing appropriate pieces from whoever possessed them. But it was up to Teresa to provide plenty of food and *chicha* for the band and the dancers and all of the relatives, *ahijados*, and *compadres* who came to the house and then to serve them with the finesse of a professional hostess, flawlessly. We worked most of Tuesday grinding sprouted corn, I using the old food mill and Teresa her grinding stones, the *maran* and *tunaw*, and boiling pots full of *chicha*. We finished all of the grinding that day, and on Wednesday Teresa continued adding the ground corn to enormous pots of water, boiling it, pouring it into the storage jars that stand along the wall at the end of the room away from the fireplace, until she had filled one large one, perhaps a meter high, and at least two smaller ones. A girl, dressed in pants as if

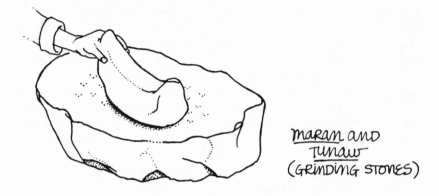

maran and
tunaw
(GRINDING STONES)

she'd come from Cusco on the truck, came to the house at one time on Tuesday with a cloth-wrapped bundle; she came in and opened it and Teresa bought from her some onions and carrots and a few handfuls of small dried silvery gray fish called *ch'ini challwa*. Another young woman came a little later, and Teresa invited her in and gave her a bowl of soup and they talked. Teresa explained to me that her mother was also making *chicha* for a *cargo;* she stayed only long enough to eat her soup. Then there was a very shy little girl—I never learned why she had come—who Teresa said to me later was *manan mamitayoq* (simply, "one without a mother").

Wednesday was less hectic. I labored for hours in the morning cutting *yuyu* leaves, a whole carrying-cloth full. A little tedious, gathering the stems into large handfuls with the slender white threads of the roots upwards, cutting the roots from the bundle, and then cutting through the whole bunch a couple of times, as I have learned to do watching Teresa, trying to hold the knife as she does. My hands ended up blistered from gripping the dull knife. But with a certain small pride, I sat in the sun and cut the whole armload myself: Teresa had left the task to me, confident that I could do it, and well enough that the results would meet her rigorous standards for the festival.

In midafternoon when the adobe of the oven had dried enough from Tuesday's rains, we began making bread, mixing the dough, heating the oven, letting the bread rise. This time Baltazar used flour that had been ground from their own wheat: Daniel and Hugo had taken it on horseback Saturday, staying the night at the mill at the old hacienda called Wayninki. Gary and I bought lard from Juana at the shop, which Teresa melted over the fire and Baltazar mixed into part of the risen dough later with some sugar; and we offered what was left of the dry yeast that we'd brought from Cusco to use instead of *qonchu*—most of it had been used, in the end, to make bread for us all. It had turned out beautifully, much to

Baltazar's pride: made with the bleached flour from Cusco, the yeast instead of *qonchu*, and the lard we bought from Juana in Ricardo's store, it came out of the oven like puffy, golden biscuits, and broken open, they were soft and white inside. We divided the bread with them, including the fancy ones that Baltazar had made—*caballos* and *wawitas*, braids and baskets and shapes like bunches of bananas—and we gave some of ours to don Andrés and Celestina, who raised them to their lips to kiss them in thanks, and some to Pascuala, who took me inside and gave me a bowl of soup when I brought them to her.

On Thursday Teresa and I started cooking just after breakfast. I ground *tarwi* beans in the food mill, a bucketful, and Teresa cooked *mot'e* and potatoes and made *uchukuta*, a very hot sauce of ground dried *ají* peppers and onion and piquant herbs, and we peeled and cut onions and carrots into slivers and cooked the carrots. It felt like Thanksgiving: the whole morning in the kitchen, Teresa a little frantic, making sure that everything was done; and in midmorning, people began to arrive, the musicians first, then relatives and *compadres* and *ahijados,* and she warmed clay pitchers full of *chicha* by the fire to serve generously to everyone. The last thing she cooked was the little fish—they must be anchovies—she had bought from the young woman from Cusco, frying them in lard and then rinsing them. When the sky cleared, the men and some women who had brought *chicha* sat outside drinking *chicha* and *trago.* Baltazar, absent most of the morning, arrived with a bass drum borrowed from the school, a drum which Gary ended up carrying down, having gone to look for Baltazar and found him. (Gary has wryly begun to refer to himself as the *asnu* [the mule]: Baltazar now uses Gary's back and legs and arms to do things, like carrying the enormous drum, which he normally can't; their relationship is, happily, a simple one, a willing friendship, not charged with debt and obligation as relationships between men of the village are—Gary is an outsider, so Baltazar feels free to ask or even expect the favor, and Gary really doesn't mind having become Baltazar's arms.) There were two flute players and a man with a small drum—they had played for a little while in the *comedor* over their *chicha*—and eventually a man to play the bass drum. There was also a young man who was going to dance with the younger boys as an *ukuku,* a highly stylized representation of the Andean spectacled bear. And the boys, the dancers, began to arrive and were outfitted: two *ukukus,* Daniel and the young man, a "bull" and *torero* and one bashful boy who found himself dressed as a woman, in a *bayeta* skirt and a shawl and *montera,* the traditional hat which is flat with a fringe and which no one here wears now, and with a thin scarf over his face like a veil. The "bull" was instructed how to behave like a bull—he wore around him a hoop wrapped with hide with a bull's head attached, which he held in front of him, guiding the horns with his hands on the hoop—to duck the bull's head and charge the *torero's* pink cape and to threaten and chase innocent bystanders, which he later did enthusiastically.

Teresa served *mot'e* and plates full of hot ground *tarwi* garnished with carrots and onions and the little fishes, which are eaten whole, heads and tails and all, and taste briny and sharp because of the fine bones, and the *yuyu hawcha* and hot pepper sauce. Gary and I were called inside to eat with Celestina and Teresa and Baltazar, who ate only a few mouthfuls, in the kitchen. The band went out of the yard and up toward the plaza, playing with more enthusiasm than expertise, followed by the procession of dancers. Then the women lifted jars full of *chicha*, the mouths of the jars stuffed with corn husks, onto their backs—the jars held in place with ropes threaded through the handles of the jars and tied around their shoulders—and, with collections of enameled tin cups gathered in their outer skirts, followed the others.

On the plaza in front of the town hall, the event proved to be a fierce competition between *ayllu*s: between bands and dancers and between women serving *chicha*. When we got there, the town officials, the schoolteachers, and the men who bore *cargo*s, along with some of their male kin and *compadres,* stood or sat in chairs in front of the town hall door. On one side of the door was "our" band, that of Ayllu Nayhua, and we women sat along this same side of the area in front of the door. Another band came soon to stand near ours, another team of dancers—boys dressed like ours—and another group of women with *chicha* jars, who sat along the opposite side. As the bands played in turn and the dancers performed, women poured endless cups of *chicha* which were carried to the men in front of the town hall by a man who was allowed no rest, running constantly between the women and the men, and were passed among the women. Teresa did not serve: the women sitting at her side tipped the jars to fill the cups, and it occurred to me later that neither she nor Baltazar appeared in public actually performing the work of the *cargo,* as if to demonstrate or confirm the network of kin, by blood or by ritual, upon whom they can call for support and aid within the *ayllu,* the strength and loyalty of those ties. It also seemed to me that, in serving her family, and us, in the kitchen, separated from the performers and guests, she made it clear that she was not just feeding a group of people but honoring and thanking those who would represent her and Baltazar and the *ayllu* in the events that followed.

The contest, in all of its aspects, developed to a furious pitch as two more bands, teams of dancers—these much different in character from the groups of boys—and entourages of women bearing *chicha* entered it. At first, the women had served mostly the men and women of their own

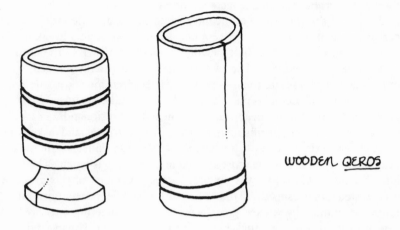

WOODEN QEROS

*ayllu*s, but as the festivities progressed, they began serving the other *ayllu*s as well, trying to outdo each other in hospitality and generosity and sheer quantity of *chicha* served: by the end, there were women sitting near me (and so I found myself once or twice) with a vessel of one sort or another—tin cups with colored yarn tied around the handles as identification, plastic glasses, wooden *qeros*—in each hand, trying as desperately as good manners allowed to get someone else to drink the *chicha* they'd been served.

The two new teams of dancers had an almost sinister quality about them. The first came into the plaza from the road and crossed its length to the town hall; the band of flutes and drum stood in a line in front of the men gathered before the town hall door. The new dancers were three men in soldiers' olive-drab uniforms and black boots, wearing goat masks—the skin of real goats' heads drawn over their own—who were called simply *soldados* (soldiers), and one man dressed as a woman, wearing a deer mask—again, the cured skin of a deer's head—a role which Baltazar called not *qoya* (woman), but *saqra* (devil): an evil character rather than a good or neutral one. They danced a dance of Carnaval, the *soldados* feigning sexual assaults on the "woman." Their actions were crude and aggressive. The second group descended the street at the end of the churchyard and crossed to the town hall, dancers dressed in the same costumes as those of the previous group, but younger men, adolescents. The musicians, a harpist and a man with a concertina, came up to the town hall playing loudly before the band that accompanied their predecessors had stopped, and a man from the new band walked up to them defiantly and roughly pulled a flute from a musician's hand, ordering them to stop. The women had all moved to the side of the plaza and sat under the tin-roofed shelter, built for passengers waiting for the trucks but never used, to get out of the rain that had begun to fall, so I didn't see much of the performance of these dancers except occasionally, through a break in the crowd, a glimpse of a "woman" lewdly mauled or thrown to the ground under a heap of *soldados*. The two new groups eventually merged, with our older *ukuku* joining them—he was treated even more roughly than the "women"—dancing to the music of the harp and concertina. I got up after a while to venture near enough to hear the music, and a *soldado*, one of the older, more disorderly group, came to me and asked me through his eerie goat mask for a *bailecito* (a little dance). I shook my head but he took me by the wrist and led me, resisting as much as I dared, into the dance. Gary too was invited, by the "woman" of this group. I was treated more respectfully than I feared I would be, not handled but at times surrounded by wicked goat faces, men's eyes peering into my face beneath their horns, or snuck up on from behind; and I suspected that gestures were made out of my sight: there was a lot of inexplicable laughter among the crowd of watchers. Gary finally disengaged himself and rescued me, led me to the side, and Celestina soon came to escort me to my proper place with the women. Baltazar came over after a while and admonished me in a generously fatherly way that those men were all drunk and I would do better to stay there with the women. I was afraid I had embarrassed him and like a dutiful daughter said, Yes, yes, right here, and stayed there, even though I couldn't hear the music or see the dancing, drinking more *chicha* than I had thought I could, until we all went home.

Between the performances of the first two and the second two groups of dancers, there had been a pause for an official ceremony, voices booming over the loudspeaker, the words so muffled by its volume that I couldn't tell at all what was being said. Gary told me later that he and the schoolteacher and one of the town officials were asked to offer blessings to the *apus*—Aqchakar, Aphitu, Ankhara, Qarukalla, Qeruru, Sullkan, Seratachan, Tauka: all of the peaks which stood around us—and to perform a divination for the year's corn crop with kernels of corn. Apparently, Gary made a favorable divination—the kernels are dropped from the hand like dice, and the divination is read according to how they fall—and recited the names of the *apus* faultlessly, thanks to Baltazar's drilling, and this drew impressed comment from the schoolteacher and from the governor, which in turn impressed Baltazar as an expression of approval from the community officials.

After the second performance, the crowds in the plaza dispersed, and our dancers, musicians, women with empty or near-empty *chicha* jars, relatives, and *compadres* and friends returned to the *comedor* at Teresa and Baltazar's house to continue drinking and dancing to the music of the

record player until quite late, the celebration uninhibited now by any vestige of the responsibility of the completed *cargo*. I slipped out as early as I
could, finding myself in a corner between two drunken men: kin or *compadres* or not, they were drunk and I was uncomfortable there. We slept
that night in the massive presence of the bass drum, stored in our house
for the night, which occupied most of the limited space of the little
storeroom.

Later, I was told, one of my two drunken companions from the corner
of the *comedor* had beaten his wife in the street just outside the compound after an argument with her over his lost flute. I was asleep and
didn't hear their children crying or the commotion of the neighbors trying
to intervene and calm him. In a few days, the flute was discovered among
the dry corn stalks stored for fodder in the *comedor*, in the corner where
we had been sitting.

Baltazar, having apparently resolved that our observance of the holiday
should continue as long as the *chicha* lasted, announced the next morning that we would rest that day and drink *chicha*, and this we proceeded
to do. By the midafternoon of a peaceful, lazy day, we were sitting outside
in the sun with don Andrés and Celestina, drinking *chicha* and talking
while Teresa and then Celestina laboriously washed *quinua* for *merienda*
(the afternoon meal). *Quinua* is a high-altitude grain, as fine and pale as
sesame seed, and has a bitter taste unless it is thoroughly washed; it
foamed as they scrubbed it between their hands, so that I wondered if
they had actually put soap in the bucket to clean it. Teresa cooked it like
rice and garnished it with slivers of carrot and onion and lovely sweet
little fried cakes, which were special and so everyone gave either whole
ones or halves to somebody else, especially to the children. Gary bought a
bottle of *trago*—he had offered to buy one to contribute to the previous
day's celebration, but Baltazar had persuaded him to wait—and we
drank it together, sitting outside; toward sunset we moved into the *comedor* to drink and dance to scratchy records played on the little record
player. It grew later and later, and still we hadn't exhausted the supply of
chicha. I danced mostly with Teresa and Celestina but a couple of times
with don Andrés: he is a real gentleman and, dancing, has a sense of his
partner and of style which I have not experienced in dancing with other
Quechua men; he held me by the hand and guided me, turning me
around. Andrés finally managed to slip away, having tried to do so a
couple of times: once, he and Celestina had both disappeared, and it took
both Daniel and me to bring them back, only after I had eaten several
potatoes I had difficulty swallowing after all of the *chicha* and had stuffed
my pockets with more that they insisted that I take, which I couldn't
bring myself to make even a pretense of being able to eat. I tried to escape

once from the celebration, but Teresa came and found me, reading by the light of one quiet candle, and brought me back, and we continued to dance to a point of exhaustion, precariously near the onset of the state of delirium which too much *trago* eventually, inevitably, brings about.

We seemed in the following days to have earned much more the confidence of Baltazar and Teresa through the small parts we played in the fulfillment of the *cargo* and in the public festivities—Baltazar has said several times recently that we are like a son and daughter of the family and has urged us to enjoy the privileges of that status: to sit close to the fire if we are cold, to ask for *chicha* if we are thirsty rather than waiting to be offered a drink as a guest would.

The festival was our first real, graphic demonstration of what the *ayllu*s are and how they function. The concept of *ayllu* is one that has been extensively explored and analyzed by scholars in the fields of Andean ethnography and Quechua and Inca ethnohistory, in large part because, while the *ayllu* is clearly a critical element of Quechua social organization (and *was* clearly a critical element in the social organization of the Inca empire), the term *ayllu* is used by the people of different regions to mean different things. The first phrase of the definition offered by the dictionary we rely upon with utmost faith (the *Diccionario Quechua Cuzco-Collao* of Antonio Cusihuamán) is: "ayllu, unidad étnica de las comunidades campesinas" (an ethnic unit of *campesino* communities). This is sufficiently cursory and neutral—except perhaps for the word "ethnic"—to be relatively safe in the furor of debate over what an *ayllu* is. But it doesn't tell us much. The second part of Cusihuaman's definition is the single word "familia" (family) and in some villages, the *ayllu* is in fact a kin group, all members related to each other in some way. But not in 'Tambo. When Gary asked Baltazar one day if the members of Ayllu Nayhua were all his *parientes* (his relatives), the response he drew was something equivalent to an emphatic "*Those* S.O.B.'s? You must be joking!" In other places, the term refers to something like a neighborhood— a community within the community or the community as a whole. But this is apparently not the case in 'Tambo either. 'Tambo is divided into two moieties, or halves, though this term refers neither to the proportion of the population which belongs to each half nor to their geographical distribution. The moieties are called Hanansayaq and Hurinsayaq— which mean, roughly, upper or superior part and lower or inferior part— and everyone in the village belongs to one or the other. The moieties are further divided each into the five groups which are called the *ayllu*s, and these stand in an established hierarchy to one another. But although the names of the *ayllu*s are mentioned in some context almost daily, no one seems to be able to tell us precisely what, in 'Tambo, an *ayllu* is.

According to Baltazar, *ayllu* membership is fixed and inherited or adopted by marriage; and each *ayllu* possesses land, which is also inherited by individual members of succeeding generations along with their membership in the *ayllu*. Each *ayllu* has an established number of workers—Baltazar says that, as *segunda* of Ayllu Nayhua, he now has possession of the list of names of all of the workers of the *ayllu*. *Ayllus* in 'Tambo seem to be, in practical effect, groups of workers that are called into action to carry out community work projects, like cleaning irrigation canals or repairing the road after the rainy season (or building houses for *abuelitas*), and to celebrate festivals—but the members of his *ayllu* are not those a man necessarily calls upon to help him in his fields or to support him in the fulfillment of *cargos*. The *ayllus* seem to function in public, village-wide activities, and the division of all available workers of the village—this means all of the men both old enough and young enough to perform hard manual labor—into *ayllus* serves as a standardized means of dividing labor, spatially and temporally, and of delegating the responsibility of celebrating all of the saints' days that must be observed during the year.

On Saturday, Gary went down with Baltazar, Hugo, Daniel, and Jaime, and an *odre* full of *chicha* slung over the back of a horse to do *ch'ampa*, the process of breaking up clods of earth in preparation for planting with a scratch plow and team of bulls. I helped Teresa along with Leonarda, who worked only when her mother was watching and sometimes not even then (but with the haughtiness and sense of importance of an eleven-year-old girl who finds herself with the distinct advantage of greater knowledge than somebody else possesses, she carefully studied my technique and offered stringent criticism and little-appreciated advice), make *yuyu hawcha* which, accompanied by *mot'e*, hot pepper sauce, thin, flat omelettes of eggs and flour, and the last of the dried fish, would feed the workers. When it was done, she gave me some to eat and I prepared to help her carry the meal to the field, but she told me to stay because it was going to rain, which I had assumed because of the heavy, iron-gray clouds that gathered during the day and had taken into account. I was surprised and disappointed, but Teresa was insistent and I gave in; I stayed inside—it rained most of the afternoon—huddled under a sleeping bag against the chill and damp, and read a whole book of Agatha Christie stories borrowed from someone in Cusco and felt a little guilty because I was the only one who wouldn't get wet that afternoon: even though Leonarda hadn't gone with Teresa either, she would have to go out to the pastures outside the village to bring the cattle home. But mostly I felt left out, hurt by exclusion from even the misery that everyone else would suffer; I didn't want to be pampered that way. They all returned in the early dusk and we gathered in the kitchen, where Gary sat close to the fire with Hugo and Daniel, and Teresa gave us cups of heavily sugared coffee to drink and pieces of bread and *mot'e* and handfuls of leftover *hawcha*. In place of my mood of desolate abandonment of the afternoon, there was now a heartwarming sense of companionship, of welcome, almost of belonging, odd as we are. It was a feeling that persisted the next day, Sunday, the day of rest, a long, quiet, rainy day which we spent visiting each other, Hugo and Daniel or Baltazar coming over to our house to talk, or Gary and I sitting in the kitchen with Baltazar and Teresa and the boys, Teresa and I spinning and Baltazar telling stories and explaining things to us.

5. Todos Santos

Baltazar baked bread all day on Thursday and Friday and Saturday before the first of November, the fiesta of Todos los Santos—the day of All Saints; from the plaza, you could see the thin column of smoke rising among the eucalyptus trees around the oven. As he began to heat the oven for the first batch, he asked Gary for a cigarette so he could blow its smoke into the mouth of the oven to drive out the *mal aire* ("bad air"), or *machula*s as he said it first, the spirits of the ancestors or old ones: the oven, like a *chicha* jar not used for a while, can shelter *mal aire*. We plunged into the work, Gary feeding the fire alongside Baltazar or Daniel, sometimes alone, and I working with the women shaping breads and with the children bringing boards laden with unbaked bread in relays to the oven from the *comedor*, which Baltazar had cleared again for baking bread for the holiday. We worked till a little after dark each day and began again the next morning. On Saturday, Gary and I had gone home and started to get into bed when a young woman knocked on the door and asked me to help her carry her bread to the oven. I went out to help, though I carried only one board, and waited with them for a while as the bread baked, until it started to hail. Not wanting to abandon them when they had specifically asked me to help, I waited a while longer until I was convinced, perhaps mostly by misery, that I was not needed and was possibly even in the way, and the ground was covered so thickly with hail that it looked as if it had snowed and my skirt and shawl were soaked and melting hail was dripping from the brim of my hat; I was standing with my face against the wall of the oven's still-roofless shelter, hoping that it would shield me from the hail. I went home and went to bed. A little while later, the young woman came in with four pieces of warm bread for me—an offering of thanks—a little embarrassed because we were in bed. It struck me as extraordinarily generous since I hadn't really helped very much and had deserted them at the moment of greatest hardship, even though each family we had helped had given us a few pieces of bread in gratitude, so that we had collected much more than we knew what to do with. I thanked her as much and as sincerely as I could in Spanish, hoping that she understood.

Sunday was the day of Todos los Santos, and we should, supposedly, have been observing the holy day, the day of All Saints, but people began to arrive again early in the morning to make bread. Baltazar, Daniel, and Hugo worked until late afternoon, though I quit hours earlier, tired finally of being given contradictory commands by Baltazar and Daniel and sometimes even, infuriatingly, by six-year-old Jaime—and Gary quit soon after. I took over to don Andrés and Celestina five small breads and a large one in the shape of a coca leaf which we had been given and sat in their house with them for a while. When I went in, only Andrés was there, and he conquered his charming shyness and embarrassment enough to give me a plate full of potatoes from a pot on the fireplace, some of which, enough so that I wouldn't seem ungrateful, went into my pockets when he wasn't looking. When Celestina returned, she promptly gave me a little jug of *chicha,* and Andrés vanished, though he came back soon with a bottle of *trago* which Celestina warmed in a cup placed on top of the *chicha* jug over the fire, and we drank, out of a tiny cup—of bone, I think, or wood, very fine and thin with a worn design engraved on it. Señora Pascuala came in, then Baltazar came and went, and finally Gary came over to rescue me: I had made several attempts to leave but failed each time as one hand or another pulled me back by my skirt. When we did at last go, I went back to give Pascuala some bread as well and another of the "coca leaves" we'd been given: at Andrés and Celestina's house, it had been apparent that she had been crying, and I wondered if she had bread for her husband's grave. We are told that people traditionally clean the graves of their dead, replace the crosses that guard them, then go to the cemetery taking bread and drink and sit by them in vigil for a day, the second day of Todos Santos, drinking *chicha* and *trago* in their honor.

We helped a little more with the baking until finally the last batch was done, and then we all went up to the house of Mariano and Felícitas, just above Baltazar and Teresa's compound, to drink with them. They had arranged a *mesa* (a sort of altar)—a carrying cloth covered with various objects and food, flowers and cups of *chicha*. The foods placed on these *mesas* are special things, like pineapples or candy or soft drinks or favorite foods of the dead person who is mourned. They poured a few drops of *chicha* on the ground before the *mesa* as a blessing before they drank. We left them, we and Baltazar and Teresa, and returned to Baltazar and Teresa's kitchen to continue drinking: it is traditional also, apparently, to get very drunk, though I can't tell whether it is a token of sorrow for the loss of loved ones or a mechanism, since everyone cries when they're drunk, for the expression of that grief which is held inside, denied, for the rest of the year or a response to fear of the spirits of the dead, the *almas*, who return at this time. Toward dusk, Juana came into the house, so drunk she was literally reeling, and pleaded with us all to come and drink with her and Ricardo—they lost a child, an infant, during the past year, and this would be the occasion of the first visit of its *alma*. She left, and after a while Gary and I, since no one else seemed to be going to accept her beseeching invitation, went up to their house. They too had established a *mesa* with candles burning among the cups and flowers. Don Andrés and Celestina were there, and we danced with them all, bodily supporting both Juana and Ricardo or helping them up from the floor if they fell. At last I stopped dancing: Jaime and Orlando were sleeping—only a child could have slept in the midst of the din of the record player and the wailing of the mourners—but Eloy was sitting in a corner crying, probably understandably confused by the commotion, and I took him in my arms on my lap and held him, stroking his hair, until he fell asleep. When we left, I laid him on the bed with the other boys.

We went home, back to the kitchen, where Señora Asunta and Hugo had joined Baltazar and Teresa just before we'd left. Todos los Santos is also traditionally a time to arrange marriages, and this seemed to be the beginning of Asunta's courtship of Hugo's family. They were deeply absorbed in their discussion, and I took over the serving of the *chicha* from a jug by the fire, which thrilled me with a sense of honor and acceptance—the first time I had ever served the *chicha*, Baltazar affirming, "She knows, she knows"—and Gary the serving of the *trago*. The conversation degenerated into tears all around; even Hugo was crying, and Leonarda came in and started crying, and finally I cried, influenced by the *chicha* and *trago* and the room full of strong emotion, whatever it was. Eventually I slipped out, and then Gary; he said Sebastiana came before he left.

The second day of Todos los Santos is the day when people go to the cemetery to sit by the graves of the dead, and we assumed that Baltazar and Teresa would go, and Baltazar had said that we would go with them.

Fairly early in the morning though, Ricardo came by, and a little later Baltazar and Gary went up to his house to drink again. I gave Teresa an aspirin for her headache, and when she felt better, we followed them. We sat in the yard of their compound all day, drinking. I helped Juana and Teresa prepare *tarwi* for the afternoon meal. Hugo came after a while, and don Andrés and Celestina came, and Señora Asunta and a couple of other people whom I don't think I knew and can't remember now anyway. Late in the afternoon the women began dancing together and sometimes persuaded Gary to join them, and sometimes Hugo danced with Señora Asunta. It became apparent that no one was going to the cemetery; when Gary asked them if they were, having hoped to observe the ritual, he was told no and decided to go himself. His decision inspired an atmosphere of trepidation, and soon after he had gone, the women convinced me, urgency ringing in their voices, to go after him and bring him back. Haunted by a vague fear I didn't understand, I started down the path toward the church under the leaden sky and followed him into the churchyard; before going to the cemetery, a family goes to the church to ring the bells of the *campana* for their dead. I crossed the churchyard to the bell tower. As I reached it, a man stood in the doorway through which I had passed into the churchyard and shouted to me not to go up, not to go in there. I felt deeply frightened, not understanding all of his words shouted across the diagonal length of the churchyard in the twilight, not knowing why I shouldn't go in. But Gary called to me from the *campanilla,* and I went in and up the earthen stairs. There were two men in the open chamber with him, the great old bells looming shadows in the center of the twilit space, and I stood there for a few uneasy minutes, only long enough to tell him in English that they had all said he shouldn't go to the cemetery, though I couldn't tell him why, and that I thought he shouldn't go because it was a private place, a private ritual, and as an outsider he would be intruding upon that very solemn and important privacy. He said he was going anyway, and I left him, the strange feeling hurrying me down the stairs as if it were hands pressing against my back. Not used to walking by myself in the village, I wasn't sure where to go, whether to return to Juana and Ricardo's house or to go home. I met Celestina coming down the path as I started up toward Juana and Ricardo's house, and she beckoned to me to come home with her. Glad of her familiar presence, I followed her to her house, where she gave me something to eat. Then I let myself into our house and sat there in its dim interior for a little while, filling myself with its silence and solitude before I decided to go back to Juana and Ricardo's house. I was welcomed there and given *chicha.* Gary had not come back. Still before dark, he returned: he had gone to the cemetery gate and had watched the people going in with their *chicha* and *trago* and bread but had not gone in, feeling finally that he did not belong there. The gathering in the little yard of Juana and Ricardo's house, which in the course of drinking had been gradually forgetting his departure for the cemetery, seemed to breathe a final, small sigh of relief, and the atmosphere relaxed once more. Soon after darkness fell, Baltazar and Teresa and Gary and I returned home.

6. Corn planting

Rainy season morning, early November: it rained all night, and when we woke in the morning, a cloud was drifting through the village, trailing a veil of fog like thin smoke through the streets between the houses. The tops of the mountains of the Otra Banda are hidden, and there are clouds far below us in the river valley.

You leave behind, when you come here to live this way, a lot more than familiar surroundings: your cat and your favorite walks and a beloved unmatched pair of lovely old engraved crystal bowls; you are forced to leave behind also a lot of assumptions and standards ingrained to the depth of instinct which simply don't make sense here. I thought about this the other day, as we were preparing food to take to the men planting Baltazar's corn field: I sat for perhaps an hour or more peeling carrots and cutting them into tiny slivers to be used as a garnish, after having spent most of the day peeling beans — peeling beans!—with my fingers, breaking most of my fingernails in the process. At home, you would buy the beans in a can or at least already peeled somehow, and if you didn't have a food processor, you would use some simple implement like a grater to shred that quantity of carrots, or you probably wouldn't do it at all: you would find some alternative or might simply decide that the result wasn't worth that much time and effort and would simply do without. Here, there are no alternatives, and you can't do without. I thought of it again when we left the field yesterday just before dusk for the hour-and-a-half walk back to 'Tambo. The field, in Manzanapata below Qolqeuqru, is far enough below 'Tambo that you can feel the difference in altitude in the air, the humidity: the air has enough weight, enough substance, to carry the rich scent of flowers, the sound of myriad insects. The field is more than six hundred meters below 'Tambo, along a rough trail of loose stones in places, often very steep. We climbed from late daylight through the treacherous twilight and on into the darkness with only a half moon lightly veiled by cloud by which to see. It seemed crazy to me, but here, there is no consideration of danger or caution—there can't be, really: you simply go home after a day's work, and it happens to be a daunting climb of an hour and a half through dusk and darkness. No alternatives: what other possibility is there? The only danger one fears as darkness falls is *mal aire*, against which the Quechua protect themselves, as we did that night, by chewing coca and by blowing cigarette smoke into their hats and putting them quickly on their heads and blowing some down their shirts or sweaters.

We began preparing for the planting on Tuesday, when Teresa and I spent the day grinding corn and boiling pots of *chicha*. The planting of corn is clearly one of the most important occasions of the year, an event laden with social tradition. Baltazar went to Qoipa last week on his horse, armed with a bottle of *trago,* an indispensable agent in making deals, to arrange for four teams of bulls to be brought by *compadres* or friends there. He said there would be twelve or fifteen men working: again the blood-kin and ritual-kin—*compadres* and *ahijados*—that one calls on for help. On Wednesday, with enough *chicha* made to fill two *odres* (the big skin bags) we prepared food: those beans and carrots and a couple of pieces of some unidentified and unidentifiable meat which Teresa had dried in the sun the day before and now boiled; and after dark, when I had given up and gone home, my back aching from squatting all day on the floor, Teresa cut *yuyu* greens for a pot of *hawcha.*

The men—Baltazar and Gary, both of the boys, the husband, Nicasio, of Señora Asunta, and another old man—left in the morning at about seven after an early breakfast, with the two big skin bags full of *chicha* and an enormous sack full of seed corn on the horses and, on Hugo's shoulder, the long scratch plow which usually hangs above our door. Teresa put me to work peeling potatoes. Soon, a woman came whom I had seen before at the house, an older woman, Dolores, from Qolqeuqru whom I think is Teresa's or Baltazar's aunt, bringing a guinea pig—its neck, I was thankful, already wrung. As I peeled the potatoes for the *hawcha,* she cut them, and Teresa scalded, cleaned, and gutted the *qowi,* with somewhat less ceremony than I had observed at Pascuala's house, though she followed the same procedure. It was skewered and stuffed with diced potatoes and some of the entrails and leaned on a roof tile in front of the fire, its liver and kidneys and the stomach stuffed with potato

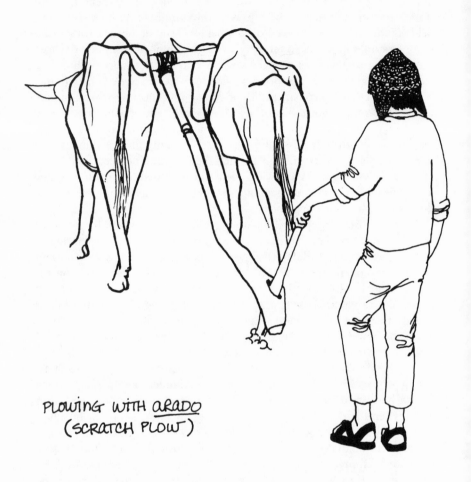

PLOWING WITH *arado*
    (SCRATCH PLOW)

placed in the coals in the front of the fireplace. Teresa gave the organs to Dolores and me to eat; the stomach was saved for the men. The *qowi*, when it was done, was unceremoniously hacked into pieces, as I had seen before. (Later on at the side of the field, I was served the head, which I could not bring myself to gnaw on, even to taste, and had to conceal surreptitiously in my pocket and offer to Sandor, who accepted it with deep canine gratitude, under cover of darkness.)

One by one, as we were working, other women came—Juana (and the children), Señora Asunta, Felícitas, and another older woman who I assume is the wife of the man who went with the others to plant. Thanks to Teresa's skillful organization, the operation was relaxed, the children the only source of disorder, and when everything was clearly in control, Teresa began serving *chicha*. When we had finished all of the innumerable little tasks of cooking, there was a tremendous amount of food: *mot'e*, cooked potatoes with hot sauce, *yuyu hawcha*, ground *tarwi* beans mixed with onion greens, and all of the beans I had so laboriously peeled, now cooked; little cakes of flour, water, salt, and a little *chicha*, fried in lard; the meats, the slivered onions and carrots, and the dried fish I had brought Teresa from Cusco. We were each given a plate of all of this, and each of us respectfully passed her plate to at least one other woman for her to take a token bite before we ate ourselves. Most of the women—all in fact I think—ate their *hawcha*, some *mot'e* and potatoes and discreetly dumped the rest into their skirts to save for their children; I, wearing only one denim skirt in which I couldn't carry anything—they draw the hems of their outer skirts up to their waists, and twist the heavy fabric at their backs to make a sort of pouch in the front—found myself forced to eat all I had been served and was terribly embarrassed, afraid that I appeared to be a glutton. There was nothing I could do: I couldn't give it back—one never gives back what has been graciously given to her—and it would have been indiscreet if not rude to walk out the door with my plate to take it to my house. Everything was quickly packed, and Señora Asunta and Dolores set out ahead of us carrying huge burdens of food. Teresa served the women remaining each a *copita* of *trago*, and then we followed, I carrying a smaller burden—only the *tarwi*—and Teresa just a small plastic jug full of *trago*. We walked very quickly, sometimes running, until we caught up with Dolores and Señora Asunta just above Qolqeuqru. We passed through the edge of the village, defying a couple of fierce little dogs, and on down the path to the field.

When we arrived there, we sat for a while as the men continued to work: one of the men hadn't come with a team of bulls and plow, so the work had gone more slowly than Baltazar had hoped—he had wanted to finish in one day. While we waited, we drank some of the *chicha* the men had brought that morning in the cups they had brought with them: three cow's horns with zigzag lines etched on them, and two wooden *qeros*, all vessels I had never seen at the house. When the men stopped, they sat in a half circle on the ground near us and served themselves and us more *chicha*. The *mot'e* and potatoes in cloths were placed on the ground within the half circle, and as the men began to eat and the women to fill plates with the other foods, the men, represented by Hugo, returned to us each handfuls of *mot'e* and potatoes. Each man was served a plate half *tarwi* and half *hawcha*, with two of the little cakes, meat, and a generous handful of onion and carrot and fish; they didn't, among the ten of them, eat even a third of all we had brought. When they finished they began again to serve *chicha*, first to us, the women, in thanks, and Teresa filled their bottle with *trago* from the jug we had brought and they served this as well, giving each woman two *copitas* before serving themselves. Teresa arranged more plates of the food that was left, tying them in cloths with *mot'e* and potatoes, and gave them to the other women and the men from Qoipa whose wives were not there. We all drank in rounds until we'd finished the bottle of *trago*, and the men returned to their work. The women packed the food that remained, the pots and pails and spoons, and we sat and sipped *chicha* and picked flowers—fabulous big flowers like lilies, growing on bushes—for our hats until they had finished. In the late afternoon, they completed the section they had been working on and came to the edge of the field to load the horses, saddling them with heavy cloths and piles of sheepskins, packing the rest of the seed, the blades of the plows, the short-handled hoes, the skin *chicha* bags; and we began the long walk up. The men from Qoipa with their bulls and Dolores and her husband from Qolqeuqru left us at forks in the trail to go home. We stopped about halfway up, as it grew dark, to rest and quench our thirst, to protect ourselves against *mal aire* with cigarette smoke and take mouthfuls of coca. We stopped once more to rest briefly at the top of the trail up the mountainside, then went on to the road into 'Tambo. Señora Asunta and Nicasio came back to the house with us, where we unloaded the horses and retired to the kitchen to drink yet more *chicha*. Gary and I finally gave up, leaving them to continue talking into the night, probably about the marriage Señora Asunta wants to make of her daughter Sebastiana to Hugo; Sebastiana herself came in before we left. She is very young, hardly more than a child—maybe fifteen or so, though she carries herself like a woman—and sturdy and solid, with a smooth, broad, and impassive face with large features, pretty, in a very Quechua sort of way.

We have been watching the gradual initiation of Hugo, who is eighteen, into young manhood. He returned from three months of work in the gold mines of Puerto Maldonado in the jungle just about the time we arrived in 'Tambo, and though his face is that of a boy, he was quiet then, almost sullen, and somehow clearly not a boy anymore. Baltazar and Teresa do not yell his name the way they do Daniel's and Leonarda's when they want them to come and seem to respect an independence and right to decide for himself which, even to us who hardly know him, seem new-born. We have watched them urge him to drink *chicha*, offering him a cup in his turn when the adults drink; at first he often refused it, or tried to, and made faces at its taste when the cup was forced upon him by his parents. Now he accepts it quite naturally. On the day of Todos los Santos, I saw him for the first time drink *trago*, grimacing at its bitter fire the way a woman does. By the end of that day he was serving the *trago*, a man's privilege, and he drank with the men, though hardly as much as they, and served again on the day of the corn planting.

The night of Todos Santos was the first time I'd seen Señora Asunta at the house in connection with Hugo, though I think she'd been here before since Gary and I arrived, before I began to sort out all of the new faces and names. Todos Santos and Easter are the times of the year when marriage arrangements are made: the final agreement is reached, often after long negotiation, when the father of the young man pays a formal visit to the family of the young woman, arriving in the middle of the night with that indispensable bottle of *trago*, to ask for the hand of their daughter for his son. Todos Santos was the time Asunta chose to initiate her courtship of Hugo and his family. Her daughter Sebastiana is one of two girls who would like to marry Hugo: the other girl, Susana, lives in Wayninpampa, an hour's walk away from 'Tambo and thus at a certain disadvantage, and has begun her courtship by sending to Baltazar a record of a song the words of which I don't understand but which they listen to attentively, without talking—to remember her by, as she wrote on the label of the record, as if she too courted father rather than son—and another to Juana, Hugo's eldest sibling living in 'Tambo. We hear differing reports from everybody except Hugo, always reticent, about which of the two girls Hugo prefers and why. From Baltazar's point of view, marriage to Susana would be better because she will inherit more land from her mother and because her parents are somewhat wealthier than Asunta and Nicasio and will therefore be more generous in providing for the young couple as they begin their new life together. Nevertheless, the reciprocation of Asunta's attention seems to be a display of abundant, almost exaggerated, hospitality by Hugo's family. Upon her recently more frequent appearances, she is forced to drink more *chicha* and *trago* than anyone else and is offered more food. At the field where we planted the corn, when the men were served, Hugo somehow returned to her two full plates of food, and I saw Teresa sit down before her and give her *copita* after *copita* of *trago*, overriding Asunta's protests, refusing to drink herself.

7. My birthday

The other day, when we were cooking for the planting, Juana's little boys, Jaime, Eloy, and Orlando, were scolded rather severely for knocking the new flowers off the *tumbo* vine outside the house with a stick: if the flowers are picked, of course, the vine won't bear its rare and highly prized fruit. But the flowers are spectacular, long, green tubes with a flare of deep pink petals at the end, tantalizing, too much temptation for a small boy with a stick to resist. This morning, Jaime and his friend Agapito—the son, about Jaime's age, of Mariano and Felícitas—came into the yard, their hands full of stolen flowers, *tín tín* flowers, much like the *tumbo* flowers, with which they proceeded to replace the vine's lost blossoms, carefully tying them onto the vine with its own coiled tendrils and, looking around, satisfied with their subterfuge, quickly left the yard.

November: a month which at home I love, wearing it comfortably like a favorite old shirt, for some reason; the raw edge of winter. I wish for it, that familiar November, longingly: the hard, gray skies and bitter metal cold, the brittle branches of deciduous trees stripped bare, scraping the sky, the flocks of Canada geese honking overhead—and the comforting warmth of a wool sweater and a fire in the fireplace. But it is difficult now to evoke its feeling. Here it is late spring instead of late fall, early winter, and, the threat of the rainy season temporarily abated, the afternoons are often clear and hot, the sun blazing with unsuspected ferocity—it looks like any other sun—the air softly and thinly, sharply, scented with flowers, a perfume like vanilla. In the gentle warmth of a late afternoon, standing as still as I could in the dappled light of the path below the house, I watched a hummingbird feed among the shrubs and low eucalyptus along the path: passing through the sun, flashing an iridescent emerald green, with a long, black tail forked like a swallow's and a blue-black head, the slender branches scarcely bending under its weight. Once—I held my breath—it hovered only a few feet from me, until a second winged emerald plunged from a tree and there was a silent midair collision, a surprised flurry of invisible wings, and they both vanished down the path. The tiny birds' presence, the brief skirmish, and their absence were all so sudden that I stood there for a few moments as if dazed. The next morning I saw another one, this a handsome and striking black and white, as if it were wearing a tuxedo, feeding at a scarlet cactus flower. Hummingbirds!

I helped plant potatoes yesterday. Gary went in the morning with Baltazar, Hugo, and little Eloy. It was decided, for some reason—it's part of the training of a "daughter," I suppose—that I would carry the afternoon meal to the field myself, alone, and I spent the morning helping Teresa cook. In the early afternoon, she bundled the food into a carrying cloth, and I tied it around my shoulders. She came out of the house after me with her spindle, locking the door, so I thought she had decided to come with me after all. She told me to go ahead, to hurry, and I went out of the yard and climbed the street to the plaza, where I waited for her. When she came into the street, she beckoned me to go ahead, and I obediently crossed the plaza and went on up the hill toward the school. At the top, I stopped to look for her, but she was not following me, so I walked on the road to the school and beyond, following the path to the fields of Yanchakalla. I got stuck once, just below the field where they were planting, lost: all of the hills suddenly looked alike, and I stood there, confused and helpless for a while, until the son of the governor, helping his father plant corn, called to me from a field and pointed out where Baltazar's field was. (The governor is a former big landowner who lost all of his hacienda's arable land in the Agrarian Reform. He has been planting his own fields for only a few years: before that, the "indios," the men of 'Tambo and its annexes, had planted, tended, and harvested his crops for him, as they had planted the fields of the hacienda for hundreds of years. The lands he now works were granted to him by the village. His sons have learned to work the fields only in the past season—they'd been away at school.)

I reached the field with a great sense of pride and crossed it to greet Gary and Baltazar. As I returned to the edge of the field to put down my burden, I saw Teresa coming up the hill toward me and felt my face hot with embarrassment and disappointment, feeling that she hadn't after all had confidence in me, until I realized that it made sense, that it must have

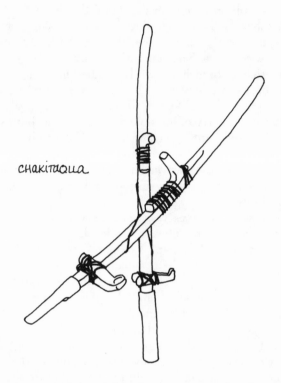

CHakiTaQLLa

been what a mother would do who had sent a young daughter alone to the fields for the first time. This conclusion seemed confirmed by the fact that Baltazar showed no surprise or amusement when Teresa appeared, though it had been he who had told me in the morning that I would come alone and had assured me that I would find the field.

The men worked a while longer, then stopped to rest, to have *chicha* and the food I had brought. We waited out a brief rain under Gary's big, blue nylon rain poncho, and then they went back to work, Teresa now working with Hugo, Eloy's attention and five-year-old's energy lapsed. Gary stopped to rest, and I worked with Baltazar to finish the last rows, Baltazar working with the *chakitaqlla* (the foot plow) and I planting the seed.

The work is hard but has a lovely and deeply satisfying rhythm. A man thrusts the blade of the *chakitaqlla* deep into the earth and presses the handle toward the ground to lift the earth on the blade. Someone walking behind, often a woman or a child, drops two seed potatoes beneath the blade and the blade is withdrawn to let the earth fall and cover the seed. The man takes a step back for the next powerful thrust, the person following him taking two steps in his wake, with the first tamping the earth over the seed just planted, bending on the second to drop new seed. Again and again.

We celebrated my birthday on the eleventh, actually beginning the cele-bration, naturally, the evening before. We were also, that evening, re-inaugurating our house: we had planted the last of the potatoes that had been stored there, and in the afternoon Gary and Baltazar removed the poles and bed of straw of the bin where they had lain from the corner of the room, and Gary and I rearranged the meager furnishings, so that now there is a lot more space, and knocked another adobe from the wall to make a second small window. In the evening, Gary bought a half-bottle of *trago,* and we gathered in our house, the children drifting in one by one. There was a feeling of family: it was the first time we had all at once been gathered in our house, and it felt natural and seemed truly to bless the house, to draw it closer into the family's compound as a place to live in, a home. The only lack, really, is a fireplace; the small kerosene Primus stove does not offer the sense of hearth that an adobe fireplace does, but that evening nobody seemed to feel that lack but me, the anxious hostess.

Teresa was in her kitchen, warming a pitcher of *chicha* before the fire, when Juana came to tell her excitedly that there were two men, *inge-nieros* (the Spanish word means engineer but has been generalized by the Quechua to apply to anyone who practices a technical trade) from the brewery in Cusco, who wanted to visit Gary and me. The message was passed to Baltazar, then to us: they were coming. We knew no *ingenieros* in Cusco, but they must have been told by the villagers that we were there and been curious. Baltazar and Teresa saw the visit as a tremendous honor, though we felt it an intrusion, and Baltazar set about directing us to rearrange the room, bringing a grain sack to lay on the bank along the wall to sit on, telling Gary to move the upended *chicha* jar, which, with a board balanced on top of it, we use as a night table, into a corner so there would be more room along the edge of the bed for the guests to sit. Teresa came in with her jug of *chicha,* but we didn't have a chance to taste it: the *ingenieros* arrived, and she hid it under her skirt. The two young men were seated on the bed with Gary. They were offered *trago,* and one of them politely drank when his turn came, though the other refused be-cause of some illness for which he was taking medication. The whole situation felt very awkward: they were typical young Cusqueño men, for whom in general my experience has not taught me a lot of respect, what-ever their position or achievements, and I did not find any reason to feel any differently about these two. Yet Baltazar treated them with utmost deference, seeming to us to humble himself to a point at which we be-came almost embarrassed for him. We knew them, the *ingenieros,* for what they are in *our* reality—often petty, self-important businessmen

with a tendency to abuse small power—as *we* know Cusco and the
world, and they are by circumstance and by their own efforts more a part
of that reality than of the world of the Quechua villages outside Cusco
and therefore should be judged by its standards; but Baltazar and Teresa
know them only as a part of their own reality—as two important repre-
sentatives of the brewery, educated men of the city, whose favor can be
both socially gratifying and possibly profitable. They represent the brewery in its dealings with the villages, where the barley for brewing is grown
by native farmers by contract: the contract forged with the community,
responsibility for its fulfillment delegated among the *ayllu*s and within
the *ayllu*s to individuals, provides for seed barley to be supplied to the
farmers by the brewery, to be planted, tended, and harvested, then brought
to Cusco to be sold to the company for some small cash profit which
compensates the farmer for his effort, one of the few available sources
of cash. I know that Baltazar hoped that he would be able to go to the
brewery with his harvest, look up one of these men, and be well received
in the office as an important man, the respect he is accustomed to in the
village; I am afraid that the only reason it is likely that they would remember Baltazar Quispe of the hundreds of Quechua farmers they deal
with is because of the presence of a couple of North American *gringos* at
his house.

So, the party was uncomfortable to me for a while, amid the turbulence
of three streams of thought crashing together, as I tried to reconcile
the way I saw these intruders in relation to Baltazar and Teresa, the way
Baltazar and Teresa must see us and them, and the way I imagined the
ingenieros saw all of us. They seemed to have assumed for themselves a
position of paternal authority in the village, which we saw as entirely
false but which no one in 'Tambo would have dared or even thought to
challenge—and wanted to know what we two *gringos* were doing there.
We feel that we need prove our good intentions and professional validity
only to the people and authorities of 'Tambo, not to a couple of self-
important businessmen who may visit a couple of times a year, and resented their presumption of any right to question us. Baltazar however,
anxious to please them and never doubting their authority, urged Gary to
show them his letter of introduction from the university, so he got it out
and they read it, and it was put away, and except for the embers of indignation smoldering in our hearts, or mine at least, the issue was closed,
everybody satisfied.

After a while, a young woman came to tell the *ingenieros* that her
mother was expecting them at her house to eat. They went, promising to
return, and the party relaxed once more into a family affair: Teresa
brought the *chicha* out from under her skirt and we served it in one of our
enameled tin cups, and we finished off the last of the *trago* and sent

Leonarda for more. When the *ingenieros* returned, Teresa urgently beckoned to us to hide the *chicha* cup, reviving all of our vicarious humiliation: why should they hide their *chicha?* We, perhaps out of some perverse anthropologists' pride, were delighted to be drinking *chicha* to celebrate my birthday and would have been glad for these *mestizo ingenieros* to know it. They brought with them, though, when they returned, a few bottles of Cerveza Cuzqueña in my honor, which in fact tasted almost sweet after the *chicha* and *trago,* and we all drank it gladly, except the *ingeniero* who had refused the *trago* earlier, authenticating his refusal as not born of distaste or disdain. I had, in the end, to appreciate their gesture in spite of myself: they didn't have to do that, and it demonstrated a good will I hadn't been willing to allow them. Before they left, Baltazar invited them to come to the house to eat the next morning.

In the morning, I wandered, a little hazy still from *chicha* and *trago* and beer, over to the kitchen to help Teresa cook: for my birthday, they had planned to kill one of the chickens and the pig to eat, with some financial compensation from us. The chicken—the rooster who had wakened us at four-thirty every morning—was lying already limp and featherless in a basin on the kitchen floor. I was put to work peeling potatotes, a task I performed with intense concentration to avoid sight of the dead rooster. This was the first experience of the day of the real meaning of my own carnivorism: this creature, whom I had not only seen alive just the day before—I had heard him crow just outside our door a couple of hours ago!—but had lived with, had been killed for my sake. I tried not to think about it, concentrating on the potatoes, to see it only as an honor they wished to show me. It was difficult to avoid when Teresa asked me to hold the chicken, partially cooked, while she cut it into pieces to put back into the soup.

We had breakfast of chicken soup with potatoes and carrots and onion, with an aperitif of *trago,* which we continued to drink afterwards, though no one had much heart for it after the night before, sitting outside in the sun. Baltazar felt for some reason that the *ingenieros* should eat in our room when—if—they came, and so we went through the entire process we had gone through before, spreading the grain sack on the bank, moving the *chicha* jar, and this time even clearing off our table and moving it over to the side of the bed so they could eat at a table. My perhaps self-righteous indignation flared again: we had never seen anybody in 'Tambo eat at a table—few even have tables. Why should we go to such trouble for these two for the sake of such a really meaningless habit as sitting at a table to eat? In the end it was ridiculous, and they must have felt ridiculous when they came and were served at this table, with Gary and I sitting below them on the bank along the wall across the room—Baltazar and Teresa were, discreetly they thought, absent—not eating, just waiting for them to finish. It was extremely awkward: we had nothing to talk about, and Gary and I had nothing to eat to accompany them, and we couldn't very well leave them there to eat alone—Baltazar and Teresa had obviously set this up, thoughtfully, on our behalf, to appear a demonstration of *our* hospitality and generosity rather than their own. Finally, they finished and we all sat outside for a while; one of them gave copies of his business card to Baltazar and to us, and at last they left, Baltazar with them as the *segunda* of Ayllu Nayhua to make a contract, and the day was ours. Almost.

Gary was called away to speak for himself before a town assembly, the opportunity he had been waiting for. He went with Baltazar and with his letter of introduction from the university in his hand to the town hall. He came back visibly shaken. He had assumed that he would be allowed to introduce himself and explain his project and its purpose and had been going over in his mind what he would say, the words he would use. But instead he was challenged. As he sat at the table in the town hall with all of the local authorities, the director of the school—a young woman from one of the local hacienda families—faced him and pronounced that there were rumors that we went out at night to excavate for gold, the gold of the ancestors, and what did Gary have to say to that? All of the good will, or at least open-mindedness, he had assumed as a foundation for what he would say vanished like a mirage in proximity, and without that foundation, it was difficult even to begin. The director pointed out that there was no official seal on Gary's letter of introduction: the original letter with the authenticating embossed seal on it had been stolen with our passports. Gary had no advantage, as if his arm were twisted behind his back. So when he came back to the house, we decided to go to Cusco the next day. The rumor was so stereotypical that it seemed simple-minded to us—I guess we had come to expect more sophistication from the people of 'Tambo. The only thing we could do was to acquire more and more convincing credentials: get letters from someone at the university in Cusco and from the I.N.C. (the Instituto Nacional de Cultura) with all of the stamps and seals and ribbons and official signatures they could want. Later we were told that the reason it was hailing so often was because someone was digging up the gold of the ancestors; it sounded to us at the time like a convenient impromptu explanation of the crop-damaging hail rather than an old superstition. We would not return to 'Tambo without the letters.

This decision reached and Baltazar and Teresa informed that we were leaving, we put the problem as far from our minds as we could to enjoy the day. The sun shone lazily, though much of its vagueness may still have been in my mind from the *trago* we had drunk that morning. Teresa came out of the house with a pot full of potato peel and vegetable scraps and broth for the pig. Thinking that this signaled its doom, like the last meal of a condemned man, I went into our house to avoid witnessing what I could not bear to see. But she only caught the animal and tied it by its hind leg to a stake, though it screamed as if its end were indeed at hand. Later, when Baltazar returned from some errand, they began to prepare to kill the pig. I didn't know how to escape awareness of the deed: the screams of its capture had been much more than audible inside the house, and I couldn't very well just leave. I braced myself to be present during the slaughter but should have known that, if I was present, I would have to help. I did: they needed my hands to help hold the struggling creature, its head covered with a cloth, its mouth held shut, as Baltazar pierced its throat with a knife and to hold a bowl to catch the blood which pumped from the wound. I had had, I was glad now, enough *trago* to be at least partially disengaged from reality, and with some effort of will, I managed to separate myself emotionally from what we were doing. I stood and watched with a detached though still horrified fascination as the carcass was scalded and the hair pulled off, watched it cut open and the entrails removed and, standing by Teresa at the basin under the tap outside the kitchen as she cleaned them, numbly offered a hand when it seemed that help was needed.

Gary and Baltazar went to heat the oven, and the sharp spicy scent of the burning eucalyptus wood was somehow a relief, cleansing, clearing head and heart. I brought to the kitchen some potatoes which Andrés and Celestina had given us, to cook in the cavity of the carcass, and cut them while Teresa ground *ají* peppers and garlic and a sharp herb called *wakatay* with her grinding stones, to rub the skin with. We fried the potatoes and filled the *lechón* with them—I could think of it now as a *lechón* instead of as a pig, considerably transformed from the state in which I had previously known it. When Daniel came home from school, he made dough for bread, a contribution to the meal on their part that Gary and I hadn't known about: a lovely surprise. When everything was done cooking, we all had a meal of *lechón* and potatoes and fresh warm bread to soak up the rich, spicy sauce; the meat was difficult for Gary and me to enjoy, rather tough, and many pieces had the skin with a few hairs still on it. But we knew well what a treat it was for everyone else and were gratified by their enjoyment, and the potatoes and bread and sauce were wonderful.

It was late afternoon when we finished the meal, and don Andrés and Celestina were invited to come over then to eat. They ate *lechón* and drank *trago* with us, then disappeared, to return with a bottle of *trago* for me and a pitcher of warmed *chicha;* the bottle even had a festive bit of red yarn tied around its neck as a present. The record player was brought out and the music began. Juana and Ricardo came with another bottle of *trago*—this one real *trago*, real cane liquor, not diluted alcohol—and Señora Asunta came bringing more *chicha,* and finally Sebastiana arrived. We drank and danced till all of the *trago* was gone and continued, drinking only *chicha* then. I was deeply moved by their thoughtfulness and gifts and that everyone seemed to be enjoying the celebration. Even so, I was exhausted by the long day's various traumas and all of the drinking and dancing and was grateful that I was allowed to sneak away and go to bed and glad that they went on dancing—I could hear the scratchy *huaynos* playing until I fell asleep—enjoying each other's company. It had been a good birthday.

8. San Andrés, barley planting

Gary took a taxi out to the university in Cusco to speak to a professor there whom he has known for years who agreed to write a letter of recommendation for him, which he could then take to the director of the I.N.C. And then we went to the Aero Perú office and bought tickets to Lima: we would make ourselves once again completely official by getting new passports to replace our stolen ones. Our only "official" form of identification for the last two months has been the police *denuncia* which records the numbers of our lost passports but bears no indication of the length of our visas, our permission to be in Peru even as long as we have been. With even the people of 'Tambo questioning our credentials, we would feel much more confident if all of our papers were in order; too, it would be one more document to show to the village authorities of 'Tambo. The experiences of friends, other anthropologists and archaeologists, had taught us that endeavors such as obtaining letters and permissions from any bureaucracy in Peru, including the I.N.C., could take weeks, even months: we might as well get everything taken care of at once, unwilling as we were to return to 'Tambo without what we hoped would be convincing credentials.

So we flew to Lima on the seventeenth of November and passed several mornings fretting with the procedures of acquiring new passports and visas: the American Embassy was as friendly and efficient in a familiar North American way as we had hoped it would be, and even at the Peruvian office of immigration, once we had finally been directed to the right man after the customary odyssey from one office to another, we secured without problems new visas—diplomatic visas as we had had before, which don't require renewal, as tourist visas do, by leaving the country for forty-eight hours every ninety days—in less than an hour. In the afternoons, when many of the offices were closed, we walked or sat at the tables of sidewalk cafés in Miraflores, drinking coffee, watching the expensively dressed people in the streets, the fine cars. Cusco seemed, when we returned, very quiet and unsophisticated after the days of offices and crowded sidewalks, taxis and tangled traffic, and very much like home.

We remained in Cusco until Tuesday. We didn't receive the letter of reference from Gary's friend at the university until late Saturday afternoon, and Gary went with it, an almost effusive recommendation, to see the director at the I.N.C. when the offices opened on Monday morning. Our improbable luck persisted, and Gary came back with another letter in his hand by late morning, this one not quite as full of praise as the first but on official I.N.C. paper, with a letterhead and signatures and seals. We came back to 'Tambo the next morning, feeling better armed to face the rumors and suspicions.

We discovered that we had missed a lot in the short time we were away. We saw first, as we came into 'Tambo from the road above, that the new roof of the town hall, a community project funded by a gift from President Belaúnde—interested in 'Tambo as the legendary origin place of the Incas—had been completed, the new red tile clean and bright in the morning sun. As we came into the yard from the street, we found too that the roof of the shelter for the oven was also finished, crowned with its *taytacha*, a wooden cross decorated with brightly colored flowers cut from plastic bags, a small bottle hanging from one of its arms, an ear of corn in its husk from the other, symbolizing plenty, and learned from Baltazar that its completion had already been celebrated—without the oven's official godparents! In the yard were spread large pieces of meat to dry in the sun, in the air a sickly, sweet smell of rottenness laden with clouds of flies: one of the cows, the one that had fallen before we left, breaking a horn and injuring its hindquarters somehow, had fallen again and been killed. It had been more than a week: the smell confirmed it, and we couldn't bring ourselves to eat the meat we were served as soon as we arrived. The community had also received the seed for the contracted crop of barley from the brewery—three large bags of it were stacked in Baltazar's *comedor*—and everyone was preparing for sowing.

Barley is an intrusive crop, not a native or traditional one, but it is the only real cash crop for many communities in the highlands around Cusco, like 'Tambo, and therefore has, at least here, acquired all of the behavioral importance of corn. It is planted with scratch plows and bulls and teams of men with the small crooked hoes called *kuti*s, like *lampa*s but

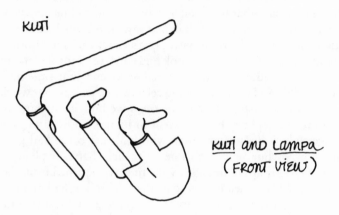

kuti

kuti and lampa
(FRONT VIEW)

with a narrow blade, on communal lands which belong to the *ayllu*s, by
men of the *ayllu*. Some may also be planted independently as a cash crop
on individually held land, if one has free land not planted in subsistence
crops, such as land lying fallow after a crop of potatoes. And some may
be planted by community organizations, like the soccer team, to raise
money for uniforms and equipment or various community projects. As
bulls and men are required, the same procedure is followed as to secure
help for the planting of corn, the *chakrayoq* (the owner of the field) calling on kin and ritual-kin, and help is rewarded in the same way: women
cook bountiful meals with meat, working together all morning, and there
is *chicha* and *trago* in abundance. To our minds, as anthropologists, who
tend toward a romantic wish that cultures could remain somehow pris-
tine, this element of commercialism is dismaying: the planting of barley
in Baltazar's and then Ricardo's fields completely overshadowed in our
family even the celebration of the day of San Andrés, November 30, when
large crosses, also called *taytacha*s like the small one on the roof of the
oven's shelter, wound with blue and pink cloth and lavishly decorated
with flowers, are carried to mountain- and hilltops around the village to
watch over the crops during the growing season. This one, among the
many festivals which seem to be observed simply by drinking too much
and which is recognized by public ritual and even a pilgrimage throughout the countryside around the village, Gary had badly wanted to see.
From Baltazar's field in Yanchakalla, we heard the music of *quena*s and
drums, as the procession of men bearing the crosses set out through the
streets of the village below, and the ringing of the church bells.

The day of San Andrés is also, of course, the *día santo* (the name day or birthday) of dear old don Andrés: he said that he would be eighty years old, though I am sure that this is an approximation and he may be somewhat older or younger than that; Baltazar says he has no documents, and by the time one is that elderly, anyway, one's exact age is no more than a matter of interest. Helping Teresa cook and carry food for the planting of Baltazar's barley field on the day of San Andrés and Juana the next day for Ricardo's, I missed nearly all of the celebration, except that we shared with Andrés and Celestina a bottle of *trago* we bought for him, on the morning of the second day before I went to Juana's house, and gave him two oranges which Teófilo, the man who built the oven, had given us, brought from Nayhua when he came up to help Baltazar plant, which Andrés raised to his lips in thanks. By the time we returned from the field on Monday and I returned on Tuesday, the celebration had already progressed too far, everyone too drunk—including eighty-year-old don Andrés—to drink or dance more; it wasn't certainly the drinking I was sorry to have missed, but I had looked forward to dancing with Andrés.

One day I had helped Celestina begin the preparations for his birthday: we spent the whole day sitting in the sun in front of her house, breaking corn from the cobs for *chicha*, sipping *chicha* as we worked, until my hands were raw and blistered. In the early afternoon, don Andrés came into the yard leading his old horse—whose bones show through his flesh as if it were no more than a drape of some thin fabric, like silk—loaded with firewood. Andrés untied the burden and let it fall to the ground; he seemed upset about something. I could see from where I sat that a place in the center of the long ridge of the horse's spine had been rubbed raw. I went to where Andrés had tied him to look: the skin had completely worn away, leaving a large open wound. It looked bad. I shook my head in commiseration and returned to my work with Celestina, not sure what I should do: we have medicines, antiseptics and germicides, but I didn't know whether or not I should interfere. It was an ethical problem, as doctoring must be for an anthropologist: I was certain that they had some method of treating the wound, but I hated the thought of the trauma and hardship of loss of their one old horse if their treatment failed and the creature was debilitated or died. I waited, tormented by internal debate. My inclination was not to interfere. It seemed to me like interfering with the course of nature, a system that maintains its own laws, into which I feel that no one has a real right to intercede in any manner except as a natural, native element of the system. I and our medicines can in no way be a natural, much less native, part of the cultural "system" of this community—but I watched as Andrés went into his storeroom and brought out an old battery, and Celestina brought another from somewhere, and with a rock he pounded on them to break them open. One at last broke, and I watched in some horror as he carried it to the horse and emptied the black powder of dry acid onto the wound. The muscles of the animal's back twitched convulsively. I jumped to my feet, putting together some of my few Quechua words to cry, "¡Hampi kanmi! ¡Hampi kanmi!" ("I have medicine!") and rushed to our house to fumble through our bag of non-prescription medicines and first-aid supplies until I found an envelope of cotton swabs soaked in a betadine solution and brought it out to where the horse was staked. My unfamiliarity with injuries made the wound look worse to me than it may have been, and I was afraid that applying antiseptic was a pitifully small measure to take, but nonetheless I felt better when I had cleaned away the battery acid and stained the wound with the iodine in the solution: at least I had killed a few germs. In gestures, I instructed Andrés to cover the wound to keep the flies off, and he tied a piece of sheepskin over the creature's back with a rope around its belly. They thanked me profusely—I imagine they had more faith in my medicine than I had—and I returned to my work and my *chicha*. I have learned since then that horses so commonly have raw patches on their backs—though not usually perhaps as bad as this one—that the word for them, *khiki*, is used as a generic, affectionately pejorative name for horses.

All of the men in the late afternoon are splitting firewood, enormous logs of eucalyptus: when they are done, there is a great heap of fresh-cut wood, tumbled like matchsticks. I carry the sticks by armfuls into the house and hand them up to Teresa, standing on the bank in front of the fireplace to put them onto the poles that span the room just under the ceiling, to dry above the fire. Men never carry firewood into the house, whether they bring branches from the mountainsides outside the village or split logs in the yard, but simply leave it in the yard outside: it is a part of the woman's domain, the domain of house and fire.

Baltazar told us once, when we were talking about putting the roof on the oven house, that a house is considered to be a woman, sheltering, protecting, and that the roof is her shawl or carrying cloth. In practice, the house belongs to the woman of the family, whether she has inherited it from her mother or her husband from his father: she is the one who cares for it, always being sure that the door is locked when no one is there, who tends the fire, and in many ways a husband behaves like a guest in his wife's house, always thanking her when he leaves after a meal. One day Baltazar came home after working all day in the fields, and Teresa wasn't home. The door to the kitchen was closed but not locked because I was there nearby in my house. But Baltazar would not go in and pour himself a cup of *chicha*, though he was clearly exhausted and his back and leg ached and he was thirsty; he would not even open the door. He sat outside, on the ground, looking rather sulky and resentful because Teresa was not there to attend to him, until she returned and hurried inside to stir the fire.

One day, finally, we rested, after all the days of the hard work of planting, having worked with remarkable diligence through Sunday, which is usually observed as a day of rest—a practice instigated by the Catholic church—through San Andrés and the second day, the *corcova,* of the celebration of Andrés' birthday. We stayed around the house. I cleaned an arroba of wheat we'd bought from Andrés and Celestina, sorting through it grain by grain to pick out tiny pebbles and microscopic bits of twigs and dry leaves, to take to the mill at Wayninki the next day. And Baltazar braided a strap, for the camera Gary had bought, from the hide of the cow that had died, which he had treated by soaking it in a solution of urine and soap, a trick that Chumbivilcano leather workers—the people renowned in Peru for their leather work—use: it stank but made a beautiful strap, a tight braid of six strips of hide like the bridles they make for the horses, with a knot and loop at each end to attach it to the camera. In the afternoon, Teresa made a dish called *sankhu,* a food which Baltazar describes as a food of the Incas: toasted wheat ground with some corn into a flour, then mixed with a little sugar and water or *chicha* to make a slightly moist meal which sticks together in clumps which are eaten with the fingers. The sugar and *chicha* enhance the natural sweetness of the wheat, and it is delicious, with a fascinating texture. Baltazar said that the Incas made *sankhu* of corn on the day of Inti Raymi, the festival of the sun, June twenty-fourth, when they offered it with prayers to the sun—all of which Baltazar seems to have learned from the contemporary, highly commercialized version of Inti Raymi, when the Inca ritual is enacted with great pageantry at Sacsahuaman in Cusco for the benefit of tourists who come from all over the world and wet sawdust represents *sankhu* in the offering to the sun. Yet it made sense, as we ate the *sankhu,* that it would in those days too have been considered something very special, worthy of an offering to the sun; Teresa seems to make it, with her infallible sense of occasion, on rare days when people are just sitting around, perhaps a little bored.

While we were eating, in the late afternoon, it began to rain and then to hail heavily, the small hail called *chimallaku;* large hail is called *chikchi.* Hail at this time of the season is a threat to the young crops, the tender, frail plants just emerging from the earth. The two little boys, Jaime and Eloy, stood in the doorway of the kitchen, blowing through pursed lips into the whitened air outside as if to blow away the hailstorm. The hail was still falling when we had finished eating, and Teresa went outside and unearthed an old clay pot, the asymmetrical kind used for toasting and popping grains, from a heap of old junk near the water faucet and laid it upside down in the yard near the fence toward the west. Then she came inside and took ashes from the hearth, carried them outside, and with them drew a cross of ashes beside the overturned pot which resounded with the pelting hail, a deceptively gentle, hollow sound.

Gary and I walked to Wayninki on Friday, carrying the load of wheat— now more than thirty pounds, with the portion of grain that Baltazar and Teresa had contributed, plus gifts to us of wheat from Celestina and from Señora Dolores, for whom we had brought from Cusco sugar and matches—wrapped in an old poncho of Baltazar's which Gary uses, the bundle wrapped on Gary's back, two corners of the poncho encircling the grain, the others drawn over one shoulder and under the other and tied across his chest, the way a man carries a bundle, or *q'epi*. The route is mostly along the road, a gentle grade down toward Qoipa, though at the end there is a trail leading down from the road into a narrow valley with a stream in its bed, rushing toward the Apurimac, and a climb on the other side up a steep slope to Wayninki. The hacienda stands alone on a rough outcrop of rock on the mountainside, with great cacti blooming with enormous, sweet-scented flowers growing around it, and huge old eucalyptus; there is a sense of luxurious spaciousness, the house not crowded among others as in the villages but surrounded instead by its own fields and pastures—what remains of the great hacienda after the Agrarian Reform—a few walled or encircled and shaded by the eucalyptus. The adobe buildings—one of them of two stories, whitewashed, with glass in the windows, and curtains, even wallpaper, visible through the windows, with a walled garden of flowers and vegetables—form an open rectangle: there is a sense too of the contrastive luxury, the grandeur that must have reigned here, aloof, proudly separate from the life in the villages around it, though it is now much humbled. The family Nuñez remains powerful around here—Lucrecia, the director of the schools of 'Tambo, is of this family by marriage—still living a life somewhat apart and more worldly and sophisticated than that of most *campesinos,* though it has been forced like other hacienda families to adopt the patterns of *campesino* life, to adapt to the exigencies of life in the Andes without the support of great wealth and political power. Just before we left the hacienda, a woman, a friend of the Nuñez family, rode a horse into the courtyard full of chickens and ducks and dogs and cats. She had driven the hacienda's horses back from pasture somewhere near 'Tambo. As she talked to the woman of the house, the horse stood quietly. Its coat was smooth and gleaming, obviously brushed, its mane cropped evenly along its neck, its feet shod, and on its back was a real tooled-leather saddle, with silver trappings and stirrups, instead of the complex pile of cloths and skins with simple wooden stirrups which usually serves as a saddle in the *campo*—and a real bridle, studded with silver, a bright medallion across the horse's forehead. This beast too bespoke a different life, a proud life once taken for granted.

The mill, which, even though I knew it was operated by a gasoline engine, I had romantically envisioned as a great masonry structure housing enormous grinding stones, was a machine, built in Spain or Brazil or somewhere, attached by a wide heavy belt to a North American Briggs and Stratton engine, housed in one of the adobe buildings around the courtyard. The woman was alone there, her son gone to Cusco for a few days, and she didn't know how to operate the motor, so we had to do it ourselves, Gary starting it up with great difficulty by pulling a handled cord like that of a lawnmower engine. None of us knew the adjustments to be made to the machine to regulate the grind, so the flour we ended up with was coarse, unsuitable for making bread: it would have to be ground again. We finally persuaded her to trade some already-ground flour for ours, because we couldn't wait for her son to return on Monday to re-mill it, and started back after sharing a plate of food and *mot'e*, and several cups of *chicha*, which she offered us and with an invitation to come to the celebration of her husband's birthday in May to take photographs. And gifts of several pieces of bread—they have an oven as well— and three lettuces and an onion from the garden, which I delivered to Teresa.

On Saturday, we planted wheat in a field just below Wayninki, on the 'Tambo side of the stream. I set off with all of the food in the early afternoon ahead of Teresa, and since I knew the way, she didn't catch up with me until I was just above the field. It was a lovely, bright afternoon with clouds gathering, big, white thunderheads, all around the horizon as if caught on the peaks of the mountains. The men stopped to rest soon after we came, and we all ate and drank, the men talking and joking. I listened and contemplated the quiet mountainsides, the hacienda Wayninki, as still as if abandoned, the villages of Qoipa and Ayusbamba across the valley. When the men returned to their work, Teresa too went out into the field to pull up weeds and work with Jaime's little hoe, leaving me to sit there feeling quite useless. I followed her into the field and began pulling up weeds and tough grasses and, when she stopped to rest, asked her for the hoe she'd been using and went to work with it, breaking the earth where the seed had been scattered but where the cattle-drawn plow couldn't reach. I enjoyed the work, back bent under the sun, hands blistered by the handle of the hoe, the rich smell of damp earth rising from the broken ground under the blade as I turned it over the seed; a wonderful feeling I've never had of connection with the earth, cooperation with it to make things grow.

The work went quickly, the rest of that field and the small section above the road, the hoe taken from me finally by Ricardo when he finished with the plowing and had released the bulls to graze, with the implication that it was improper for me, a woman, to be working in the field with a hoe. I felt slightly hurt and indignant—I wouldn't have gone out to help in the field if it hadn't been for Teresa's example—but I have begun to see that, as they grow older and their children are grown, women seem to be freed to some extent of some aspects of the role of *woman,* no longer bound at least in casual situations by certain standards and restrictions which apply to younger women; also, the field was one Teresa had inherited from her mother, her land in effect, and it may have been proper for her to work in that field and not for me. Anyway, I sat idly and watched again, and then we all sat by the edge of the field drinking *chicha* and *trago,* as the clouds spilled over the mountains, darkening the late afternoon sky. By the time the *chicha* was gone and the cattle rounded up, the horses loaded, a light rain, almost no more than a mist, was blowing in the air, driven by a strong wind.

We started back, the long line of us—the men, the boys and some of their friends, Leonarda and Teresa and I, the horses and cattle—climbing the very narrow and winding and deeply worn path to the road. The rain still blew in the air, never enough to wet us, but enough to cool us after the hard work, and we reveled in it. Across the river, over the Otra Banda, rain fell in leaden sheets. The sun from low on the western horizon flowed up the Apurimac valley, reflecting from the mountainsides, from the clouds, diffused by the rain. The bend in the river was a cauldron of diaphanous gold, the mountains lit by the sun like the walls of a rough golden bowl, the air, full of rain laden with sun, like molten gold: it was phenomenal, and Gary and I, walking ahead with the horse on the road, stopped, our breaths all but taken away, and stood there awestruck in the road until the others began to catch up with us and we hurried on, a little embarrassed by our ingenuousness in the face of such spectacular beauty, a beauty which they, accustomed to grandeur, hardly seem to notice.

9. Virgen Concebidayoq

We went to Cusco for a couple of days in December, to bathe and to look for mail—the letters from family and friends in the States which keep us tenuously anchored in that other, more familiar world—and to buy *ají* peppers and onions for Teresa to make *uchukuta*, the very piquant hot sauce which enlivens what would otherwise be a very healthy but bland diet of grains and potatoes. I am afraid that we have created a near-addictive desire, almost a need, in our family for *uchukuta*, a condiment which most Quechua families in the highlands must usually do without. Though some families have small gardens which produce a few onions, they seldom produce many, and so onions, great crops of which are grown in the flat fields in the valley of Cusco, must usually be brought from the market in the city; and *ají* is grown down in the lowlands near the jungle in the Urubamba valley and must also be bought in the market in Cusco, except—in 'Tambo—when vendors come to the village for the festival of Natividad. *Uchukuta* is therefore an expensive luxury, since most people don't have money most of the time even to travel to Cusco and don't have a couple of live-in *gringo* anthropologists with an unnatural desire to bathe' now and then to bring occasional supplies from the city.

In this season, the journey to Cusco and back becomes more and more a trial, an ordeal fraught with hazard. As it rains more frequently and harder, the road grows worse and worse, washed away little by little where water runs across it or blocked by fallen rocks and mudslides, scored by deep rain-filled ruts or a half-foot deep in mud, slick as ice.

There are moments I wish I were even nominally Catholic like the others and could pray with a genuine sense of hope to Saint Christopher, take my hat off and cross myself when the truck lurches and teeters on the verge of a steep fall into some river valley. I have always enjoyed a certain sense of danger, but now I realize that the dangers which thrill me are ones which depend entirely for their quality on me, are under my control, or lack of it: situations which test courage or fortitude or skill, when if I fail, then the danger is real. But I have no control at all over the pitching of the truck over the unpredictable roads, no communication with the driver, can't usually even see the road to be prepared for the shocks that come, and therefore find my heart in my throat and feel a fervent desire to pray . . . This trip was made even longer by the failure of the brakes as we were coming down the hill into Yaurisque, which was remedied by substituting urine, readily available, for the brake fluid we needed, which was not: it worked. And then we ran out of gas not far beyond Yaurisque, a problem not rectifiable by turning to the same resource. Gary and I even considered walking to Cusco from where we were stalled, so ill-fated the journey seemed—safer on our feet—about twenty kilometers we figured, maybe four hours; we could be there by six or seven that evening, *if* all went well. But another truck came—San Martín, slow but dependable, though each time you see it on the road, creaking and swaying, you swear it highly improbable that it will make the trip again. It was crowded, but there was just room for us to stand against a wall. We reached Cusco about five.

Baltazar and the boys were gone when we got back to 'Tambo, Baltazar and Hugo down at Manzanapata doing *hallmiyoq*—the first hoeing of the small corn field. Daniel had gone to Huaynacancha to dance as an *ukuku* for the festival of the Virgen Concebidayoq, the Virgin of the Immaculate Conception, December eighth. Leonarda was out with the cows at pasture. We sat for most of the day doing almost nothing, reading, helping Teresa a little. When Baltazar returned, we ate, all together except for Daniel, who had gone the day before, Tuesday, and wouldn't return until Friday. We gave them the framed picture of Saint Francis—traditionally portrayed in a monk's brown robe and with a halo, his foot resting on a blue globe, helping Christ down from the cross—who is the patron saint of bakers, which we had bought for our godchild, the oven. Their delight was plain, like that on the faces of children on Christmas morning, and they admired it for a long time, pointing out different aspects of the picture to each other—and we felt secretly like the parents of those children on Christmas morning. We made an altar out of the picture the next morning in the *comedor* where the bread is made: a piece of sky blue paper tacked to the adobe wall—up high, out of reach of the little boys—as a background for the picture and a shelf underneath with a lacy skirt of pink plastic around it which Hugo cut from a plastic bag, to support a can of potato flowers and a candle. I had bought strawberries in the market in Cusco for the occasion of this little benediction, had carried them in my hat, holding it against my chest to protect them from the perils of the rough five-hour truck ride as best I could, and Teresa made *chicha frutillada: chicha* mixed with *trago,* flavored with crushed strawberries and some sugar, warmed in a pitcher in front of the fire. It was delicious. We blessed the work table in the *comedor* with it, under the eyes of Papa Dios and Saint Francis: we took off our hats and Baltazar said a sort of prayer in Quechua, and we each sprinkled a few drops of our first glass of *chicha frutillada* over the table, poured a little on the ground at each of its corners, and then drank.

Teresa had been cooking all morning, had started in fact the night before, as if for planting, and we didn't know why: if we had been going to plant, we would have set out early in the morning. They had been planning to go to Karhuakalla that day to meet the dancers returning from Huaynacancha to 'Tambo but had decided that we would go on Friday instead. So Teresa's intensive effort in the kitchen remained unexplained and, to us, ominous: if we are not allowed to know what is going on, it usually means we are to be excluded from whatever it is. Only after we had eaten and Teresa had packed up the food and filled jugs full of *chicha* and the horse was brought to be saddled did Baltazar tell us that they were in fact going to Karhuakalla that day, right then, not to return until tomorrow. They were going to stay the night with his nephew, which meant, because there is no communication between villages four hours' walk apart and the nephew had no way of knowing that they were coming, that Baltazar and Teresa would go there prepared to be good and welcomed guests, with food and *chicha,* and his nephew, once they were there, would be obliged by the customs of Quechua hospitality to insist that they stay. If this was the reason why Baltazar and Teresa didn't want us to go with them, we would have understood perfectly: we'd have felt awkward in our own culture intruding upon relatives with such unexpected and odd guests as we would have been in Karhuakalla and therefore rather resented the ruse they seemed to have felt necessary, allowing us to believe that we would all go together and saying nothing to us until it was unavoidable; though, to be fair, I suppose that they, knowing as little about us and our ways as we do of them, had no reason to assume that we would understand the situation. And, of course, it is possible that it had nothing to do with that at all, and the reason was much more complex than this.

Part of our bitter disappointment at times like this, when we are left out, is caused by the fact that when Baltazar and Teresa are not here, we have very little to do in 'Tambo, so much a part of the family's activities have we become. We learn from everything we are allowed to participate in or even just to observe, from the most mundane activities to the most exotic; we learn nothing from sitting at home. And we have found that it is usually a useless effort to go to visit other people, except on Sundays when almost everyone rests at home. On other days, either no one is at home, or you find yourself awkwardly in the middle of some event in which, by your presence, you oblige the people you came to visit to include you. So we end up sitting in our house or in the yard, as we did the rest of that day and Friday morning, idly reading books or writing, wishing we were in Cusco where at least we could go out for a cup of coffee in a café.

Hugo went both days to help Nicasio, Sebastiana's father, plant barley: somehow, at some time, a choice has been made—Hugo will marry Sebastiana. The decision will not be made formal until Baltazar goes to talk to Asunta and Nicasio about it on January sixth, his birthday, the day he has chosen to pay this call. (But how was this decision arrived at, and *when?*)

We had suggested to Baltazar as they were leaving that we would walk out to meet them on the path in the direction from which they would come with the dancers when they returned early on Friday afternoon. Baltazar had said that was fine; we would bring the camera, and he is ever enthusiastic at the prospect of being photographed. I helped Celestina for a while, cooking a meal to take to Andrés in the field where he was working, and about noon Gary and I prepared to go. We were halted before we left the yard by Leonarda, who insisted very definitely that her parents were not going to return until the *next* day, which we recognized, of course, was entirely possible in spite, once again, of what they had told us. We were again bitterly surprised—we thought, How naïve we are! Will we never learn?—though we weren't certain whether to believe her or not, whether for some reason of her own she simply didn't want us to go. But Celestina confirmed it, and all we could do was accept it as true. We went back to our house, unlocked the door, unpacked the things we'd been going to take with us—raincoats and books for a wait—cursing and complaining. Why can't they simply tell us what is going on? Why do they seem to feel they have to manipulate us like this, like children? We had thought this was over. I returned to Celestina's house to guard from the chickens the sprouted corn and wheat she had laid out to dry in the sun, while she carried Andrés' dinner to him. When she came back, Gary and I went for a walk, down to the stream called Misk'iunu (Sweetwater) just below the village to read: there is a grassy hillside which faces the afternoon sun, with the chatter of the water falling nearby to gently fill the air and calm the soul. Unfortunately, we ran into Leonarda and Jaime, pasturing the cattle in the little fenced meadow just above this refuge, and, not in a mood to tolerate anyone's company but knowing that it wasn't fair to take it out on them, endured their seldom-peaceful presence until finally we heard a child's shout from above, to which Leonarda responded. She reported to us, without revealing a trace of awareness that the news contradicted what she had told us not long before, that her parents had returned and wanted the key to the lock on the kitchen door, which Teresa had entrusted to me and I was keeping in my pocket. Damn it! We sent the key home with Leonarda, petulantly resisting our natural inclination to rush to welcome them home as if nothing was wrong, feeling generally deceived and abused, not knowing whether they had not instructed Leonarda to tell us that they wouldn't return when they had told us they would, to prevent us from even going out to meet them, and sat reading sullenly until we had each finished the chapters we were reading. Then we strolled back to the house and greeted them then as wholeheartedly as we could, hoping only that things would return to what we have learned to feel is normal.

A week or so later, the situation seemed more hopeful. We baked bread from the flour we'd brought back from Wayninki, a candle burning on the altar beneath the feet of Saint Francis, and in the afternoon baked some for a young woman to offer to the workers helping her father, a *compadre* of Baltazar, build the walls of a new house. A woman died on this day; we heard the church bells toll periodically. For a number of days afterward, people talked about it: she had been bitten by a spotted snake, and when she died, a toad jumped out of her mouth. Sunday morning Baltazar left early for the woman's funeral. He was gone all morning, and we reckoned that he would be out all day drinking, which proved to be true. In the afternoon—a big, broad afternoon, dead still as only the middle of a warm, sunny afternoon can be—we went for a long walk, out to Qeruru to see the cross that had been planted there on the day of San Andrés. As we were walking along the narrow path that cuts straight across the side of the mountain about halfway down, following the line of its crest, a large rock came hurtling down the long steep slope from above, bounding away from the earth upon impact with outcrops and ridges, gaining momentum with the force of gravity. We heard it, but the sounds of its approach did not add up to a whole, recognizable impression until it bounded across the path ahead of us and careened crazily down the slope below, leaving in its wake only an echo in our ears of the whistle of its passage through the stillness. The calm of that sunny mountainside suddenly shattered by a sense of danger, we stopped and looked up and knew—the quick mental calculations of surprise—that the rock hadn't

just somehow come loose and started rolling: it had been sent on its ca-
reening course deliberately. Someone was trying to hurt us. Neither of us
spoke. In moments, some mechanism of instinct assessed the significance
of that certainty and all aspects of our immediate situation—the lack of
shelter, the angle of the land above us—and then, without a word, we
went on, our hearts pounding. We heard the second rock before we saw
it, like the first: dull thuds when it struck earth, a clatter against rock, the
rustle of its swift passage through the brush. It swept across the path only
a foot or so in front of us. We froze, shielded somewhat from view from
the top of the mountain by a tall, straggly bush, again looked up, now
frightened and angry, and again saw nothing. We went on quickly, tensely
alert, like hunted animals, fugitive. When the third, bigger than the
others, more than a foot in diameter, hurtled down the mountainside at
us, there was no shelter, and we did not stop. We came to a herd of cattle
and horses and told ourselves that it was just some child, pasturing these
animals, trying, unable to know that we would do them no harm, to keep
us away from them, which made sense but did little to allay the fear and
anger which the sense of immediate danger had brought nor the intuition
of malice which shrouded us like a pall. We had passed beyond the crest
of the mountain and the slope above us now was gentler and the momentum of a rock would fail before it reached us, so we climbed on and up to
the prow of land where the *taytacha* stood, decorated with flowers, now
brown and withered, and a long, fringed sash. When we looked back we
saw a group of children as we had suspected, but the two who were
working their way down toward us from the crest were boys well old
enough to know that a rock tumbling down a mountainside could badly
hurt or even kill someone in its path. When they were near enough to
hear him, Gary shouted at them in reprimand. They stopped, but we were
certain that, over that distance, they couldn't have felt the force of our
anger: we should have waited till their curiosity led them to us to speak to
them. We walked out to the end of the ridge to sit in the sun as we had
planned to do and study the landscape, the fields and pastures below us,
the deep valley of the Apurimac and its tributary, the Molle Molle, the
point of their confluence just hidden by the mountains. But we couldn't
enjoy it. The boys came as near to us as the cross, where they stood innocently shouting questions at us: What was our dog's name? (Sandorcha
had come with us.) Did we want some *chicha?* Would we take their pictures? We alternately tried to ignore them and shouted back at them that
we couldn't hear them, that they should come to us if they wanted to talk:
we wanted to know who they were. We gave up at last any hope of peace.
Gary shouted that yes, he would take a photograph of them, so that they
wouldn't run away when we approached them, and we climbed back toward the point where the cross stood. When we reached them, Gary

scolded them furiously, threatening to report them to the authorities in 'Tambo and to the schoolteachers, now that we knew who they were, though actually we didn't recognize them and, in the heat of emotion, didn't think of asking their names.

We left them rather stunned, speechless, by the vehemence of our reaction and followed the path across the mountainside back toward 'Tambo, feeling somewhat better; the anger had been a catharsis for fear.

The following morning, as Baltazar and Gary and Hugo were preparing to go down to work in the corn field at Manzanapata, the governor came to the house accompanied by a young man. I saw them from the doorway of the kitchen where Gary and I were eating breakfast and assumed it was a slightly inopportune social call or that they had come to request help for some task. When I went outside, I greeted the governor and shook his hand. He asked me if we had gone to Qeruru the day before. My heart sank: maybe it was forbidden to approach the cross or to photograph it. Gary came out of the house, and the governor repeated his question to him and added that the young man with him accused us of having stolen the sash that hung around the cross. It was suddenly obvious that he must be a relative—if not a father, perhaps a brother or cousin—of the boys we had reprimanded, and they, taking our threat of reporting them seriously, felt they had to discredit us before we got them into trouble. It would be easy enough to discredit us: we were *gringos*, strangers, and there had already been doubt about our motives. Gary pointed out angrily that it was ridiculous, what would we want the sash for? and said that the man was welcome to come into our house and search for it if he wished. The young man mumbled, never meeting anyone's eyes, and the governor explained that he now claimed that we had also been seen excavating there; he had apparently decided that his original accusation was perhaps dubious and wanted to back it up with another more substantial one. I nearly laughed, but I felt too numb and chilled to laugh. The least he could have done was to invent something more original than an accusation of excavating for gold: the first *gringos* who came to Peru, the Spanish conquerors, stole gold, nearly every ounce of Inca gold—cups, jewelry, reliefs and plaques, statues, masks—to melt down into bullion and coin, so that almost none of the metalwork in gold survived. All it seemed that they wanted was gold: it was believed that they ate it, needed it to sustain life, they required so much of it, a suspicion corroborated by the Spanish themselves. And it is still somehow believed to be the ultimate motive, beyond tourism, of all *gringos* who come to Peru, four hundred and fifty years later.

He still refused to meet our eyes or even the governor's. Gary said that they should go, the three of them—he, the young man, and the governor—out to Qeruru right then to see the evidence, and then if our accuser wished to file a *denuncia* against us to enforce his accusation, we could go to court in the provincial capital to settle the problem. The governor declined—said he had work to do and suggested that they wait until tomorrow. But we protested that, in a day's time, someone could go and remove the sash and dig an excavation to provide false evidence against us; we assumed, perhaps naïvely, that no one had had the foresight or courage or time to do that the day before, after we'd gone, or that morning. Gary insisted that the man come with him to the *alcalde* to solicit his participation as witness, but Nicasio, the *alcalde*, said that because Qeruru was nearer to Pumatambo, the matter did not come under his jurisdiction. They returned to the governor, who had gone home. It was plain now that the accuser didn't want to go to Qeruru and see his accusation blatantly refuted, as we gambled that it would be, and the governor, Gary told me, finally called the man a liar and told Gary to go home and not to worry about it anymore. Don Carlos, the governor, had seemed skeptical about the validity of the accusation all along—I had even thought I had heard an insinuation of sarcasm in his voice when he'd first told us what it was—and I imagined optimistically that he took at least a little pleasure in denouncing it. We worried about it all day anyway. The way rumors spread here, we could not doubt that all of 'Tambo would hear of the accusation, valid or not, but probably not of the governor's reaction. When Gary went to talk to him on Wednesday though, don Carlos said the man hadn't come back, and the affair seems now to have died uneasily away.

One day, Gary helped don Andrés plant his barley fields, land right up on top of Apu Aqchakar, the mountain on which 'Tambo is built, nestled into the hollow of one of its flanks; I helped Celestina cook. After the remarkable organization and efficiency of Teresa's kitchen, the preparations seemed—and were in fact—painfully slow, rather poorly planned, and we didn't reach the field until quite late, three-thirty, by which time, Gary told me, Andrés was quite angry with her, though of course he said nothing when we arrived. I felt embarrassed for her and for Andrés: the special meals brought to the field are an important offering of gratitude for the help of the *chakrayoq*'s kin and *compadres* and should arrive just when the men begin to feel their hunger. The men helping Andrés had had to work from early morning until late afternoon without eating. The next day, when the planting was completed, we reached the field about one o'clock.

Each of those two days, Andrés came out of his house before the sun rose above the crest of Aqchakar, with his plain wooden *qero* full of *chicha* in his hands. He stood in front of his storehouse, facing the sunrise and the *apu*, and said a prayer to it, to Aqchakar. Then he took the *qero* in one hand and swung his outstretched arm in an arc across his body, flinging the *chicha* in a larger glittering arc into the air, to the *apu* and the sun.

It rains every day now; the only thing left to wonder about is *when* in the day it will rain. In the mornings the sky overhead is often clear: the clouds are lying in the valleys far below the village—the valleys are filled with clouds. As the air warms under the sun, the clouds rise and drift up the mountainsides and through the town like a thick fog and on upward to blanket the sky. Gray. I felt fairly cheerful this morning, in spite of the fact that we have accomplished nothing constructive in the past couple of weeks, have found only frustration and confusion, even fear for our lives. But it was pretty in the little field below the house this morning, quiet green and gray, the clouds white in the river valley, with the occasional cricket-like chirp of the hummingbird in the eucalyptus and the rhythmic chop of a hoe in the little potato field next door.

This sense of well-being is as fragile as a flawed china cup, and I know it. I feel I understand now, by means of direct experience, what it is to be a member of a minority, the same experience, I suppose, anywhere in the world: you are different. We are different, absolutely, unavoidably different, to whatever extent we adopt dress, language, behavior—there is no way we cannot, still, be different. Prejudice must be a very primitive, somehow instinctive reaction to difference, conquered only by training and force of will: you *look* different from everyone else—fair skin, blond hair, gray eyes (*ojos de gato*, someone called mine once: cat's eyes)—and so you simply can't be conceived of as quite human the way everyone else is recognizably human, and your feelings cannot be imagined as the same as theirs, nor your value as a person: there are no criteria by which to judge you except *difference*. And because your number is small, nobody either fears or respects you—there is no reason to. And so, you are easily victimized: children laugh or refuse to speak to you or find nothing wrong with pitching large rocks down mountainsides at you or just throwing pebbles in the street; adults find it convenient to blame upon you, your presence, any misfortune, such as the crop-damaging hail, which falls every year, but this year it's because of you.

On a more sophisticated basis, the same is true even in Cusco, though there the difference between us and them, which here draws a reaction of uncomplicated suspicion, almost without thought, is consciously recognized and understood: you are a *gringo*, a tourist, and therefore wealthy by Peruvian standards. Anywhere beyond the main plaza and sometimes even there, a *gringo* is likely to be the victim of a variety of ingenious forms of robbery, from simple pickpocketing and the slitting of purses and bags and backpacks with razor blades—the thieves simply walk behind and wait for things to fall out—to being physically overpowered or outnumbered and one's possessions taken by force from one's hands. We no longer wonder why the tour companies keep their often middle-aged to elderly and well-to-do patrons together as a body and chauffeur them around in private buses in only the most populous and respectable parts of the city; we used to think with disdain that they were missing the most interesting aspects of Cusco. But they are safe. And there, in Cusco, as here, there is no way not to be different, noticeable, not to be a victim, and there have been times when I have cried, or wanted to, in frustration at the injustice, the sense of violation, and times I have simply wanted to pack up and go home, all the way home.

We understand of course, rationally, the mechanics of the reaction to difference and that it is difficult for the people of a village to understand why two *gringos*, that breed known to them only as tourists and wealthy, would come to a place like 'Tambo not as sightseers, to look at the nearby ruins and the mythical origin place of the Incas and go away again, but to live as they live, in earthen houses without plumbing or electricity, and even help them in their work, the hard and necessary work of planting and raising and harvesting the crops, work from which we receive no benefit which they can comprehend, which means anything to their lives: we have no land for them to help us work in this system of cooperation and reciprocal labor, and these crops will feed their families next year, when we are gone. The concept of anthropology naturally doesn't make sense. We are apparently *not* spending the days of our lives, as people must, to produce food or to earn money (many sons and daughters have left villages to work for wages in Cusco or Lima, so they do know of making a living that way, and Gary's profession of university professor does mean something to them, but still, he is *here* and not there teach-ing). How do we support ourselves? They can't imagine some organiza-tion giving someone money to come and help them plant their crops. So they grow suspicious.

Don Carlos had suggested to us that we show the town authorities our official letters of introduction, which no one since the assembly in the town hall had asked to see, so that they could legitimately answer for us when townspeople, like the young man who had accused us of stealing the sash, came to them. Gary was asked to present them at an assembly to be held in the fields on the day of the community-wide *faena* to plant the crop of barley for the brewery. That morning, Teresa and Juana and I worked all morning in the kitchen: Teresa, as the wife of the *segunda* of Ayllu Nayhua, was preparing to feed all of the workers of the *ayllu*. I very nearly wasn't allowed to accompany Teresa to the fields in Paqopata, for when everything was ready, she packed my *q'epi* and directed me to go to

Hugo's field, where he too was planting barley, his first crop, and to hurry back to the house so I could watch the chickens and the pigs, which had gotten into the neighbor's potato field next door the previous afternoon. Baltazar had told me that morning before he left, using the familiar second person singular form of the Spanish verbs as he spoke to me, so that he clearly meant me and Teresa and not "the women" in general, that we would come later to bring the meal and an *odre* of *chicha*, so I had assumed that I would go with her and had begun to look forward to it: I had never seen the operation of a *faena* and had never been to Paqopata. Also, I felt it was important to be there so that Gary and I would present a united entity and to demonstrate to the community that I also worked and didn't spend my time out looking for gold while Gary worked in the fields. My astonishment and disappointment must have shown plainly on my face because Ricardo, who had returned with the horse to fetch the big *chicha* bag, said, "Or do you want to go to the *faena?*" I answered him, feeling hurt and indignant, that yes, I wanted to go to the *faena:* I wanted to take food to my husband and wanted to be there when he presented his papers. He explained this to Teresa and Juana, and they spoke to each other in Quechua too rapid for me to understand. I asked him to explain to me why Teresa didn't want me to go with her, when now I always accompany her to the fields, but he didn't respond. Finally Juana said directly to me in her awkward Spanish that all of the men of the town would be there and I said, "Yes?" and she added, "But everyone will see you." I said again, "Yes? They'll see Gary too." She must have thought that this blunt statement of fact, implying their objection to my company, would convince me, and when I remained apparently innocent of the implication, she reluctantly abandoned this line of reasoning. I looked to Ricardo. He said, "But the assemblies are always in the morning. It's all over now," a reason which I was convinced—rightly—that he had just invented for the purpose of the argument. I looked at them for a minute and then said, "All right," put down my spindle, demonstrating in gesture the confusion of hurt and anger I hadn't the vocabulary to express in words, and went to lock the door of my house. I felt I had been reduced to the stature of a kitchen slave whose presence was acceptable in relatively private situations when it was useful but an embarrassment in public, useful or not. I felt that if Baltazar so generously insisted to us that we are now a son and daughter to them—and indeed we have come to do more work than their own sons and daughters to help them now—that for the sake of honesty or at least of our feelings, they ought to stand by this sometimes-drunken declaration in public as well; at least not so clearly demonstrate embarrassment at our presence. Sometime, I thought—perhaps, again, naïvely—they have to get used to us. Don't they?

While I was out of the kitchen they discussed the problem. Perhaps

Ricardo explained to Teresa and Juana what he understood of my reaction, for when I returned and bent to lift the bundle that Teresa had packed for me to take to Hugo, he said, "No—you're going to the *faena:* Juana will go to Hugo." I said no, it was fine with me not to go with Teresa, but they insisted. This was the first time I had ever contradicted Teresa's plans, ever made known my own desire and intent, and I think now that it must have impressed Teresa that I had such definite feelings and the integrity to express them, having given little indication of either before. She packed the load from my bundle into another one for Juana to take and divided the rest into three nearly equal burdens for me, for Felícitas who had come to help, and for herself. Yet, while we were outside filling the *chicha* bag and securing it with ropes onto the back of the horse, Ricardo continued the attempt to discourage me from going. He told me that there would be eight hundred men working—another fabulous invention: the entire population of 'Tambo, men, women, and children, is only eight hundred and fifty or nine hundred. The *alcalde* had told Gary the day before that eighty or ninety men would be working. I said, "Eight hundred?" He nodded. Then he said, "And there are a lot of ignorant people. They'll talk. They'll talk nonsense, say stupid things." I thought wryly, So what's new? and wondered what they could say except that I had been there, as a proper daughter of the family would be. And I tried to explain to him that that was exactly why I felt I should go, so that people would see me as well as Gary, see me working like any other woman, perhaps understand a little better my purpose and Gary's, and therefore be less ignorant and suspicious. I'm not sure I convinced him.

The walk to Paqopata was lovely, the *q'epi* not too heavy, the path varied, neither all uphill nor all down: up through the village and toward Yanchakalla, but where the path which we climb to the fields of Yanchakalla leads up the mountainside, we followed instead a branch that continued level along its side and eventually into a marshy valley, where it crossed a small river on a bridge of logs brokenly covered with adobe and sod, and up to the fields, about forty minutes' walk. Ricardo had preceded us with the *chicha,* so when we reached the field, the men of the *ayllu* were already sitting in the sort of horseshoe formation called *kuskan tiy,* traditional for taking more formal meals in the field (*kuska,* meaning together, and *tiy* from *tiyay,* to sit), the opening of the arc downhill, with the eldest and most important men at the top and each man along the sides sitting between the legs of the man behind him, each on his poncho, all facing downhill. The women's carrying cloths with *mot'e* and cooked potatoes heaped on them and bowls of *ají* sauce were placed on the ground within the arc; the women all sat together outside its curve. The men were drinking *chicha:* one man sat outside of the arc with the *chicha* bag beside him, and a young man conveyed the *asta*s (the drinking horns) which the first filled to the other men in turn. As soon as the *asta*s were returned to him, we were served, Teresa first. Baltazar took his place at the top of the horseshoe.

Teresa served the meal in a manner which I imagined to be more like the way meals must have been served in the field before the advent of inexpensive and easily carried enameled tin plates. Because there were so many to be served, she filled only a single plate, which was carried into the center of the arc as the *astas* had been by a young man who filled the hands of each man with food from it; Teresa supplied a full plate when the first was emptied. Each man was served twice but, full of *chicha*, they ate hardly more than half of all we had brought. Near the end of the meal, the president and the *alcalde* came to take roll, standing with Baltazar before the men, reading out the name of each of the workers of the *ayllu* from a small notebook, and making marks in it as each man did or did not respond. A place was made for them along the side of the arc, and the two young men sat and Teresa served them from a plate which they shared. Then they rose, thanked us, and went on to another *ayllu*. Finally, a last round of *chicha* was poured and it was time to return to work. The men gradually began to leave the formation, always standing up inside it and walking out through the open end: one should never leave the group except by this route, nor anything be passed or reached for to or from the outside, out of respect for the center, where the food is received.

The men worked, stopped to rest, and worked again until they finished at the top of the field above us. Then, everything packed and loaded onto horses and our backs, the men and very few women of all the ten *ayllu*s descended the hill to where, at the bottom, the president and the *alcalde* convened the disastrous assembly, the men standing in the grassy pasture below the fields, each with his poncho tied over one shoulder and the crook of a hoe or a pick over the other. I sat some distance away with Teresa and Felícitas and another woman, who served us *chicha* from a plastic jug. As I watched the assembly, too far away to hear much but the confusion of shouting, I longed to stand beside Gary within the crowd of men, to add one more voice to our defense—the only other besides Baltazar's—but women do not take part in most assemblies. As he stood in the center of the large group of men, all of the hostility, rumors, and accusations which, except for that one, have never been spoken directly to us were hurled at him, everyone shouting at once. The *alcalde*, Nicasio, quieted them, Gary gave him the letters, and Nicasio read them aloud and then explained them in Quechua. The uproar began again: How do they know that we are the people the letters refer to? Where is our identification? I sat restlessly, straining to hear, composing in my mind an eloquent and moving little speech about how we had come to Peru for the same purpose for which their children go to school—we had attended, invited by the schoolteachers, the elaborate graduation ceremonies at the school on Friday (achieving, we thought, a measure of social success) and had been impressed by the respect and importance the people of 'Tambo attribute to education—to *learn;* about how nobody in the United States knows what life is like in Peru, the life of which they are in fact very proud, and that of course we could go to see Machu Picchu or Mauk'allaqta and Pumaorqo like all of the tourists, but those aren't the real Peru: *this,* their lives, is the real Peru. I thought, If only I could say something to them; but it probably wouldn't have made much difference. The reaction to us by the people of 'Tambo is by this point an instinctive one, not rational, and probably inevitable, something we will just have to endure; the problem not one that will respond to eloquent speeches or carefully reasoned arguments.

Afterwards, Gary came toward us a little pale and shaken, a little angry, with Baltazar and Ricardo and some of the other men of the *ayllu,* the more open-minded ones I supposed, who were willing to accept us more readily than others on the basis of Baltazar's belief in us and support. We drank *chicha* from the bag, talking about the United States, Gary and I answering their questions, responding to their curiosity as eagerly as scolded children anxious to please anyone who will give them friendly attention; and about air travel and tourists. We started home in the still-blazing late afternoon sun. I found myself soon far ahead of everyone, propelled by a tight-wound coil of tension: Gary had quietly explained to me all that had happened, and it was clear that this was a breaking point. He had decided to leave the next day—Monday—for Cusco, return with our passports to 'Tambo on Tuesday, and come back on Wednesday. We are leaving on Thursday for several weeks in Nazca. This would mean three consecutive full days of difficult and exhausting travel to and from Cusco and back again, to be followed by two more to Nazca, but seemed necessary to him. Baltazar later convinced him to make notarized copies of the documents instead, send them to him and to the authorities of 'Tambo on the truck, and bring the passports when we come back from Nazca. We thought sadly, as we sat with the family later, that though we have won enough of the affection of Baltazar, Teresa, and the children to know that they, privately, will miss us as we will miss them, they will probably be rather relieved not to have to cope with the problems we present for a while.

We left for Cusco the next morning. We are sending the officials notarized copies of our new passports with the truck driver; they have copies of the letters—stamps, seals, signatures and all. We seem to have reached that point in the evolution of human relationships, friendships, marriages, or the relationship of an anthropologist with the particular people he lives with, when after the initial fascination of discovery wanes, the stress of inevitable difference becomes too great, and each partner in the relationship must finally confront those differences and understand them if the relationship is to continue. We are prepared to deal with difference: that's what, as anthropologists, we are here for. We only hope that now, during the time we are away, the people of 'Tambo will be able to do so, without the distraction of our presence. There were tears in Teresa's eyes when we left the next morning.

Interlude

C hristmas Day in Cusco. We spent the afternoon of Christmas Eve strolling among the crowds in the streets and around the plaza. The market has spilled out into the city: lining the streets that circle the plaza, now closed to traffic, there are vendors' stalls, several deep, selling decorations and crèche scenes, fireworks, toys, dolls, and *panetones* (special Christmas breads baked in tall round loaves with raisins and candied fruit). And traditional, typical foods: stuffed potatoes and *rocotos rellenos,* which are stuffed hot peppers like the chilis rellenos of the southwestern U.S., boiled chicken and chicken soups, guinea pigs roasted whole on spits with bright red tomatoes in their mouths, hot boiled corn on the cob served with chunks of fresh native cheese, baked sweet potatoes, and *anticuchos* (chunks of meat, usually beef heart, grilled on skewers and basted with *ají* pepper sauce). We wandered from stall to stall, inspecting the wares and sampling almost everything, one or the other of us, and came home quite certain that we'd never eat again. As a Christmas present, we bought ourselves a painted ceramic bull, the kind that are placed on the roof of a newly built house: they are supposed to bring good luck and prosperity. On our way back to our room, we were invited to share sweet Peruvian champagne and homemade cakes and cookies with the family of Señora Tupayachi, the little lady who does our laundry when we are in Cusco. And then we went out to dinner, over which we sat alternately cheerful, infected unavoidably by the sight of two young fathers at another table, trying out, one after another, the toys they had bought for their children, and quietly melancholy, wishing we could somehow be transported home, where the company of family and friends and the familiar cold and snow of winter make Christmas really Christmas for us (reflecting, after the hot, tropical summer afternoon, that a year ago we woke on Christmas morning to sun dazzling on two and a half feet of snow and a temperature of twenty-six degrees below zero). At midnight, fireworks exploded all over the city, rockets and cherry bombs and fancy displays mounted on contraptions of wood and paper with wheels that spin, throwing sparks and cinders and acrid smoke in all directions—very popular in spite of, or perhaps because of, the obvious danger—sounding like volleys of rifle fire. And more this morning: we woke to the sound of small explosions from the churchyards of Santa Teresa and San Cristóbal, each just a few blocks from our room.

Tomorrow we leave for Nazca, early in the morning on an Hidalgo bus. The trip is supposed to take twenty-eight hours. We talked to everyone we knew about the bus lines to find out which one is trusted now. Any time you say you are traveling by bus, people tell you every horrendous story they know of buses going over precipices. We heard one fewer story about Hidalgo, but you never know. Andean roads were not made for buses; in fact, I'm not sure it's possible to make a road in the Andes that would be suitable for buses. Most of the big buses that ply the roads in the mountains are ones that have been retired from service on proper highways—real, paved, multi-lane highways—on the coast or in Brazil or somewhere. Anyway, if we get there, it will be nice to be warm and dry for a while. I look forward to sitting in the sun by the swimming pool at the Hotel Montecarlo.

10. Return to 'Tambo

I woke early on the twenty-third of January, the second morning of the tortuous thirty-four hour bus ride to Cusco from Nazca—this time on a brand new Morales Moralitos bus which made the entire trip without breaking down, not even a flat tire—just as the dim forms of the land began to be faintly visible through the dirty, mud-splashed window and the fog outside. A rooster crowed from a seat in the back of the bus. I watched through the window until I could see more clearly but didn't quite recognize the landscape: I thought we must have been approaching the broad valley of Limatambo but couldn't be certain and slept again until we were on the Plain of Anta, nearing Cusco then. And then we watched out the window like children, with childlike anticipation, as we descended into the city. A chill, gray, rainy-season morning, the church and cathedral towers, the red-tile roofs wet and gleaming: Cusco.

At five-thirty in the morning, still dark and cloudy, we had wished, almost, that there would be no truck going to 'Tambo. We weren't sure what we dreaded about coming back, why we were so reluctant: the physical discomforts of living in 'Tambo, which we reminded ourselves are minor, the small daily emotional discomforts, which we comprehend and are relatively easily able to cope with, or that which we have bluntly analyzed and discussed until nothing remained of it, we thought, but an abstract, intellectual problem—the general suspicion and disapproval of the population of 'Tambo. As for that, we told ourselves, we just have to wait and see, as we had told ourselves countless times during the weeks we'd been away. Though it had rained only twice, very lightly, during the week we had been in Cusco since our return to the highlands, at six o'clock—what should have been sunrise—it began to rain steadily and hard. We had been the first passengers on the truck and had claimed the most dependably comfortable and desirable places to sit, on the plank just behind the cab, next to the wall. I sat there resolutely as the truck pulled out of Cusco, chilled and wet in spite of all the clothing, the parka, and plastic rain jacket I wore: the tarp which they pulled over the back of the truck wasn't long enough to shelter us all, and you have to crouch uncomfortably, a position not bearable for very long, to remain under it if you sit on the bench instead of on the floor. I soon gave up and abandoned my place to huddle miserably on the bare floor of the truck, trying to sleep to make the time go faster, leaning against my backpack under the protection of Gary's rain poncho as he sat on the seat above me. I woke when we stopped in Yaurisque, cramped and numb. It had stopped raining.

We got off the truck, which can no longer negotiate the last section of muddy road down into 'Tambo, at Cruzq'asa, just outside the house of Baltazar's sister Vicentina. She called to us from her doorway as we climbed down from the truck to come in for *mot'e* and *chicha*. The *chicha* was good—we hadn't tasted *chicha* in a month—and the delicate and uncomplicated flavor of the boiled corn was almost a surprise, something to be savored. We sat there for a few minutes as she went about her work, then thanked her and set out for 'Tambo. Just beyond the edge of the village we met a young man and his wife who had been on the truck with us. He had been joking with Gary, after he, in silent complicity, had watched the driver give Gary too much money in change when he paid our fares, about buying a bottle of *trago* with the unexpected bonus. He offered us new potatoes to eat, and Gary offered, seriously, to buy a bottle of *trago;* this was, after all, a homecoming, however uncertain we were of welcome. The young man sent his wife with an empty bottle and Gary's money to buy it at the store in Cruzq'asa. As we waited for her, another, older man who had also been on the truck called to us. His wife had met him with a pot of soup, *mot'e,* and hot pepper sauce, all of which he offered to share with us, insisting that we finish the soup. We all shared the *trago,* to "warm us up" for the walk to 'Tambo. While we drank, another woman gave us a plate of *yuyu hawcha* and a hard-boiled egg. By the time we started walking to 'Tambo, we had eaten far too much, unable, in politeness, to refuse any of this welcoming generosity, and had begun to feel that our reception in 'Tambo might not be so bad after all; and perhaps our optimism was not just an effect of the *trago.*

Baltazar told us when he returned in the evening that day that nobody had said anything about us since we left. That all of the furor about us had been *por gusto*—for fun. Some fun. But it means, probably, that even if it starts all over again now that we're back, we shouldn't take it so seriously. We are simply the most obvious and safe target, the most interesting thing to talk about; we are the most engaging long-term phenomenon to occur in 'Tambo in a long time, perhaps ever, in people's memories, and they take advantage, deliberately or unconsciously, of the opportunity afforded by our presence to build causes, to create a sensation: to make the routine of daily life a little more exciting.

It must be some close corollary of the axiom that a watched pot never boils: that everything happens when you're not there to see it.

Daniel is gone.

The Quechua word they use to tell us about it is *chinkay:* to disappear or to be lost.

We left 'Tambo on the twenty-first of December. On Christmas morning, Daniel left home. When he woke that morning he suggested to Hugo that he might go out to Yanchakalla to see how the early potato crop was doing. Hugo was going to go out to gather firewood. Daniel was in the yard getting the horses ready for Hugo while the others were eating; when he didn't come in to eat, Teresa went to look for him, but he was gone. They thought at first that he had gone to Yanchakalla, though it was unlikely that he would go without eating first, and he didn't come back within a couple of hours—Yanchakalla isn't very far from 'Tambo—and then they discovered that all of his clothes were gone too, as were half of the four thousand *soles* that he and Hugo had saved. He didn't come back. About three in the afternoon Teresa, distraught, set out on foot to look for him and walked on the road all the way to K'airamayu, a quarter of the distance to Cusco. She didn't get home again until long after dark. And Daniel didn't come back.

Baltazar asked people who had traveled to Cusco that day if they had seen his son, but Daniel hadn't been on the truck. He said that then he had even gone to Cusco himself to look for Daniel, but without success. At the same time that Daniel left, another boy vanished, his cousin, the son of Teresa's brother Julián, and they say the boys probably went together to look for work, to earn money in Quillabamba in the province of La Convención, where Baltazar worked when he was a young man, or in Puerto Maldonado, where Hugo had worked. They also mention Lima: Daniel's eldest brother, Jesús, and his family are there. But it is unlikely that Daniel has gone to Lima: he only had two thousand *soles*, scarcely two dollars.

Baltazar asked when he told us the story, What did he lack here? Nothing! What was wrong? What did he want? Probably, I thought, nothing was wrong. He had graduated from the school in 'Tambo a week before Christmas and wasn't to go to the *colegio* (high school) in Cusco for another year, if he ever goes; it seems unlikely: few children do. I think that he must have wanted to go and earn money, prove himself, as his father had done, as his brothers had done, and was afraid that he wouldn't be allowed to go because he is the last son and because Hugo will be married soon, and then Daniel will be the only one left to help Baltazar in the fields.

Baltazar says they cried for him on the day of Navidad, Christmas day, and cried for him on Baltazar's birthday, the sixth of January. The first thing all of the children said to us as we met them one by one on our return was, Daniel is gone, hoping I think that we had seen him in Cusco or knew where he is. I am certain we will all cry for him when we celebrate Ricardo's birthday on Sunday, when *chicha* and *trago* free all of the sorrow which people here suppress so carefully, the sorrow of loss, the fear of the unthinkable: they haven't seen Jesús in ten years.

So, Daniel is gone. One of the pigs is gone (a creature I hardly miss: I wish they'd give away the other two, who now sleep in Sandor's place just outside our door). The trader from Espinar came and, in exchange for some amount of barley, wheat, and corn, Teresa bought new, white wool to spin. Juana is pregnant—I thought I had heard her say so before we left; she has mentioned it several times since we've been back. They celebrated Baltazar's birthday, finished most of the hoeing of the fields, and Sandor has acquired a healthy population of fleas and, they tell us, tangled with a puma: he still bears the scratches on his nose. And in the meantime, everybody seems to have forgotten or forgiven our sins.

Life simply goes on; it has for more than a month now without him, and since they told us about his disappearance, nobody has said a word about Daniel. Not even the children.

The weeks away from 'Tambo, in Nazca with another professor and a group of students from Gary's university, refreshed in us our sense of identity as North Americans, sharpened our memories of our life at home in the States, reminded us of what it is to be accepted, to *belong*. The sense of adventure that carried us bravely into 'Tambo when we first arrived does not recur now: we are too aware of the relative deprivation, both physical and emotional, of life here. I feel somewhat less ambition, rather less willingness to subject myself to awkward situations, which for me at this point, so insulated have I been, means virtually any situation outside our adoptive family, who know why I'm here and how much Quechua I understand, who treat me rather indulgently like an intelligent child. We give each other encouragement, Gary and I, and tell ourselves that it's just because we've become unaccustomed to living this way, which it probably is. We won't at any rate have much time to brood about the challenge of the rest of our time here: Ricardo's birthday is the seventh, and then, very soon, it will be Carnaval. Carnaval will be a busy time—the *segundas* of the eight *ayllus* which hold land bear the *cargo* for the festival, so Teresa and I, I expect, will have a lot of work to do. The celebration of Carnaval actually begins with the Day of Compadres, two Thursdays before the first day of Carnaval, and runs through the Day of Comadres a week later and beyond to the celebration of Carnaval itself: Sunday the twenty-first is the day of Carnaval, and Tuesday is its culmination, when the celebration moves into the streets and the plaza.

In spite of the reluctance I feel, or perhaps in desperation prompted by it, I did something today that I've never done before: alone, I went visiting. I took my spindle and, for the first time accomplishing the feat of spinning as I walked, went out into the street, across the plaza and up the steep street to Juana's house. On the way, I met little Agapito, who was carrying a bundle of firewood on his back and a bunch of dahlia-like flowers, deep red, which he had brought from the *phaqcha,* where the stream, the Misk'iunu, spills across the path to Yanchakalla near the village. He asked me in Quechua if I wanted one, seemed surprised that I had understood when I answered him, in Quechua, asked me again, and gave me one, smiling at me the way a mother might smile at a baby who had spoken a first recognizable word. I tucked it into the band of my hat.

Juana had looked at the sky when I asked her if she was weaving now and said yes, she was weaving a carrying cloth, a *lliqlla,* and that she would probably weave today; weaving requires good weather—it is outdoor work, so that there will be enough light to see by to weave the intricate patterns and enough space for the long, long warp on the backstrap loom. I found her working in the yard, sitting just inside to the left of the door onto the street, yards of the warp of a brilliantly colored *lliqlla* stretching across the entire front wall of her kitchen, fastened head-high to a roof pole at the other end. I crouched beside her for a minute watching her hands as she picked up the threads of the warp to make the bands of pattern, until she politely beckoned me to sit on the skins in the shade on the opposite side of the narrow yard and instructed Eloy to pour me a cup of *chicha* from a pitcher standing near her. Apparently she had expected me, which was gratifying. I sat with my enormous cup of *chicha* and my spindle, both forgotten as I became absorbed by the rhythms of her work and occasionally chased the chickens and pigs away from the sprouted corn drying in the sun. A couple of times I returned to her side to watch, to ask any question I could manage to formulate in Quechua. Though I had thought the piece garish when I first saw it as I walked into the yard, I rather admire the boldness of her choice of colors: the broad *pampa* (the plain area) of the textile is a brilliant scarlet-orange; the patterned bands on each side of this are of contrasting colors—magenta, red, blue, blue-green, yellow, a bright and a dark green, and white, each pattern of two colors. She told me the names of a couple of the patterns, which I remembered from the weaving I had seen in progress the day we had come to 'Tambo in August and now guessed correctly, and the name of the heddle, which I only half understood. When I got home and looked up this word, I found nothing in the Quechua dictionary that was anything like what I thought I had heard. I didn't ask for any more names because I hadn't brought paper and a pencil to write them down with— rather poorly prepared for an anthropologist—and I knew I would have other opportunities. She said the wooden pieces of the loom were made from *waranway* from Qolqebamba and that Baltazar had made them for her. I learned from watching her this time that probably the only way to understand how to weave is to do it yourself, following someone's example; maybe I will ask Baltazar to make me a loom. After a while I finished my *chicha* and thanked her for it and asked her if it was all right if I returned tomorrow or Friday. She told me maybe Friday or Saturday—she would be carrying food to Ricardo tomorrow. And I left, feeling fairly satisfied with myself, though I wished I had remembered paper and a pencil.

Baltazar went to Paruro today to testify in an investigation of the death of a man, a godson of his, in Qolqeuqru: someone had filed a *denuncia* against the dead man's father, accusing him of killing his son. Baltazar came home a little drunk (as he usually is, we have learned, when he is gone all day for any reason) and recounted the whole day to us, obviously proud that he is respected by the officials in Paruro to the extent that they ask him to come and testify; he has apparently done so in a number of cases. We paid him our room and board for the month yesterday, seven thousand *soles,* and when he returned from Paruro, he boasted that he had spent five thousand *soles* inviting his friends in *la provincia* to *chicha* and *trago*—"licorcito," as he said, which might translate roughly into English as "a little drink." I wonder if this stereotype of men is universal, the stereotype of the working man who blows the first part of his week's paycheck on Friday afternoon drinking with "the boys." I wonder if Teresa knows?

Hugo and Sebastiana are now living in the premarital state of *sirvinakuy:* Hugo still eats his meals here and helps Baltazar with his work, but he sleeps with Sebastiana at her parents' house and also helps her father in their fields. Nicasio is now referred to as Hugo's *suegro* (his father-in-law). It came up somehow, I think when we were discussing the problem of the family of rats which seemed to have taken over the storeroom above our room while we were gone and had begun to make incursions into our house as well, that not only is Daniel obviously no longer sleeping upstairs, but Hugo isn't either. Baltazar and Teresa have moved into the kitchen for the duration of the rainy season, for the warmth of the dry floor—the fire keeps it dry there—and Leonarda too is sleeping there, "because she's afraid," Hugo said. We assumed that he had moved into Baltazar and Teresa's now unoccupied room or the storeroom above it where Leonarda had slept, and he waved a hand noncommittally in that direction when we asked him. It didn't strike me until later that he might not be sleeping here at all, until I remembered that Baltazar had been planning to call on Asunta and Nicasio on his birthday on January sixth. The word *sirvinakuy* comes from the Spanish *servir* (to serve) with the usual twist of the Quechua tongue which pronounces *e*'s as *i*'s and makes Quechua verbs out of all manner of Spanish words. (Even in the Spanish spoken by the Quechua, "Spanish" verbs are made out of Spanish nouns, following an etymological pattern of the Quechua language by which verbs are derived from nouns.) The word means to "serve each other" and seems to refer to the young man's service to his future father-in-law, the young woman's to her mother-in-law, perhaps to prove themselves worthy and capable spouses. In the winter after the harvest, we will build a house for Hugo and Sebastiana, and they will live together there. They may not be formally married even then: the ceremony will be planned when the parents decide to sponsor it or when they have a child. They say a baby cannot be baptized until its parents are married by the church—an odd juxtaposition of Quechua and Catholic tradition, at which I suppose any "good" Catholic, Latin American or North American, would be horrified.

Quechua Spanish: I learn it as I learn Quechua, gradually unlearning some of my book-taught Spanish—*no sirve*. In Quechua I have learned ways to plead, to complain, and to thank profusely. I have even learned how to refuse food, though this is on the very margin of social acceptability and works only because I'm a *gringa* and allowances must be made for my ignorance of proper conduct and my apparently small stomach: refusal makes people uncomfortable because it prevents the perpetuation of the see-saw disequilibrium which is the foundation of reciprocity, prevents them from either "indebting" you or reciprocating some small generosity on your part in the overwhelming proportions to which they feel perversely obliged and are accustomed to. I haven't yet learned how to refuse drink, unfortunately, except by pleading severe illness: when you say that your stomach hurts, people are extremely considerate in passing by you when serving *chicha*, but they insist that *trago* is good for the stomach. (I haven't acquired the vocabulary to attempt to explain what it must do to the cells of one's brain.) Obviously, this method cannot be employed too often for fear of coming to be considered delicate or unfit or of the hostess becoming suspicious that you don't think her *chicha* is good, so, usually, one simply raises one's enormous glass of *chicha,* says "¡Salud!" and drinks. As for *trago,* naturally, because it is potent and foul-tasting and yet necessary in so many circumstances, there exists an extensive though largely unacknowledged complex of means to avoid drinking it, ranging from simple, playful, and inoffensive tricks to elaborate ruses—most of them developed and utilized only by women. I've seen Juana dump a *copita* of *trago* quickly down the front of her sweater, for example, when no one was looking—you have to be very quick because people generally watch like hawks to be sure that you drink it—or into a neighbor's *chicha.* Unfortunately, I have not yet achieved by Quechua standards the degree of social grace required to carry any of these methods off successfully.

Leonarda has decorated the roan calf with a wreath of yellow and orange and red flowers, a crown of them around his horns: it's his birthday too, his first, as well as Ricardo's.

On Friday while Teresa and I were cooking, a young boy came to the house. He stopped by the gate into the yard, as visitors do, to call, "Tiay! Teresa Tiay!" until Teresa went out to talk to him. When she came back into the kitchen, she told me that the boy had said that Daniel was in Cusco. She told the whole story to Baltazar, who recounted it to us in Spanish that evening: Daniel and his cousin had gone to Quillabamba to work and had just returned to Cusco. The other boy came back to 'Tambo, but Daniel had remained in Cusco, staying with a family friend, one of the four Coronel brothers, who has a shop near the truck stop in Belempampa. They said that Daniel had cut his leg with an axe, a report which didn't cause as much alarm as I might have expected: it is apparently assumed that a boy Daniel's age can take care of himself, even in such dire emergencies, or else it was understood somehow that this was simply a dramatic embellishment of the original story, invented as things are in the course of retelling. But why didn't he come home? Baltazar said again that the other boys, Hugo and Jesús, had gone with his permission, with his blessing: he had given them money, bedclothes, to take with them. But Daniel had just gone, run away, not telling them where, not even saying that he was going; they couldn't even write him a letter to find out if he was all right. We gave Hugo money for the fare to take the truck to Cusco and find Daniel and persuade him to come home. Gary asked Hugo to tell Daniel that we might be able to get work for him with an archaeologist we know from the University of Texas who is digging at Pikillaqta in the valley of Cusco and needs laborers. Hugo left yesterday, and we wait, hoping against hope.

Toward noon we went to Juana and Ricardo's house to celebrate Ricardo's birthday with them. I walked up with Teresa, who carried a large pitcher full of *chicha* and a bottle of *trago*. I was ushered into the kitchen to help the women—Juana, Teresa, Asunta, and Sebastiana—shell new peas, and Gary sat outside with Ricardo and Baltazar and Ricardo's father, don Felipe, who had come from Paruro on horseback, and later a man named Federico, the *mensajero* who carries mail and messages to 'Tambo from the provincial capital like a pony express rider. Whichever man was serving *trago* outside came into the kitchen now and then to serve the women, who all tried to refuse the *copita* and ended up drinking it with a grimace.

In the early afternoon, Hugo came into the yard and dropped his red poncho near the door of the kitchen. Through the door, I could see that there were tears in Baltazar's eyes: Daniel had come back with him. Daniel was outside in the street, reluctant to come in, into the midst of the inevitable fuss that would be made over him and possibly his father's anger; he too was crying, Hugo reported. Hugo had the calculatedly casual air of a self-acknowledged hero suppressing pride in some universally recognized accomplishment. He went outside again to talk to Daniel and then came back into the yard. After a while, Daniel came in from the street, still crying, and slipped into the kitchen where he sat at the back, in the darkness away from the door. I had felt tears in my own eyes as soon as I saw them in Baltazar's, and as Daniel brushed past me, sitting just inside the kitchen door, I felt I had seldom wanted to hug someone so much: we had felt an unavoidable emptiness here since we came back and found him gone, but I had no idea how glad I would be to see him. I didn't look at him though, glancing up only for a moment as he came in, lowering my eyes quickly, not wanting to embarrass him, and his eyes avoided mine and everyone else's. He sat in the darkness still sniffling, sobbing sometimes, and every once in a while I looked over my shoulder at him, struggling with my own tears at the emotion on his face and in my throat, an emotion that charged the atmosphere and everyone there like electricity in a storm. He was always looking away, toward the wall. He looked older somehow; his hair had grown long and wavy and he wore a new felt hat instead of his knitted cap. In a little while Baltazar came into the kitchen and, choking with sobs, gave Daniel an emotional lecture about going away without his father's permission and not telling him where he was going. After Baltazar went back outside, wiping his eyes on his sleeve, Teresa, who had been out of the kitchen, came in and, also crying, gave him a mother's scolding. The little boys, Jaime, Eloy, and Orlando, came in and stood by him for a few minutes, one at a time; he was very tender with them. And when his friend Teodoro, Pascuala's son, a little younger than Daniel, came in, Teresa announced to him,

"Daniel's home!" and Teodoro's face brightened into an immediate smile which lasted only for a moment before he caught himself and then went back and leaned next to Daniel against the bed at the back of the kitchen, very casually. Juana gave them both something to eat. Once after Teodoro and the little boys had gone and most of the women were out of the kitchen, I turned around and touched his arm for a moment and said, "Daniel, it's good to see you," and he said, simply, "Sí." Finally, attention drifted back to the celebration of Ricardo's birthday. We carried on drinking and the women cooking: new peas cooked with their pods and potatoes, garbanzo beans, rice, and four guinea pigs. Daniel stopped crying and went with Hugo to play some new records on the record player in the other room across the yard. And the day progressed as birthdays here do: everyone got more and more drunk at everyone else's insistence, and after dark we danced *huaynos* and *marineras* to the accompaniment of the record player. But there was a sense of completeness that hadn't been there before, when we started, of things being right.

The next morning we talked to Daniel about the possibility of working for our friend at Pikillaqta and asked him if he would like us to talk to the archaeologist about it. He said yes, though I'm not sure his response didn't simply reflect the Quechua custom of accepting anything that's offered because it's impolite to refuse. And then he went off with Hugo to gather firewood and we returned to Ricardo and Juana's house for the second day, the *corcova*, of his birthday. When Daniel showed up later, he had been shorn: the way men here cut their hair is to cut it as close as possible to the scalp with a scissors, so that even little boys look like old men when they've just had a haircut, with almost no hair and their felt hats on. And so things seem to return to normal, except that there is an air about Daniel somehow of something precious and fragile, though everyone tries not to let him know it. And he still wears his new hat.

11. Cleaning the wheat field

Until we left 'Tambo at Christmas, I had forgotten the simple emotional comfort of spending whole days, one after another, with people you can talk to or just be yourself with, naturally; of knowing without thinking that you are behaving correctly, without having to be constantly, vigilantly *aware* because your natural social instincts do not serve—manners, gestures, the intonation of your voice even though you may speak the right language, your facial expressions; of feeling that you know what's going on around you; and of being able to understand and assess a situation accurately and have an opinion that you know is valid and that someone might be interested in. I have been through this before, of course, but when we first came to live here in September, it was an adventure, a challenge. Now, some part of me seems to feel that I've done enough—experienced enough adventure? met the challenge?—and has grown tired, I guess, of peeling potatoes and cutting up onions.

A soft, gray February morning. The world is very small: clouds have fallen over the mountains like a goose-down quilt, settling deep into the valleys. Beyond the trees just below the house, there is nothing but cloud, the spectacular backdrop of near and distant mountains replaced by one of soft, blank, seamless gray.

On Saturday, we went down to clean the field of wheat at Hak'oriki, below Hacienda Wayninki, the wheat now knee-high and emerald green. This is a process of weeding, as you would weed a garden, pulling up the unwelcome invaders with your hands. Baltazar had hired a team of boys for one hundred *soles* each for the day, and they moved in more or less a line, working uphill, over one section of the field after another. Teresa and I cooked a meal, plentiful but not elaborate, and instead of cooking meat, she made fresh cheese from milk from the cow. This is clearly not one of the most ritually important agricultural tasks, evidenced by the lack of elaboration of the meal and by the fact that Baltazar had simply hired boys for money rather than collecting his debts of labor from other men. But on Wednesday, Gary and I helped with *papa hallmay* (the hoeing of the potato fields), a task traditionally nearly as important as the planting of potatoes and corn: the work and the return from the fields are supposed to be accompanied by the music of a *lauta* (a flute) and a *tambor,* (a small drum). Baltazar worked with Gary, Hugo and Daniel, Ricardo and Nicasio, and two other men whom I didn't know though I'd seen them before. The fields are at K'airamayu, two hours' walk from 'Tambo toward Yaurisque, and at five-thirty in the morning the men came for breakfast, for which Teresa had done much of the preparation the night before; they left at six, with a big skin bag full of *chicha* and a bottle of *trago.*

Sebastiana was there to help Teresa cook. She had helped for a few hours the day before as well, beginning her service to her mother-in-law: I had seen her in Teresa's house as a guest before when Asunta was helping but hadn't yet seen her come alone especially to work. We began as soon as the men left. Teresa had begun boiling meat the day before: part of that same cow—the one that had died in November!—the meat now well dried into *charki* (our word "jerky" comes from the Quechua *charki*). Juana came, returning the pitcher, again full of *chicha,* which Teresa had brought on Ricardo's birthday. When this was gone, Teresa served her own, and we drank *chicha,* as women do while cooking for the more important agricultural events, and worked steadily until ten or ten-thirty: three dishes—ground *tarwi, yuyu hawcha,* and noodles with potatoes— and omelette-like pancakes made with five eggs Teresa had been saving and the boiled meat and *mot'e* and *ají* pepper sauce. We divided this into three carrying cloths, as well as a bundle of *mot'e* and a full plate of food to give to Vicentina as we walked through Cruzq'asa, two plastic jugs of *chicha,* one for Vincentina and one for us to drink on the way, and a bottle of *trago.*

Thirsty, we stopped part of the way up the long slope of Apu Ankhara, most of the second half of the walk, to drink. Teresa blew across the mouth of the plastic jug before she drank, reciting the names of the *apus* in a low voice, sharing the *chicha* with those powers in this manner. I had never heard her, nor any woman, do this before: only men addressed the *apus.* Perhaps it was because we were all women, no man among us, and we were drinking out among the *apus,* on the slope of Ankhara itself.

We reached the high *pampa* of K'airamayu in the early afternoon, then served the meal with all of the appropriate ceremony, Teresa hurrying Sebastiana and me in urgent whispers. Hugo brought us first horns full of *chicha,* one for each of us, then served us each two *copitas* of the *trago* we had brought and given to the men, except to Sebastiana, whom he offered only one, which he dumped quickly into her *chicha* before she could protest or prevent it (she tried to switch horns with me but, opposed by the three of us for different reasons, this maneuver failed); and then he brought us each a double handful of *mot'e.* We waited while they ate and then while they finished Baltazar's field and hoed a small one of Ricardo's nearby. *Hallmay* is done with *lampas* (the crooked hoes with broad spade-like blades); the earth in the furrows between the rows of potato plants is broken up, then lifted and heaped around the base of the plants. As we waited, I could hear a *lauta* and *tambor* played somewhere, unseen, across the hillside. I talked in Spanish with Sebastiana, who told me that she also weaves and asked me if I wanted to go with her sometime when she pastures her cows: it is in the fields when they are pasturing their families' animals that girls learn from each other and practice the complex patterns which they will later learn to weave into the fabric of carrying cloths. In spite of the gradual improvement of my Quechua, it is wonderful to meet a young woman whom I can really talk to, and I harbor a hope that, as she becomes part of the family, we will become friends. We talked about our families, about marriage and having children, about cooking and weaving.

It had been, so far, a lovely day, with only high, white clouds in the sky, but as the men worked and we waited, a front of heavy, dark clouds approached from the east, turning mountainsides one by one black with their shadow, nearer and nearer to us, like ominous slow footsteps. As the men finished Ricardo's field, it began to rain, lightly at first, mixed with hail, then harder and harder. We huddled together beside a boulder, away from the direction of the pelting rain, under sheets of plastic (which the Quechua call *maylun* or *baylun,* a word which, I realized as the result of a puzzled etymological analysis, comes very simply from the word "nylon"!) and Gary's big rain poncho, while the men finished the *chicha* and *trago.* When these were gone and the rain had eased, we started back, miserably cold and wet, across the marshy *pampa,* up the mountain on paths that ran with torrents of rainwater, and over a hill that was white with hail, as if it had snowed. The stream below Wayninpampa that we had earlier crossed stepping from rock to rock without wetting our feet was now a rushing river of icy water across which there was no way but to wade very carefully, the water well above our ankles and tumbling white, so we couldn't see where to put our feet.

At home, most of the workers and Sebastiana sat with Baltazar and

Teresa and the boys in the kitchen around the fire, drinking more *chicha* and *trago* to warm themselves. Gary and I declined Baltazar's invitation to join them and sat under the sleeping bags on our bed, drinking tea and hot chocolate. Late at night, after everyone had left, I heard the music in the distance of a flute and a drum. Sebastiana stayed with Hugo that night, sleeping with him in the storeroom where Leonarda used to sleep, above Baltazar and Teresa's now disused bedroom. In the morning when I got up at dawn, I could hear their voices, talking softly, the door half open. Asunta came irritably to fetch her daughter soon after.

I am often questioned about our evident lack of children. Women are surprised that we have none and often seem concerned or sympathetic, as if something is wrong. We explain to them that we are waiting until we get back to the United States; that it is difficult, if not dangerous for the child, to travel with a baby such distances—literally inconceivable for them—as we travel from the United States and back; and that we've only been married for three years, which in North America is not an unusually long time for a couple to remain without children. But here, where no young couple would by choice remain childless for any length of time, the decision we say we have made and our apparent unconcern are difficult to comprehend. Yet, though a family without children is considered a tragedy, the desirability and convenience of some means to magically control birth at some point, beyond which more children would be difficult to support on a particular family's resources and there might not be enough property for all of the children to inherit sufficient resources to support their own families, is naturally recognized. They know vaguely somehow, as if by rumor, about birth control pills and sometimes ask us about them in the context of these conversations, a certain phrasing and tone of voice belying incredulity. Women often try, more than half seriously I suspect, to persuade *gringos* they meet in the cities to take their "extra" children with them back to the United States or Europe. Even Ricardo and Juana have asked us several times if we couldn't take Orlando with us when we go; we explain to them, savvy as they are about documents through experience with us, that it is legally impossible. We joke about it now. And now that Juana is pregnant and Hugo's marriage impending and they seem to have accepted, more or less, our explanations, the teasing and joking are more frequent. On the second day of Ricardo's birthday celebration, there was a long session of teasing; Ricardo asked me, his implication obvious, "Doesn't he know how?" I condemned us to more teasing and laughter whatever answer I offered: the men had a wonderful time; the women could probably only guess at what was going on as all of this was deliberately in Spanish. Juana often brings it up, our lack of children, Teresa sometimes, and it was one of the subjects of my conversation with Sebastiana at K'airamayu. I begin to feel it would be interesting to become pregnant while we are here, to learn how differently we would be seen by the community, how differently I would be treated by the women especially, but by men as well: now, it is impossible to place me comfortably into any known category of human being—I behave and expect to be treated as an adult, but here a woman is not an adult until she bears a child. I would be a normal woman, understandable.

However, we will have a substitute child of a sort: we are to become Orlando's godparents by sponsoring his christening at Easter, when the priest comes from Cusco. This too was discussed, in various stages of inebriation, during the celebration of Ricardo's birthday. Not sure what this involves, I know only that we will buy clothes for Orlando to be baptized in and we will be present at the ceremony, which we will also, I assume, pay for, for the use of the church and the services of the priest and any other attendants. Then Orlando will be our *ahijado* (our godson) and we his *padrino* and *madrina,* and Ricardo and Juana will be our *compadre* and *comadre* and we theirs. I began to understand the nearly-kin character of the relationship of *compadrazgo,* this ritual co-parenthood, when Ricardo gently scolded me saying, "You have to serve the *chicha* when Juana's not here: it's your house too."

The next morning we walked to Yaurisque. For several days, no truck had made it even to Wayninpampa, where they usually stop now rather than attempt the last muddy descent into 'Tambo. We followed the footpath—a path that has been the way to Cusco at least since the time of the Inca Empire—that cuts across the circuitous route of the modern road, the road engineered for the heavy trucks which travel it, gentling the grades with switchbacks and avoiding steep climbs and descents by means of wide, curving detours. Some parts of the old path are still paved, as Inca roads were, with rough stones, and it is almost unreasonably straight, generally disregarding the angle of the slopes it traverses in favor of directness. In Yaurisque, after a couple of hours' wait, we caught a truck bound for Cusco from Paruro. It is the time of Carnaval, and we had been warned that children, even adults, often bombard the passengers of trucks with water, waiting at strategic positions above the road with buckets or balloons or plastic bags full of water, or in other vehicles; as soon as we had boarded the truck, we got our rain jacket and poncho out of our packs and held them in our hands, ready. There was a man riding with us who had a black automatic umbrella, which startled everybody in the truck each time he pressed the button on its shaft and it sprang open, like an enormous bat suddenly spreading its wings in our midst. We were ambushed by a bunch of children armed with buckets as we left Yaurisque and later by an entire construction crew riding in the back of a dump truck, orange hardhats full of water held carefully in their hands. We followed them gingerly, at a distance, for many kilometers while the driver of the dump truck toyed with us, slowing so that we would come up close behind them and pulling over to the side of the road so that we would be forced to pass. Finally, exasperated with the game at one of these points, our driver put his foot down hard on the accelerator, and the passengers all scrambled for whatever protection was available. It was like passing through a small monsoon, but most of us remained dry: the largest part of the deluge had been aimed, of course, at the man with the umbrella—he was asking for it.

12. Carnaval

I was visited twice, two days in a row, by hummingbirds, each time a couple, male and female. I was sitting, each time, by the loose tangle of sticks and branches which serves as a fence along one end of the yard, and the birds came to hover just on the other side of it. I heard them, the literal hum of their wings, and turned to look at them, expecting the motion of my turn to frighten them away, but they stayed a few moments: the male that metallic emerald green, but now I could see the flashes of iridescent sapphire blue, a deep, glittering azure, on its breast as the sun caught the planes of its infinitesimal musculature under the feathers; the female was plainer, an olive green, bright and glittery but not iridescent. Each time, they hovered and then sped away with astonishing velocity, along the fence and the wall at the other end of the yard, between the houses, and, turning the corner, down the path.

Día de Comadres: the Day of Comadres. On this day *comadres* visit each other, bringing *chicha* and bowls of soup, usually with meat in it, pieces of chicken—or else they send a child with soup and you send him back home with a bowl of your own soup. Juana even sent Jaime over with a little covered pail of chicken soup. But Teresa had no *chicha* to serve to her guests, so Gary and I bought a bottle of *trago* for her to serve to the women who came to visit, who almost always brought *chicha* so the lack wasn't too obvious. She also didn't cook a chicken: her practicality led her to decide to cook the chicken the next day so her family would be able to enjoy it. Her age and standing in the community must allow her to do this—not have *chicha* to serve or meat in the soup: it is the other and younger women who strive to maintain her favor and not she theirs.

A woman came to the house that day with a boy, about seven or eight, who had his arm in a sling. She brought a jug of *chicha* and a small bundle, and she and Teresa talked for a minute and then went into the house with the boy: Teresa is known for her skill as a healer of bones and muscles—her father was a *curandero* (a curer or healer). The boy's arm was broken; it curved at an odd, wrong angle just below the elbow. The woman had brought in the bundle an enameled tin cup with a piece of plastic tied over the top with yarn and a small clear bottle containing a liquid that looked like cooking oil. Teresa poured a little of this onto the boy's arm and rubbed his arm carefully, massaging it gently though as firmly as she could, with the sympathetic sternness of a nurse, and I could see that this was no primitive, superstitious cure but that her practiced hands were wisely sensitive, felt what was wrong inside, and carefully eased the bone into its place. The boy whimpered and then cried but never attempted to pull away. The woman put the tin cup in the ashes at the mouth of the fireplace to warm its contents: it held a green paste of some mixture of herbs ground and mixed with water or oil. Teresa rubbed the boy's arm with a piece of animal fat, then spread the warm paste on it thickly, and she and the boy's mother wrapped his arm in paper, bound it with a cloth held in place with a thick woven belt wound tightly around it, and replaced it in its sling.

I gave the boy a peach to reward him for his bravery in that ordeal. Peaches!—an incursion of sweetness into our good but rather adamantly bland diet livened only by the spark of ground *ají* and the other almost unbearably piquant condiments like the sharp onions and tree tomatoes and wild herbs like field parsley and cilantro and *wakatay*. Daniel and Hugo had returned in late afternoon from gathering firewood at Paqopata the day before, ate supper, and then set out for Qolqebamba, an hour and a half away, where the corn fields are, to steal peaches. It wasn't called stealing, of course, and it happens every year, and they aren't the only ones from 'Tambo and other villages too high in elevation for fruit to grow who raid the trees at Qolqebamba, but the mission had the air, the secrecy and careful planning and contained excitement, of a military maneuver. They left with two big, cloth flour sacks and a borrowed flashlight (ours; theirs never seems to have batteries, always a scarce commodity, when ours is available for borrowing): by the time they reached Qolqeuqru it would be nearly dark. If they met anybody, they would say that they had come to see how the corn crop was faring, though the hour and the flour sacks would make the story implausible and probably, surely, everyone knows anyway what goes on each year when the peaches begin to ripen. They returned long after dark and the next morning we ate peaches. There weren't many—most of the fruit on the trees was not ripe yet—but we ate them with unabashedly hedonistic enjoyment: Teresa brought out a whole big bowl full of them after breakfast, and the four of us, the boys, and Eloy and Orlando ate them one after another until they were gone. I hadn't expected it; accustomed to the restraint of eating one piece of fruit at a time, I was surprised to be offered a second, a third, a fourth, until I realized the spirit in which they were to be eaten.

Friday and Saturday were quiet, lazy days, all of us, except occasionally the boys, staying around the house as if it were Sunday. I helped Teresa cook and grind corn for *chicha* for Carnaval—she had a lot to make, two whole waist-high jars of it, because she had run completely out and Baltazar, as the *segunda* of Ayllu Nayhua, had a *cargo* for Carnaval. And I spun; just since Wednesday afternoon I had learned quickly and with a skill that seemed to surprise and please Teresa, and surprised me as well—I had demonstrated not long ago that I didn't know how to do it— to ply spun wool into yarn, so it became, tacitly, my assignment to ply the yarn for the *costal*, or grain sack, that Baltazar is planning to weave from all of the coarsely spun wool that Teresa and Leonarda and I have produced over the months. It had been at first a sort of mischievous challenge: as she had been preparing on Wednesday afternoon to begin the work herself, Teresa handed me the enormous bundle of doubled threads and the big spindle and said, "All of it!" So I did it; I took to it quickly, learning and enjoying the motions and rhythms, different and faster and less frustrating than those of spinning raw wool, and it became *my* job. I finished one large ball of plied wool, as big as a large melon and tightly wound, in a couple of days.

One day Baltazar and Gary and the boys went down the path to the pasture to cut brush to build a new fence: the one that stood along one end of the yard was bare and ragged and leaning, and a lot of it had been used for firewood—a year old, it was the driest wood available, and it was just outside the kitchen door. They hauled an immense pile of green brush up the path and stacked it outside the yard, and in the afternoon Gary and Baltazar built the new fence, tall and solid and green, supported by posts which stand wedged into holes in the earth with rocks, the thick mat of leafy branches held between long, thin withes wired to the upright posts. The yard now has an unaccustomed green privacy, like an arbor. As if to deny the leafy wall that now cuts off the yard from sight and some communion with the neighbors, Celestina came over after it was completed with a large pitcher of *chicha* for the two laborers, and we all sat in the yard and drank together. The greenness and a lot of the privacy won't last long, though, because the bull calves like to eat the brush of which the fence and the greenness and the privacy are composed.

The day of Carnaval, Sunday, was gloomy and dank, and a fine mist fell; being outside was like being in a cave or the damp cellar of an old house, the walls close and wet around you. Don Felipe, Ricardo's father—though we learned from Baltazar that he isn't really Ricardo's father: his father had died or abandoned the family, and Ricardo and his siblings had subsequently been raised by their older brother, Felipe (we had thought when we met him on Ricardo's birthday that he didn't look enough older than Ricardo to be his father)—had invited us to come with Juana and Ricardo to his house near Paruro for Carnaval.

We set out from their house about eight-thirty in the morning, I carrying the food Juana had prepared, our *q'epis*, along with two enormous several-gallon jugs and a smaller plastic jug full of *chicha*, on the back of Baltazar's horse which Gary and I had brought with us for Ricardo. We followed the path up to Cruzq'asa, then across an edge of the *pampa* beyond the scattered houses and into a high pass, a broad saddle between Ankhara and Seratachan. Seratachan is flanked by a mountain called Apu Tirena—the only *apu* characterized as female—remarkably different and distinct from craggy Seratachan, with all of its rocky bones exposed among the scrubby vegetation; Tirena is smooth and covered with short *puna* grasses, gray-green and silvery blue-green. At the base of Apu Tirena there is a large, squarish boulder with a smaller boulder close beside it, which Ricardo pointed out to us: they are thought of as a mother, Qoya Tirena, and her baby, and the small oddly shaped boulder does look like a baby, its head tilted slightly to the side, one leg folded, the other drawn up to its chest, cuddled against its mother.

We reached Felipe's house, descending to it from above, even though it is in land still too high for most cultivation, around it on the hillsides only pasture and the grassy ridges of long unused potato fields, a vista all green and gray of the valley of Paruro beyond it: far below, the edge of the town of Paruro could be seen. The single, small house stands on a prow jutting out over the valley with the land sweeping back away from it, down into a shallow valley, back up to the mountaintops not high above it, the slopes populated by herds of cattle and sheep and horses. This place, which Ricardo called *la estancia*, is Felipe's *chosita*, a seasonal residence (*chosita* means "little hut") where he lives in the summer with his animals. He explained to me that the land had been part of a great hacienda, that he had acquired it when the hacienda had been broken up by the Agrarian Reform. A young man was racing wildly about an open space near the house on a clearly unbroken horse.

There were a lot of people already there, mostly men, to whom we were never really introduced, learning a few of their names only through their conversations with those who knew them and called them or toasted them by name; we never learned whether they were siblings or more distant relatives or simply *compadres* and friends of Ricardo and Felipe. We sat on a rise just beyond the house toward the valley, and Juana and Ricardo served the food and a bottle of *trago* we had brought. I helped the women peel potatoes—a task at which I am gradually becoming fairly proficient even by Quechua standards, thanks to daily practice and Gary's sharp pocket knife—for *t'impu,* the traditional Carnaval dish. *T'impu* is a celebration of the season, made of whole *ch'uño* and *moraya* (the two forms of dried potatoes) and whole, large new potatoes and whole new cabbage leaves and chunks of mutton—a sheep is killed the day before Carnaval because Carnaval is considered to be the birthday of all sheep and so they cannot be slaughtered on that day—all boiled ("to boil" is *t'impuy* in Quechua) and served in bowls with the broth, or the vegetables and meat simply in cupped hands, and usually eaten with the hands.

We drank the rest of the day, all of the men contributing bottle after bottle of *trago;* Felipe's wife (whose name is among those I never learned) doesn't make *chicha* there at the *chosita*—there is no storage space for the huge amounts of corn which would, besides, have to be hauled up from the valley, so there was not a single *chicha* jar in the house and all of the *chicha* we drank was from the huge plastic jugs we had brought: plenty but not too much. We sat on the rise just beyond the house talking, watching the men take turns demonstrating their skill as daredevil horsemen, racing toward us on the half-broken horses from a point just above the fall into the valley—more than one of them fell off their mounts, though I suspect that none felt the pain of their bruises until the next morning—and, Gary and I at least, admiring the astonishingly beautiful landscape, still all green and gray. The *t'impu* was served mid-to-late afternoon, and then, as the drinking resumed, the record player was brought out and we danced the *kashwar* (the traditional dance of Carnaval), everyone holding hands together and dancing in a ring, our faces white with flour which Gary and I had brought from Cusco and I had been persuaded to rub or throw into people's faces—an act which guaranteed enthusiastic retaliation in kind—like strange masks, eyes wild with *trago* against the pallor of the flour. Then we danced ordinary *huayno*s and danced until we were forced inside by the growing dark, and the *trago* was served until everyone fell asleep in their places, all of us stretched out side by side, literally like sardines in a tin, in the tiny house.

We woke, one by one, at dawn; someone turned the record player on at what seemed its full volume, awakening un-gently those who still slept,

and began serving *trago,* joked about as being medicinal and which indeed most accepted as if we were children being administered cod liver
oil, no one allowed to refuse. It seemed for a while that all we would do
that day was eat: we were given, in succession, cups of heavily sweetened
maté, *t'impu* from yesterday, fried liver with onions, fried mutton with
onions, big chunks of fresh cheese and *mot'e.* We moved outside into the
wan sunshine to let it heal bodies abused by the quantities of alcohol we'd
drunk (five more *copitas* of *trago* already) and were given bowls of soup
with the ubiquitous potatoes and pieces of sheep intestine—there was
fortunately a dog lazing in the sun beside me who gladly accepted whatever I could not bring myself to eat—and then big cups of warm, fresh
milk, straight—literally—from a cow and sweetened with sugar. That
cup of milk and the admirable though failing effort of the sun finally
made me feel a bit more whole, and wholesome, and healthy.

With lassos in their hands, the men went down into the enclosed pad-
dock below the house to mark the youngest cattle: they were to be
branded, with Felipe's crisp FA. A fire was built in the center of the corral
beneath the overhang of a large boulder, and the men set about roping
the yearling calves one by one, flinging the lassos, some quite expertly,
over the horns of an animal, letting it struggle until it quieted and stood
still, when someone slipped a rope around its legs. They threw or pushed
each animal over onto its side, turned its horns into the earth and held
them there to still its head, and with two men leaning hard against the
ropes which bound its legs, another came and pressed the hot brand
against the hide of the creature's shoulder: there was an acrid smell of
burned hair and flesh in the air for a moment. A cup of *chicha* was
poured into the raw wound, and the calf was released.

When all of the young animals had been marked, the cattle were
herded together; gathered, they huddled together as if to commiserate
now that their ordeal was over and some had been through it, burned
shoulders still aching, and some, not remembering last year or the year
before, had escaped—a feeling perhaps of incomprehensible persecution
seeming to draw them together. And the men, don Felipe first, each
poured a cup of *chicha* and tossed it in a dull arc under the now-sullen
sky over the backs of the herd. Felipe flung one more cup over them as
they were driven out of the corral through the gate. The men, high-
spirited from *trago* and the intense concentration and effort of their
work, now played with the lassos, roping each other, most of their endeavor directed toward one white-bearded old man—his beard was unusual, its whiteness exceptional and startling: most Quechua men have
virtually no beard at all and pluck the few hairs that grow on their chins
with tweezers bought in the market in Cusco—whom they roped and

pulled to the ground, rolling him onto his side as if they would brand him too. He bore all of this with what we had learned was a characteristically easy good humor, as if he were accustomed to such pranks. After a brief rest and more *trago*, a few of the younger men rounded up a yearling colt and filly and branded them. The women, during all of this, sat together beside the house, watching and sipping *chicha*. The men all joined the women, and after a while—and more *trago*—Gary and I gathered our things into my carrying cloth and his poncho and left, displaying necessarily firm resolve against the protestations of the young men: one more drink, one more dance—for the record player had been brought out again, onto the *pampa* beside the corral, and was blaring music into the mountains and out over the valley. From the hillside above the *estancia*, we watched the sheep herded into another pen, held for a few minutes, then released. The whole event had been for us wonderfully pleasant and relaxed; we had been accepted as easily and casually as if we had not even been strangers, much less a couple of *gringos*. Nobody even asked what we were doing living in 'Tambo.

The pass was bleak and barren and windy, a thin, cold mist driven through the air, and the valleys filled deeply with cloud. For a mile or so we could see nothing but the mountaintops flanking the saddle and the peaks in the distance, as if there were nothing left of the world below thirteen thousand feet.

Tuesday was the major day of the celebration of Carnaval in 'Tambo: the day the *segundas* of the *ayllu*s did battle. People began to gather at Baltazar and Teresa's house in midmorning, the first to arrive a funny little old man with a wizened face, don Francisco from Nayhua, whom they called, gently, *sunsu* (the Quechua interpretation of the Spanish *zonzo*: dim-witted or slow) because he is a little deaf, so that everybody always shouts at him and his Quechua is unintelligible. He seemed to like me immediately and whenever he could would talk to me; to whatever he said I could only answer, Yes . . . yes . . . uh-huh . . . , hoping that it would never be an entirely inappropriate response. Francisco was to play the drum to accompany Baltazar's dancers to and at the site of the battle. Teresa and I and Sebastiana spent the morning peeling potatoes for our own *t'impu*. Teresa used only new potatoes, for which we were thankful, because *ch'uño* and *moraya* both have a rather musty taste and slightly rubbery texture, and even Baltazar admitted that he doesn't like them. We were interrupted once by the woman and the boy with the broken arm, and Teresa gave him the same treatment as before. She seemed concerned because the boy's arm looked rather worse than better: it retained its vaguely grotesque angle and appeared swollen and bruised. This time I

gave him one of the chocolate cookies Gary smuggles into town for sur-
reptitious snacks; fortunately, none of our little boys were around to see
me do it.

Sebastiana was so efficient and eager that, once the nearly interminable
task of peeling potatoes was done, there seemed to be nothing for me to
do, so I went to sit with the men and few women who had gathered in the
comedor. Baltazar was bragging—we had told him that my parents
might come to Peru and that we were thinking of bringing them to 'Tambo
to meet our Peruvian family—that the father of Señora Julia—a lawyer from the United States!—was coming to visit him. The men seemed
to have enough knowledge of lawyers somehow to be, in Baltazar's esti-
mation, satisfyingly impressed. Old don Francisco had decided that he
wanted both me and Juana to come to live near him in Nayhua and
jokingly (I think: his face and expressions are inscrutable) offered Gary
all of his land to farm and suggested that he build a house in Nayhua. The
t'impu was served and eaten, and we moved outside into the sun.

The musicians and dancers were all present now: Francisco and a man
named Agustino who plays the *lauta* (a cane flute) and a third man who
played a longer, deeper-voiced *lauta;* and a youngish man and Sebastiana's
younger brother Teodoro to dance. Baltazar set about preparing them,
and everyone else, for the festivities: he served a lot of *trago, copita* after
copita in succession, to the older dancer, who hadn't been drinking with
us all day and so, apparently, had to catch up with us; somewhat less to
his musicians; and to the rest of us another *copita* or two. His sister-in-
law Juliana, the mother of Jesús' wife, was serving *chicha;* a wry, middle-
aged woman, she watches out for me on these socially important occasions: I am her newfound namesake, more or less. The dancers dressed:
the man, who in costume would be called the *alcaldín,* wore a man's
pointed *montera* and a poncho tied closely around his shoulders and
chest and carried a *vara* (a ceremonial staff of wood bound in silver) and
a *waraka,* a woven sling. Teodoro was dressed as a woman called the
waylaka, in a skirt and a carrying cloth worn as a shawl and also a *montera,* but of a woman's flat, fringed style. He carried a large, white flag,
the *bandera,* with a spray of flowers and green ferns tied to the top of its
pole. Children brought flowers for everyone to fix in their hatbands. As
the dancers performed in the yard to the musicians' accompaniment,
Baltazar further prepared them and the rest of us as well: he went from
one person to another and, ignoring all protest, smeared each face with
flour. Hugo ceremoniously wound strands of colored *serpentina* around
our necks and then, mischievous with a can of improvised red paint but
not as ruthless as Baltazar had been, painted as many cheeks as he could;
people ran from him when he approached or struggled with him, and red
paint was spilled everywhere. Someone painted poor Francisco's face en-

GIRL WEARING
MONTERA

tirely a deep forest green, even his lips and teeth, and a sympathetic group gathered around him to help wipe some of it off. There were green smudges on the skin of his drum.

Finally, everyone headed off toward the plaza, the women after the men, except Teresa and me. We filled two small jars with *chicha*, stuffed the mouths of the jars with corn husks, and searched the yard for pieces of rope to carry them with. We gathered cups, identifying bits of red yarn around their handles, into a carrying cloth, locked the doors, and then we too set out for the plaza, leaving the *chicha* jars and bundle of cups in the yard. We found the women at the top of Calle San Juan, just below where it reaches the level of the plaza, watching; Baltazar, his musicians, and his dancers were nowhere to be seen. In the center of the plaza, a *chachakuma* tree had been sturdily erected—the *mallki kumpay* or *mallki mithay* (*mallki* is tree, *kumpay* to knock down, and *mithay* to split or shatter). To one side, two young men stood holding up a record player and its speaker; around the tree a great number of people, including most of 'Tambo's most eminent citizens and officials, danced the *kashwar*. Crowds of children clustered at the edges of the ring, some with balloons full of water in their hands, as threatening as bombs with the fuses lit. The tree was decorated with loose coils of *serpentina* and water balloons and presents or prizes provided by the *carguyuqs*—old 45-rpm records, bags of coca, sweets, bottles of soft drinks. One by one, couples stepped out of the circle of dancers and moved toward the tree to pick up an axe that lay on the ground and swing a couple of strokes at its trunk and then re-join the *kashwar*. At last the tree came down; there was a riot of people, dancers and children eager to retrieve the prizes from the tree, in which people were knocked down—none hurt—and the records and some of the bottles of soft drinks, of course, were broken. The felling stroke of the axe had been delivered by Angélico, the son of the governor, winning him and his partner the *cargo* to erect the tree next year at Carnaval.

We retreated to the house, the women and the men who hadn't disap-peared with Baltazar, to drink some *chicha*. One of the women had cap-tured a broken record; it bore the inscription "Recuerdo de Angélico Araujo Nuñez," the young man who had felled the tree. Someone sent it whirling through the air onto the roof of the *comedor*.

After a couple of cups of *chicha* from a pitcher Teresa had brought from the house, two men picked up the *chicha* jars and, tying the ropes around their shoulders, carried them out of the yard, followed by the rest of the men. Teresa relocked the door of her house and I tied the carrying cloth with the cups in it around my shoulders and, all holding hands in a line, the women followed them up Calle San Juan and across the plaza, where some men sat on benches of planks supported by adobes in front of the shops and drank with the village officials, and up the street at the end of the churchyard. At the corner of the churchyard we turned toward the cemetery and stopped several yards from the intersection; we sat against the wall with our *chicha* jars. Then commenced another battle of *chicha,* as we served the men of our own *ayllu* and the women and men of the others, seated across the intersection from us, and they served us; our hands were filled with a succession of enameled tin cups, plastic glasses, little ceramic pitchers and wooden *qero*s. Soon we heard the flutes and drum, and Baltazar and his entourage came up the street toward us from the direction of the cemetery, the dancers leading them, Teodoro waving the graceful flag, turning with it, and the man—the *alcaldín*—holding the silver-bound staff before him, with the sling, held in his other hand, looped around its end. Sometimes he snapped the end of the sling against the ground, its report as sharp as the crack of a whip. They halted beyond us, nearer the intersection, and Baltazar took his stand across the street from us. The musicians gathered nearer the corner along the wall against which we sat. Two other groups of women arrived with *chicha* and sat near us.

The dancers stepped into the intersection and danced as the three musi-cians played. After two or three songs, they retired and the dancers of Ayllu San Miguel, also dressed as *alcaldín* and *waylaka*, performed. Though according to Baltazar each of the eight landholding *ayllu*s was supposed to be represented by dancers and musicians, only these two, the first of each moiety, were; Baltazar explained to us later that the other *segundas* had not fulfilled their *cargos*—these are among the very few festival *cargos* that are not voluntary: they are a required duty of the man who holds the position of *segunda*. The two groups alternated several times, and then the true battle of the day began: Baltazar and the *segunda* of the *ayllu* of San Miguel faced each other in the intersection, armed with slings and stones, and began, in earnest, a duel, the blows of the stones released at full force drawing gasps and discreet cheers from the crowd of observers. The duel lasted only a minute, and neither participant seemed really to win; Baltazar threw his arm about the neck of his opponent and forcibly drew him over to us to be served *chicha*. He was then led away, now feigning resistance in turn, to drink the *chicha* of Ayllu San Miguel. The music began again, and the dancers, their relationship slightly altered now, returned to the center of the intersection: now the *alcaldín* of each pair held the banner and the "woman" the sling. With the sling, she beat the backs of the man's legs as they circled each other warily: these blows too drew gasps.

About dusk, the women rose and we danced a *kashwar* in the intersection as Baltazar's musicians played, the women singing shrilly, a song about Carnaval, the time when grown people play like children. Then, hands still joined, we descended the street to the plaza, crossed it—stopping in the middle to dance briefly in a circle—and returned home as a light rain began to fall. We ate more *t'impu*—Sebastiana had been tending it during the afternoon. I sat in the kitchen with the children, reluctant to join the adults whom I knew would continue drinking now until they couldn't anymore; but Gary and I finally slipped away without being noticed. Someone later recognized our absence and sent Sebastiana to fetch us, but she didn't insist and apparently they managed without us for the rest of the evening.

We rose only a little later than usual the next morning, and I went to help with the cooking. There was already a large group of people filling the warm kitchen, people who had slept there all night, like the musicians, and Ricardo and Juana and Sebastiana who had returned that morning from their own homes. Teresa was serving a folk cure for hangovers—a concoction of onion and hot pepper and every piquant herb available mixed with cubes of fresh cheese—passing a bowl around the room for each one to take a few mouthfuls. One of the men, at what seemed to me cross-purposes, was serving *trago*—but it was Carnaval. The men went into the *comedor* while we made soup for breakfast and served it, and finally we joined them there. The musicians played and we danced, as the *alcaldín* and *waylaka* had danced the evening before: each dancer wore a *montera* which he or she passed on to the next dancer, and the man of each couple who danced carried the *bandera* and the woman lashed his legs with the sling, urged on by enthusiastic cries of "¡Más fuerza! ¡Más fuerza!" ("Harder! Harder!"). When the sun at last broke free of the clouds, the party moved outside. Don Andrés and Celestina danced, Andrés handling the *bandera* with the grace of a bullfighter, Celestina merciless with the *waraka*. Sebastiana served a lunch she had made, and finally Baltazar, about three in the afternoon, began to saddle his horse: we had been planning to go to Cruzq'asa to the house of his sister and his brother-in-law, Vicentina and Honorato, to mark the herd of sheep, though Gary and I had thought this plan forsaken by that hour. We straggled away, Gary and I, Baltazar and Teresa, and the musicians— or at least Francisco and Agustino, the flute player—abandoning, with little ceremony, the rest of the party, who sat bemusedly in the sun, suddenly without music or refreshment.

We followed the musicians like a parade, wearing *serpentina* and flowers, our festive passage preceded by the music of flute and drum. Along the way we stopped to drink *chicha* from a very small wooden *qero*, which Baltazar said his godfather had given him, and from it later *trago*: it was the perfect size for *chicha*, a big mouthful and a little more, but full of *trago* it was dangerous. When we got to the house, no one was home except the children, though we knew they'd been expecting us. (Lord knows *when* they had expected us though, and if I'd waited since early morning, I thought, I too might make a point not to be home when we arrived late in the afternoon.) We sat down outside the house anyway and drank *chicha*, served now in horns, from the plastic jugs we had brought with us. Finally Vicentina returned, and Teresa offered her some *chicha*— a little dig at the absent hostess: here we had been, sitting at her house, having to drink our own *chicha*. Vicentina accepted it and then hurried inside to warm *chicha* for us. And then Honorato, who had been detained of course by the people he had been drinking with, arrived.

Toward dusk, when Honorato's daughter had returned from pasturing the sheep and had driven them into a tiny corral, just big enough to contain them, at the end of the yard between the two buildings of the compound, Baltazar rose and filled the small *qero* with *chicha*. Alberto, Honorato's son, brought Baltazar *t'ankar* flowers, long, magenta bells nodding from a short stalk; Baltazar took these and the *qero* and went to the gate of the corral and, reciting the names of the *apus*, said a blessing to each as he intoned its name in a mutter and dipped a few drops of *chicha* from the *qero* with the flowers. Then he flung the *chicha* over the backs of the animals in the corral. Each of us performed this ritual in turn, even the children (and the *gringos*), and we sat down to drink again, in earnest, both *chicha* and *trago*—served in the little *qero*—calling to people passing on the road to join us. The rest of the evening was, of course, all drinking and dancing, until everyone collapsed.

In the morning after breakfast, we completed the marking of the sheep. They were herded into another tiny corral attached to the other end of the house, and with Gary's pocketknife and very little ceremony, Baltazar cut small wedges from the edge of one ear of each struggling animal. We were all crowded into the corral along with the animals and around its gate, including again the children. And as each ear was clipped, Baltazar dropped the bit of flesh into a clamshell filled with *trago*—the little *qero* had been, not surprisingly, misplaced during the universal inebriation of the night before; the full clamshell was a much more manageable amount of trago to swallow—and gave one to each of us to drink, even the two little girls, Vicentina and Honorato's daughters, the shepherdesses, for whom I felt deep sympathy: even adults who are used to it can't drink *trago* without a deep shudder. Two sheep were not marked with the notch that would identify them as Baltazar's. They were gifts for the shepherdesses. We sat in welcome sunshine until midafternoon, drinking peacefully and talking, and then, as enormous dark clouds crowded into the sky, Gary and I started home, assuming—rightly—that if we didn't simply go we would sit there until almost dark when the trip home would be difficult: Baltazar and Teresa didn't get home until nightfall.

It had been, aside from the festivities of Carnaval, a strange time, full of what might have been omens. As we returned from Felipe's *estancia,* descending the path into 'Tambo, we saw a group of people standing together in a yard, most of them dressed in dark clothes, but one in startling white, holding a staff with a cross at its end; as we neared the plaza, we heard the tolling of the *campanilla:* the gathering had been a funeral. As we entered the yard at the house, our eyes were drawn to the empty sky above the red tile and thatch of the roofs by a knife of black: a condor, immense and unhurried, passed over us, and a second higher above our heads, both in slow, languid loops, lower and lower and then, drawing back, higher, beginning their descent again. We had never seen condors before, in the wild, and pointed dumbly into the sky, exclaiming to Hugo, "Condor!" Hugo, hardly glancing at them, said casually, "Oh, they always come when somebody dies."

That night, on the eve of the battle of the *ayllus*, unable for some reason to sleep, I lay amid the warmth of our sleeping bags on the hard bundles of reeds on our bed, reading by candlelight. Hours after dark, everyone in the compound asleep, a sudden noise on the balcony of the storeroom above our door startled me so I jumped—I knew that sound instinctively from years of living with cats in houses with wooden floors, but this one was *big;* then a brief squawking and flapping from the chickens who roost on the railing of the balcony; and then Sandor's voice with a frantic, slightly hysterical note in it, barking furiously. I thought, puma!

and was frightened, too frightened to dress and go out to see if the chickens were still there, reasoning that there was nothing I or anyone else could do even if I had wakened Baltazar and Teresa and told them that a puma had carried off a chicken—except Sandor perhaps, and he was doing all he could. Much later, I woke to the sound of Sandor's bark after a long quiet, a stillness. He barked that same furious, frantic bark until dawn. When we opened our door in the morning, there were white feathers everywhere, and only one of the three fat white hens and the little black laying hen sat on the rail. In the mud before the door were the prints of the paws of a large cat, each impression broader than the palm of my hand. Across the yard in front of Pascuala's house were more feathers, the paw prints of the cat and Sandor, and, caught on the top of the high gate that closes the narrow passage to Pascuala's door, a tuft of soft, white belly fur.

It took hours for the presence of the puma, and the shock of the loss of the hens, to dissipate like a heavy, clinging fog in the excitement of the holiday.

On the road back from Cruzq'asa, we met a man who had news of yet another death, that of a young man, a musician, who had played the violin. He was going to tell the man's godfather, who lives in Wayninpampa: the man had died suddenly, unexpectedly—for he had been healthy (they always say this, denying to themselves and to any listener that there was any clue that something might have been wrong)—from drinking *chicha* that was too cold, they said, his stomach in death distended. In 'Tambo, we passed below the house of his family; in the yard, people cried and moaned and wailed under the lowering sky, darkening with clouds and crashing with thunder. The bells of the *campanilla* tolled again, mournfully, until dark and early in the morning; and in the gloomy afternoon, a long procession led by the sacristan in white, others wearing dark hoods or veils, wound down the hill toward the church and beyond it to the cemetery, bearing the coffin to its burial.

And the prodigal son is errant again, but this time with his papa's blessing and a pocketful of his mother's money for the truck fare to Cusco and the train fare down the valley to Quillabamba. Daniel left Sunday, the seventh of March, to spend the night in Cusco before going on to Quillabamba in La Convención, in the lowlands down the Urubamba beyond Machu Picchu. All day Monday we speculated, as Teresa and I spun and Baltazar fashioned a new *chakitaqlla* for Gary: he would be leaving Cusco now, he must be at Machu Picchu by this time, now he is in Quillabamba . . . He said he'd be back for the potato harvest at K'airamayu in April.

13. *Puna yapuy*

Fleas! They're everywhere now, and everybody seems to have them. March is the season for them, and Sandor, who is otherwise a fine and noble creature, almost the only dog I've seen in Peru who even looks like he's got some part of a recognizable breed in him—though I'm sure his lineage is far removed from the union of collie and shepherd he looks like—supports a thriving population of them, with whose tenancy he is generous. Following the example set by Teresa, who on every sunny day lays the collection of sheepskins and heavy woolen blankets her family sleeps on out in the yard and assigns one of the children—or sits there herself—to sit by them and watch for the fleas drawn out of the fibers by the warmth and to catch them and crush them between two fingernails, I laid our sleeping bags out in the sun on a stack of firewood and was, well, in a way not terribly surprised by the number of shiny, hard-shelled little creatures hiding along the seams and zippers of the down bags: I haven't been able to sleep for several nights because of their bites. A little dismayed, though; I've never had fleas before. Most North Americans, who buy flea collars and flea powders for beloved pets, are, I suppose, rather naïve about fleas and have maybe *seen* fleas on their cats or dogs, or perhaps only observed the resultant scratching, but have probably never found them in their own bedclothes or in their clothing. They are accepted here, in their season, very matter-of-factly: no fuss is made, except over Sandor, who has earned the nickname Piki-wasi (Flea-house) and who is brutally driven away whenever he comes in a door or sits down near someone; the poor creature must feel somewhat persecuted, having

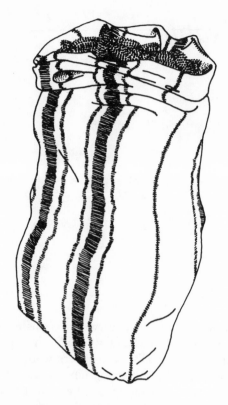

COSTAL WITH CORN

to suffer the torment of itching and receiving not sympathy but treatment even more callous than usual. The bedding is laid out in the sun, and everyone at some time snatches up the hem of her skirt or the cuff of his pants to turn back the fabric and search for the annoying intruder, muttering, "Piki . . . piki . . ." But they say that a lot of fleas now means that there will be a good harvest: you have to admire a people who can find something good about a major infestation of fleas.

I haven't gone back yet to watch Juana weave, nor have I gone with Sebastiana when she goes out to pasture her family's animals, the flow of ordinary events completely disrupted by the madness of Carnaval. But the day after we returned from Cruzq'asa, I sat and watched Celestina and a friend of hers—an old, white-haired woman who wears an old-fashioned dark brown *bayeta* skirt, a hand-woven shawl, and no shoes—stretch the simple warp of a *costal* (the large heavy woven bag in which produce is carried and stored). This one, like most *costales,* is of coarsely spun, undyed wool: stripes of natural brown-black wool on an off-white background. Then I watched for several days as she wove, one long length to be folded in half and sewn firmly up the sides. There is none of the complicated *pallay*, the complex picking up of threads that makes the pattern of a carrying cloth, involved in the weaving of a *costal*, and, undistracted now by my desire to learn *pallay*, I began to absorb the fine, simple rhythms of the weaving itself, and I began to imagine myself weaving the *costal* Baltazar and Teresa are planning, for which I am plying the yarns.

I sat by Celestina with a small pitcher of *chicha* by my side and my spindle in my hand, both of us working peacefully in the sun in front of her house, and it was a perfectly natural situation, two women sitting together working, except for the lack of conversation. I'm not sure what Celestina and I would talk about if I spoke fluent Quechua, but if I had been a young woman of the village, there would have been—I am beginning to understand—an endless flow of gossip.

For the first time, I have achieved something which actually elicits surprised comment and praise from other women. One morning Leonarda, showing off, picked up my spindle and began to spin, saying slyly in Spanish, "¿Así queremos?" (which, translated roughly, in that context, was "Is *this* what you're trying to do?"). After she left, I determinedly continued what she had begun: a strand of wool not much thicker than sewing thread, mine a little finer even than her careless, taunting example. I had seen Teresa spin wool that fine and simply thought that someday, if I continue spinning for the next thirty years, I might spin like that. But—and this too I am learning: how to *learn* in Quechua—I find that the way to learn anything here is just to do it, and keep doing it until you can do it well.

Women seem unable to resist taking my spindle from me and showing me how to do whatever it is I am doing, even when they have just praised my work. With older women, I let them, hiding my reluctance—for example when Celestina, whom I dearly love, took away my new fine thread one Sunday when everybody was drinking *trago* because their son had come to visit and she was very drunk and her spinning was irregular and about twice as thick as mine—out of deference. But when Leonarda begins to take it away, I refuse: it's very hard for me, trained as I have been in a North American, a Western, cultural tradition which celebrates the talent and achievement of the individual, to let go of my work, to relinquish control over it, as if someone were going to judge the final result. But I have learned that sufficiency and not perfection is the standard here for most spinning at least—whenever someone watches me spin, I am always urged *not* to undo and correct mistakes, but simply to go on. Spinning here is not an art, as we North Americans now conceive of it and as it is for me, learned out of curiosity and desire rather than necessity, but simply a chore that must be done. Exceptional skill is generally the result of a lot of involuntary practice in combination with a particular facility, not of an effort to achieve excellence, and is not audibly noted and admired. Spinning is only preparation for the real art of weaving, in which skill and a fine result *are* admired.

The woman and the boy with the broken arm came back today; the boy came with his younger sister in the morning, as if to make an appointment, and Teresa told him to come back in the afternoon. Teresa had spent most of the day making *chicha*, grinding corn and, this time, sprouted wheat as well, the pots boiling over the fire. The boy and his mother waited a few minutes until she stopped grinding and had shoved a few more sticks into the fire. While they waited, the woman unwrapped the boy's arm and, following Teresa's instructions, made the boy urinate into a cup; she rubbed the boy's arm with his own urine and wrapped her sweater around it until Teresa was ready. Teresa rubbed fat onto the broken arm—lard this time—and began to massage it: it is healing crookedly. Now there is only a trace of bruise near his wrist, on the inside of his arm, but the bone just below his elbow protrudes unnaturally, and his broken arm doesn't seem to bend as his other arm does, though that may be only the result of stiffness from disuse. Teresa seemed dissatisfied with the results of her ministrations and rubbed his arm hard, and the boy cried plaintively, heartrendingly: the bones are healing, they may be crooked, but they are healing, and now Teresa's gentle but insistent efforts to push them into their original places are efforts to alter the configuration of the boy's body, and it hurts. She worked for a long time, talking to his mother about how he uses the arm when he plays, whether he sleeps on it or not—a doctor's questions—stopped massaging it and prepared to wrap it, then, dissatisfied, began again. The boy never tried to jerk his arm away, but he gradually leaned away from her, drawing away involuntarily from the source of the pain, and I sat behind him to support him. Finally, the woman added a little of the contents of the two small bottles—which may, I think now, also be urine, at least one of them—to the cup of green herbal paste, nestled it into the coals for a minute to warm it, and helped Teresa smooth it on the boy's arm and wrap it in paper and the cloth, the belt, and the sling as before. I decided I have fallen into the role of the nurse: the boy accepts me easily, unaware of anything in the blindness of his pain but comforting hands and a body to lean against, and only realizing afterwards that I am the one who was there and gentle with him. This time, like the nurse handing a kid a lollipop after an injection, I gave him a piece of sugar cane and four smuggled crackers.

I assured Gary one morning with a certain confidence that a woman wouldn't ask another woman to walk a long way to a field with her only to keep her company if she didn't actually need her help to carry food. And indeed Juana didn't ask me to accompany her when I went to help her cook that morning. What she and Teresa tried to talk me into was going by myself, just me, accompanied only by Jaime, although it was Ricardo's land our menfolk were working—because her hand hurt from a burn. I couldn't quite figure out why this would keep her from carrying a *q'epi* on her back and walking, even a long way, and I had been out to the new season's potato fields at Pantiwayqo with Sebastiana the day before, when the men were working Hugo's new field, and it was a long, difficult walk and my legs and shoulders still ached that morning. So I took off my *ojota* and showed her the bandage I had put on my toe to pad some unidentified injury, which I hadn't taken the time to look at closely, and told her it hurt and I couldn't walk to Pantiwayqo. It must have looked convincing enough to make Juana give up her hope of avoiding the long walk, and I was glad because it honestly hurt enough under the pressure of the rubber sandal to make me limp slightly. When Teresa and I got home, she asked me about it, so I took off my shoe again and the bandage this time and we inspected the wound. It was red and slightly swollen, but we could see nothing to cause the pain. Teresa pressed the area gently with her fingers, massaging it, and I winced now and then. I thought she might offer some elaborate treatment like that she gave the boy with the broken arm, but she decided it was a *kiska* (a thorn) and asked me for a needle. She probed with it, gently, for a few minutes, then gave up, saying it was inside and she couldn't see it. I couldn't either but took the needle from her and continued the operation myself and at last extracted the fairly impressive point of a thorn. Almost more than for the relief of the pain, I was glad there had been some tangible, recognizable injury, familiar and understandable, so that Juana would know—if Teresa knew, Juana would—that it hadn't only been a carefully planned excuse, which, considering the length and difficulty of the walk to Pantiwayqo, the largest part of which seems to be uphill both going and coming back, a phenomenon possible I think only in the Andes, would not be an unreasonable suspicion.

Juana and Teresa and I went out one day to dig up new potatoes from the fields near the village, in Yanchakalla. Now, as we are just beginning to reap the harvest of this year's crops, women and children bringing bundles of new beans and peas from the fields when they come home with the animals, we are beginning to prepare for the coming year's crops. The men are working next year's potato fields, turning up grassy earth into ridges called *wachu*s in which the potatoes will be planted— earth which has lain fallow for six years and must now receive the sun and rain until planting time. The potato lands in the *puna* are held by the community and are allotted, each year to each man at a town assembly, from a specific area which, in a careful system of rotation, has rested and renewed itself long enough to support a new crop of potatoes. In the *puna*, the work of turning the earth is called *puna yapuy;* they have also been opening fallow fields in lower lands, *purun yapuy*, for the crops of corn and barley—*purun* is the word for land which is uncultivated or has lain fallow. In *purun yapuy*, the earth is simply turned randomly, not into the furrows and ridges which, in the high, cold *puna*, trap heat and moisture to nurture potatoes.

Puna yapuy is a beautiful dance with the *chakitaqlla;* performed by a well-coordinated team, it is stunning, mesmerizing to watch. Two men, each with a *chakitaqlla*, work up the rows from the bottom of the field to the top. For each chunk of sod that is turned, the men in unison thrust themselves slightly off the ground to allow their left feet to land on the footrests of the plows with the force of their whole weight behind them, the blades at the ends of their shafts tearing through the tough roots of the *puna* grasses; a second thrust drives the long, narrow blade to its hilt into the earth. Then the men, as a team, bend, drawing the handles of the *chakitaqlla*s down toward the earth, the leverage which pries the sod from its foundation. A man called the *rapachu* (from the word *rapay*, which means to turn over clods of earth with the hands when plowing) turns the great chunks of earth over first to one side to build one ridge then to the other to form the ridge beside it—an inglorious job: he is constantly bent, creeping, step by step, his hands in the often muddy earth, up the rows in the wake of the *chakitaqlla*s. Those dancers turn slightly with each fresh thrust, toward the ridge to which the *rapachu* will turn the slab of earth, the blades of their plows entering the earth in the line of a slight arc that curves gently away from the *wachu* toward the top of the field. Unless a blade strikes a rock, there is never a pause: the rhythm is exhilarating, hypnotizing.

Puna yapuy, like all of the tasks involved in producing the potato crop, is ritually important: if this task is not done, a family will have no potato field the next year. Great teams of men are assembled through *ayni* (the system of reciprocal labor) to attempt to finish each *chakrayoq*'s field in a single day: no one wants to walk the two and a half or three hours uphill to the *puna* to complete a little section of land on another day. The *chakrayoq* provides *chicha* and *trago* in great quantity, and the women cook special meals to be carried to the workers and usually bring more *trago*. The men, at the end of an exhausting day and before the weary journey home, often sit and drink until *chicha* and *trago* are gone. Baltazar and Hugo performed a marathon of *puna yapuy*, going on Monday to receive the assigned lands and mark them out by digging rows at their borders and going on succeeding days to work Hugo's, then Ricardo's,

land, then that of a man who had helped Hugo for two days in Yanchakalla, then Baltazar's brother-in-law Honorato's. On the last day, I walked
to Cruzq'asa to help Vicentina cook and carry the meal to Pantiwayqo
(we rode the truck, on its way from 'Tambo to Cusco, most of the distance), and Gary and I, planning to go to Cusco the next day, returned
together to 'Tambo that evening, arriving weary and thoroughly soaked
and chilled by the cold, cold rain, which had begun to fall in midafternoon
and had not let up since, and miserable; the wet rubber of my *ojota*s was
slippery and my feet had slid in them, chafing painfully against the sharp
edges of the hard rubber straps until they had cut through my skin. But
the other men went back to Cruzq'asa with Honorato and Vicentina and
spent the night and all of the next day drinking. Ricardo's brother, Agripino, who had been helping with the *yapuy,* had come from the *estancia*
for two purposes, neither of which was specifically to help Honorato: one
was to break Baltazar's new horse which, at the age of five, had never
been ridden. The other was to arrange his own marriage to Honorato and
Vicentina's eldest daughter, Isabela, who is fifteen—it was negotiated by
Ricardo, acting as Agripino's father. The negotiations were successful,
and so this, as well as the day of rest—it was Sunday—after the long days
of grueling work, required hearty celebration.

3 APRIL 1982, CUSCO

Dear Elizabeth, Your house is lovely! The photograph *is* very American, terribly American, poignantly so for me: that broad North American–plains light, the brittle shadows of bare branches on white
clapboard. Most people at home, without really thinking about it,
would not understand how much it is possible to miss *bare trees:* trees
here never change through the seasons. Bare winter trees. But the seasons do change, thank God: these days—three or four now—have an
autumn feel, a high china blue sky (the Spanish word for this blue is
celeste), big white clouds, a great dry wind in the eucalyptus above the
house (on the road from 'Tambo, we pass through a deep grove of
eucalyptus, and above even the grinding of the truck's engine, you can
hear the sound of the wind in the rigid, knife-blade leaves, like the
sound of a Chinese bamboo wind chime heard from a distance, profoundly soothing). The air is cool and crisp and clear, the night almost
bitter cold and studded with stars in unfamiliar constellations. The
stars look enormous. And the harvest begins this month; though
we have had new peas and beans and new potatoes, brought in
small bundles from the fields, now the crops will be brought in to be
stored away.

On the truck there were people from Tahuay, in Chumbivilcas on
the other side of the Apurimac River, to the south. Chumbivilcas is

sort of Peru's Wild West: it is always referred to as La Otra Banda—
The Other Side. They ride horses, a necessity: the mountains there are
rugged and there are few roads. The people on the truck had ridden
for a day to come to Cruzq'asa, a village an hour above 'Tambo, their
nearest connection with a road to Cusco. The men wear enormous,
brilliant red ponchos with flamboyant borders with patterns—instead
of the tight, complex geometrical designs—of big butterflies and
flowers, men and bulls and horses, and long white scarves. They wear
felt hats like everyone does, but often instead of a ribbon band they
wear an *honda* (a woven sling) and the sides of the brim are turned
up and held in place with a leather strap. People here say they are
crazy; even their horses are crazy, even their cattle. There is a nickname, Walaychu, especially for men from Chumbivilcas, sort of like
calling someone Cowboy: a suggestion of rugged eccentricity and
willful independence and self-sufficiency.

I watch a cat, an old, battle-scarred tom, stalking a territorial rival,
a young, careless gray tabby, on the roof across the courtyard. People
in Cusco make a distinction between *roof* cats, essentially feral, and
house cats, who never go up on the tiles. No matter how much you
like cats and how sincere you are with them, roof cats are unap-
proachable, though one day when we were sitting quietly on the beds
reading, the old tom came in the door, gave us a long hard look of
appraisal, and then prowled around under the desk and shelves by the
window near the door for food. He found none and left, giving us
another cool look over his shoulder. Closest we've ever gotten to him.
(This letter feels sort of distant and uncommunicative somehow. Is it?
It's maybe just the day, which feels too big and empty: not used to the
sky being so far away, after months of living under the rainy season
clouds . . .)

'Tambo from across the *quebrada* of Misk'iunu.

'Tambo seen from the road above the village at sunset.

Looking down through 'Tambo from above the church. The belltower is in the center of the photograph.

Teresa, Baltazar, Daniel, and Hugo with Sandor in the *canchón*.

Andrés and Celestina posing outside their house.

Baltazar in the fields after a day's work, with Teresa in the background.

Hugo saddling a horse outside the family's compound.

Baltazar and Teresa relaxing in the yard with Juana and Ricardo's twin daughters, Nancy and Elisa, born after we left 'Tambo.

Leonarda weaving.

Daniel helping to construct an altar for the festival of San Juan.

Sebastiana and me at the potato field in K'airamayu.

Hugo at the *era* during threshing.

Juana in the yard of her parents' house.

Juana and Ricardo on Ricardo's birthday. The small pottery vessels are Inka artifacts found in the fields around the village, which they use to serve *chicha* on special occasions.

Jaime preparing straw for rethatching the roof of Baltazar and Teresa's kitchen, with Leonarda weaving in the background.

Juana with Eloy and baby Hernán, born in 1985.

Orlando.

Andrés, Celestina, and me.

Celestina and Andrés.

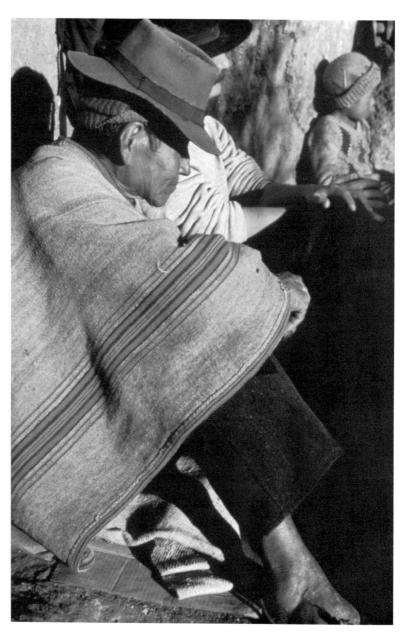

Don Andrés.

14. Teresa comes to Cusco

We had arranged for Teresa to come to Cusco on the twenty-eighth of March to visit us. She hadn't been to Cusco since August, and then she had come with Baltazar, not alone. When we met her at the truck stop it was obvious that she's not accustomed to the city: her face was drawn and tense, and she crouched slightly—it seemed a defensive posture, hunted. She had traveled on the truck with a young man, one of four brothers of the former hacienda family Coronel of 'Tambo, who are friends of theirs, and had a large bundle and the last fat white hen to sell. We accompanied them to the Coronels' store, on Calle Belén just above the bridge—they sell *trago*, in quantity—and we left them, planning to meet there in the morning. It was a strange feeling to meet the truck, faithful San Martín, and search the faces of others who had made the trip instead of climbing wearily off ourselves, to be in those streets I have known only at five in the morning and in the haze of exhaustion in the afternoon, arriving from 'Tambo, when we head immediately for the post office. My orientation in those streets during those liminal passages of arriving and departing has always been to or from 'Tambo with little bearing to Cusco, and they seemed very foreign now to the heart of our Cusco, our little room; when we travel to or from 'Tambo, even that room, our home in Cusco, becomes a part of the journey, alien, the lights unnaturally bright and harsh as we leave hurriedly in the middle of the night; or when we arrive, with that strange feeling you have when you come home after being away for a while, as if your home had a life of its own while you are gone, about which you know nothing. But now these streets became for me a part of Cusco.

We met the young man Teresa had traveled with on the street before we got to the Coronels' store the next morning, and he told us that Teresa had already gone down into the market and to wait for her at the store. We stood on the bridge over the lower market, which trails along the railroad tracks, and from that vantage watched her coming toward us, unaware of us, walking slowly, stopping to buy a package of noodles, bargaining and going on; she seemed to us, prejudiced perhaps, to possess a grace and dignity of bearing which the other women we could see lacked. She climbed the cement stairs at the bridge and almost walked right past us, not accustomed to recognizing *gringos* on the streets of Cusco. We went to the store with her and she left there the bundles she had collected and her basket and tied her carrying cloth around her shoulders, and we descended again into the lower market.

I'm having a proper skirt made for me: a full, *campesina*-style *bayeta* skirt. Teresa was going to help me buy the materials I need, though the *bayeta* itself I will buy from her, part of a length of undyed fabric she bought from the trader from Espinar. We went first to a woman who sells aniline dyes at a stall by the railroad tracks. I have chosen a color the Quechua call *rosado,* a Spanish word—a rich rose pink. There was a woman at the stall ahead of us, and we watched the vendor mix a formula for a brighter pink and an orange for her from the array of powdered dyes arranged, a rainbow of intense hues, in rusty cans on the counter. She and Teresa and the woman discussed colors, referring now and then to a hand-drawn color chart, twenty or thirty uneven lines of concentrated color painted on white cardboard, tacked to the wooden wall of the stall. The woman was an artist, mixing improbably colored powders to make the color she strove for as surely as a Renaissance painter must have mixed raw pigments or a master metalsmith combines the powdered silicates to make enamels. She measured by eye with a tablespoon and heaped the powders together on a scrap of newspaper laid on the brass plate of a hanging balance: the weight of a unit was that of two coins, old *sol* pieces. To make the bright pink for me, she mixed a large proportion of an earthy green powder, a bit of red powder, and a bit of clear, bright yellow, then made up the weight of the coins with earthy green. She folded the newspaper carefully, expertly, around the powder and marked each little packet with a smudge of identifying color by touching a tiny scrap of paper to her tongue, dipping it into the main ingredient of the mixture and painting it onto the paper wrapping. When she made my *rosado,* she explained to me that the cloth I will buy from Teresa is broader than the *bayeta* sold in the market and made an extra packet, then added a *yapa* (a little extra), a practice often followed by the vendors in the market—a couple of extra onions or *ajís*, an extra handful of coca, a spray of baby's breath to augment a bunch of flowers. One is fully expected to ask for a *yapa* if one is not offered: the rules of bargaining.

We followed Teresa up toward the main market above the tracks, stopping in shops to try, unsuccessfully, to find one which would sell her an arroba (about 25 pounds) of sugar and to find a large cardboard spool of crochet thread for the machine-stitched floral border of the skirt, which is done, along with the facing of the hem, by a man in 'Tambo who has a treadle sewing machine, and a spool of regular sewing thread of the same color. She seemed unwilling for me to choose the same color as the stitching on her pink skirt and on Juana's—a bright blue, which unfortunately seemed the natural choice to me—so I chose a deep garnet red. We went to another shop to buy a length of pink cambric for the facing of the hem; the young man measuring the cloth, who didn't seem to speak Quechua, or refused to, insisted on measuring out a half-meter instead of the half of a vara—an archaic measurement still used by the Quechua—which Teresa asked for, so we went to yet another shop, where the man spoke to Teresa in Quechua and measured a half of a meter and a little more to make up the half-vara she had requested. I reflected that the juxtaposition of old and newer measures must really confuse a shop's accounting.

We led Teresa out of the market in, for her, an unaccustomed direction, toward the *gringo* part of town: across the Plaza San Francisco and through the streets to our house, not far from the central plaza, the Plaza de Armas. The visit had actually been Baltazar's idea, so that they would know where we are when we're in Cusco, and also, I'm sure, to satisfy curiosity, and it seemed to us a good idea. They know of us, with whom they live so intimately, only one, atypical aspect, the aspect that is us as we live in 'Tambo, and this aspect cannot correspond to some of what they know about us: the clothes we wear and things we have, the fact that we can afford to fly to Peru and back from the United States. In 'Tambo, we try to live as they do, but they know that that life, which is all of theirs, is not all of ours and yet of the rest, the unknown aspect, of our lives, they must have little notion. We have always tried to camouflage it, to undermine the effect of the apparent, unavoidable differences, but now we feel we might owe them a chance to understand us, since they have made the extraordinary effort to accept us, comfortably at last, into their lives.

So we led her up to our room on Calle Sapphi. The Cusco traffic— which we hardly consider, used to traffic at home in even the smallest towns and having long since acquired the instincts of a hunted animal necessary to surviving a foray into Peruvian city traffic—terrified her, and she stood on every curb crying, "¡Ama! ¡Ama! ¡Ama!" ("No! No! No!")

until I told her, "It's all right now. Let's go!" and then ran to the opposite curb. Just inside the entrance to the *hostal*, we passed a group of European tourists and walked past them as naturally and casually as possible, hoping that Teresa wouldn't feel uncomfortable under their scrutiny, and they, fortunately, were too absorbed in their own conversation or didn't know enough about Peruvian society to notice her with us, to make some carefully audible comment or stare as most Cusqueños would at a *campesina* coming into a tourist hotel. We hoped, too, that we wouldn't run into the proprietors. When we opened the door and Teresa stepped inside, she said, "¿Ananau, eh?" (something like "Isn't it beautiful?"). She took off her bundle and put it on the floor just inside the door, then, without considering that she might do otherwise, sat down beside it, on the floor just inside the door, just as she would in another woman's adobe hut in 'Tambo: a woman always approaches another woman's house hesitantly, calling "Mamay . . . Mamay . . ." and being answered "Pasayki, Mamay—pasayki, Mamay" ("Come in, Mamay, come in,") until you would think she wanted to be literally begged to come in, and when she finally enters the house, goes no farther than immediately inside the door, until another visitor comes, when she moves farther inside. I gave Teresa a cup of coffee, heavily sugared, and sat on the floor by our kerosene stove—a woman's place, by the fire—until I felt sort of silly and sat on the chair at Gary's desk. We talked for a while in Quechua and at last got up to go. She asked us for a large box to carry home the four chicks she had bought in the market, which we didn't have; and a small bottle for the medicine she would buy for Hugo, whose stomach had been hurting for several days, which we gave her; and then for a bottle in which to carry kerosene: we gave her our plastic jug. Finally, she asked us to loan to Baltazar thirty thousand instead of the twenty thousand *soles* he had asked us for to help him pay for the horse he had bought. This was something of a moral problem for us: having us available to borrow money from gives Baltazar of course a distinct advantage over other people in the village, who might have to save for years to collect enough money to buy a horse. But we had already decided to loan him the money, or rather to pay him our rent for the next several months all at once, so we agreed with Teresa to bring an extra ten thousand *soles* when we returned to 'Tambo. She tucked the things we had given her into her *q'epi*, and we left.

   On the way from our house back to the market, we took her to a small, inexpensive restaurant where we often eat lunch. We had pointed it out to her as we walked toward Calle Sapphi, and she had approved of it, though from a distance. But now that she saw, standing at the door, that it was not the kind of place she knew in Cusco—the *chicherías* and *picanterías*, where villagers go, usually somewhere near the truckstop where the trucks to their villages arrive and depart: cafés with long tables flanked by benches instead of chairs (we couldn't be sure she had ever sat in a chair at a table before) and serve *chicha* as well as beer and soft drinks and simple *campo*-style dishes—and realized that we actually expected her to go in, she hesitated, and we thought she might refuse to enter. Gary proceeded as casually as he could, and I gave her a little push and followed her in. It was lunchtime, and the place was crowded with Cusqueños, and we feared, again, that she might bolt or feel too self-conscious to eat, but it began to clear out soon after we arrived as people finished their meals. We got a few glances as we came in and found a table near the window, but, we were thankful, nobody stared; maybe they thought that *gringos* are prone to do odd things anyway, like picking up a *campesina* and taking her to lunch.

We ordered a bottle of beer to share, as we often do with a meal in Cusco, forgetting that the Quechua don't drink during a meal but after and also that beer is for fiestas, whether invented or suggested by the calendar, and they wouldn't buy just one bottle of beer but as many as they could afford. Teresa was dismayed: she thought we had declared this a fiesta and were going to get drunk. But she also felt constrained to accept this hospitality on our part and bravely took the glass Gary poured for her, told us, "Salud, Mamay. Salud, Taytay," and drank it, not in one draught, but without putting the glass down, and refused any more. Minding our manners, we told her and each other *salud* before we drank but couldn't bring ourselves quite to drink our glasses of beer all at once. Gary had ordered fried fish for himself and for her—the restaurant specializes in fish and it would be a real treat for her—and Teresa had noted the fork which the waiter had brought her, saying only, "Tenedor" ("A fork"). Gary was served first and began to eat with his fingers—fish, rice, fried potatoes, and the salad which garnished the plate—to dispel any awkwardness: nobody in the village has forks—any sort of solid food is eaten with the fingers—and we didn't want her to feel uncomfortable or embarrassed, unaccustomed to eating with one. My soup presented no similar problem since most families have spoons for eating the variety of soups and gruel-like dishes which comprise most of the *campo* diet, although many people, especially older people and often women, prefer to drink soup from the bowl, eating the chunks of potato and other solid ingredients with their fingers. Gary went to the cashier to pay for the meal before the waiter brought the bill so she wouldn't know how much it had cost—we were certain that the total would have shocked her—while Teresa wrapped part of her fish, some lettuce, some of her rice and some of Gary's in a cloth which she knotted and packed into her *q'epi* to take home.

We stopped in a little supermarket to ask for an empty box, which

Teresa also managed to fit into her *q'epi,* though it looked improbable to us. We left her near the market, explaining to her when we would return to 'Tambo; she was going home in the morning. We walked back toward the plaza satisfied and a little dazed, as if we had just wakened from a dream. We felt we had demonstrated to her a hospitality she could understand without, we hoped, overwhelming her, though that hope may have been impossible to begin with: at worst the brief experience of our life in Cusco would be so incomprehensible to her that she would be unable to absorb it and it would never make any difference; at best, perhaps she now understood something about us and saw that we wish to reciprocate their generosity—both material and emotional—something she might communicate to her family. But we found it difficult ourselves to assimilate the experience; when we step off the truck in 'Tambo, we know that the entirety of the culture that we know without thought will be challenged: we have, if only by that awareness, braced ourselves for it. But how odd, how confusing, to be challenged on what is more or less our own ground, in our own cultural territory: to be made to think about whether I should wear my jeans and boots, as I always do in Cusco (I have stopped wearing jeans even for the trip to 'Tambo in the truck—it simply feels immodest to wear them in 'Tambo, and even for the few minutes before I put on my skirt, I feel out of place), and my hair unbraided; to think about whether to sit in a chair or on the floor in our own apartment; whether or not to eat with a fork in a restaurant. The hours we had spent with Teresa had been lived in some liminal world, somewhere between hers and ours. I wonder if she felt the same way.

15. Easter

These are the first days of Semana Santa—Holy Week. On Saturday evening, there were halos of small lights along the arches of the doorways of the cathedral in Cusco, red over the massive central door, white over the smaller aisle doors. On the morning of April 4, Palm Sunday, Domingo de Ramos, those doors had been thrown open, admitting the morning light into the silver and gilt splendor of the cathedral, its long, vaulted nave; outside stood crowds of people bearing palm branches who followed a procession carrying the image of the Niño Jesús, a small statue dressed in purple, borne above the heads of the crowd on a litter resting on the shoulders of four men, followed by a brass band playing something that sounded like very amateur, funeral Dixieland. We caught one dazzling glimpse through the doors of the cathedral as we crossed the plaza.

On Monday morning, the arcade along one side of the plaza was lined with vendors' tables covered with breads and cookies of all sorts, all shapes—most made, traditionally, with eggs, some from wheat flour, some from corn or potato, flavored with vanilla or orange or cinnamon. And the streets of the plaza were lined with parked cars, more cars than I've ever seen in one place in Cusco before. They were there to be blessed in the afternoon.

Late in the afternoon was the procession of the Señor de los Temblores, the Lord of the Earthquakes, a magnificent statue of the crucified Christ, eight or twelve feet high: the Señor de los Temblores is black, dark as night, and he was dressed in only a red cloth bound about his loins; red hearts and other forms fashioned of wire wrapped in red paper and covered with flowers dangled from the arms of the cross. Sometime long ago, hundreds of years ago, Cusco was wracked by a series of earthquakes which devastated the city. In commemoration of the event, religious authorities prescribed homage to a crucifix which had reposed in the cathedral for a century, since soon after the Conquest: a statue of Christ that was supposed to have been sent from Spain by King Carlos the Fifth, to which was attributed the grace that had saved all but a few of the inhabitants of the city from death in the great wave of destruction. Over the years of that century, the figure had been blackened by the soot of thousands of candles which had burned beneath it. Now that it was to be venerated, someone thought to clean the image, but such a protest was made—there was nearly a riot—for fear of altering or diminishing the power of the Lord of the Earthquakes, that the figure has remained to this day sooty black. Now, it is carried from the cathedral to the Church of Santa Teresa and back on Holy Monday, in more recent commemoration of the date when the great earthquake of 1950 struck the highlands, again devastating much of Cusco. Before the image walked ranks of citizens of the city—perhaps those who bore some aspect of *cargo* for the processions—priests, novices of the church in brown habits, acolytes in white; and after him came a censer carried by someone whom I couldn't see—only the plumes of scented smoke over the heads of the crowd. The sidewalks along his route of only a few blocks were crowded with people holding their hats in their hands: it is very difficult to find a place to stand unless you claim it early in the day, and resistance to the crowd's motion as it follows the procession is impossible. Many of the balconies above the street had been decorated, framed with purple bunting, and white sheets were hung from them; people stood on them and threw over the Christ as he passed great handfuls of scarlet flowers, *ñuqchu*, which grow in the *campo* and which people go out to gather for this day or buy from vendors in the market, and which symbolize the blood of Christ. It is said that once, as the Señor de los Temblores re-entered the cathedral, as he passed through the arch of the great central door, the earth trembled to remind the people of his power.

Good Friday: the almanac ends its description of this day with the words *ayuno y abstinencia* (fasting and abstinence), a piety which the Quechua observe for only half the day, until noon. So Teresa did not serve our usual soup for breakfast, and we assumed that they hadn't eaten anything when they awoke, their usual *mot'e* or bread and maté. Hugo attested to the fact that indeed they hadn't by succumbing to his hunger in mid-morning, driven to the extreme of cooking for himself, frying potatoes and eating them with *ají*. But Teresa and I nevertheless spent the

morning cooking: the fast is broken not with a simple, frugal meal but
with a feast. So we cooked four different dishes: two soups, one of a
squash called *lakawiti* (Teresa complained of having no *zapallo*, an enormous green pumpkin), one of potatoes and fresh beans and *machas* (mus-
sels) which Ricardo had brought from Cusco; and *arroz con leche* (a sort
of rice pudding); and *homenta* (tamales made from ground fresh corn instead of from dried corn)—like *t'impu*, another sort of celebration of season, the season of new corn. The fresh corn is ground and seasoned with
salt, folded into corn husks with a bit of fresh white cheese tucked inside
and boiled in a big pot, on a bed of corn husks and with a blanket of
more husks to keep the steam from escaping. And, exactly at noon,
having had neither food nor *chicha* (the fast includes food—especially
meat and *chicha* and *trago*—and the abstinence of coca and cigarettes,
though Gary and Baltazar had already drawn reprimand from Teresa,
whom they teased for being the *policía* of Good Friday, for chewing
coca), we ate: first the sweetened rice cooked with milk, then the two
soups, one after the other, and finally the *homenta*, several apiece. They
were unwrapped and laid on their husks before the fire to dry slightly and
were sticky and faintly sweet, the cheese melted inside. A bowl of each
soup was sent to Celestina, who sent back bowls of two soups, one of
fresh corn, in return; and some of each dish was sent to Asunta.

Late in the afternoon, just before dusk, the procession was announced
by the sharp report of a firecracker: the bells of the *campanilla,* like Papa
Dios—Christ—are believed to be "dead" from midnight of Thursday until noon on Saturday, when Christ ascended to Heaven; there was a *vela*
(a vigil) last night in the church. People gathered for the procession in the
half-light about the door of the church and along the walls of the churchyard. Led by the sacristan in a white tunic and the cantor, a group of men
carried on their shoulders a coffin-shaped frame, on the bed of which lay
the figure of the crucified Christ entirely shrouded in a cloth. At the head
of the procession, the cantor carried a staff with a cross at the top,
swathed in a purple cloth. As this group left the door of the church, the
gathered crowd fell in behind the men as they crossed the length of the
churchyard and passed through the portal at the opposite end, out into
the street, men and women generally separating themselves so that the
women followed on the left side of the narrow muddy streets, the men on
the right, as for a funeral. As they walked, they sang a hymn in Quechua,
led by the sacristan and the cantor. The procession turned east as it left
the churchyard, uphill away from the plaza, and south away from the
church at the corner into the street that runs just above the churchyard.
At each corner the procession halted and the singing ceased. The cantor
and sacristan alternately read a litany of the story of the Crucifixion and

then led the mourners in a recitation of the Lord's Prayer in Spanish, intoning one phrase, the followers responding with the next. As the prayer ended, all crossed themselves and, as the casket began to move on, again took up the hymn. The procession followed a route through the roughly paved and muddy streets that led up to the top of the village, across the mountainside several streets above the church, and down again into the plaza, with children playing and laughing among the solemn mourners and now and then an enormous sow or a couple of fighting dogs breaking through the crowd, causing a ripple of alarm and abrupt inattention. It passed through the plaza below the church and climbed the street at the end of the churchyard, entering the yard through the same portal by which it had left, crossing the yard, pausing once more before re-entering the church. By the time the procession returned to the church, it was nearly dark and a fine, sparse rain was falling; someone in the crowd carried a candle or a lamp which illuminated the faces of the sacristan and the cantor with a warm yellow light in the deepening blue-gray dusk. In the church, the casket was placed before the altar; hundreds of candles, it seemed, burned there and around the statue of the Virgin, in front and to the right of the altar, richly illuminating the great, shadowy stone-paved interior of the church, the altar, the enormous age-darkened paintings in their badly warped frames. A mass was spoken, but Gary and I left before it began, feeling that we had intruded enough into this solemn rite, and knowing, besides, how difficult it would be for us to walk home once it was fully dark.

Saturday was an ordinary day of work, the men out in the fields and Teresa and I climbing up to Yanchakalla to gather beans and a few potatoes and to cut stray barley from the potato field for the guinea pigs. But early Sunday morning, the bells of the *campanilla* sounded for the first time since Thursday. Easter Sunday is a day of celebration of awakened life; there is no formal community celebration, but the holy day is observed privately by families. We ate soup with rice and pieces of chicken in it—the poor little black laying hen, whom I had thought safe from this fate because she was so small and lean and because of the eggs she regularly provided. Leonarda brought a great handful of white daisies for our hats; between Carnaval and Easter, it is forbidden to wear flowers in your hat. Late in the morning, Eloy came to tell us that Juana and Ricardo wanted us to come and eat with them. Juana had also made a chicken soup, and as we ate with them, we talked about Orlando's christening: it had been supposed to be today, but the priest had not come to 'Tambo. So we will go to Cusco with them when Ricardo brings his early potatoes to sell, and little Orlando will be christened in the cathedral.

In the afternoon, Teresa and Sebastiana and I cooked *tarwi* and potatoes, a sort of salad of cooked, slivered carrot and potato, fresh beans and slivered onion, and two *qowi*s; while we were sharing this rather generous meal, Juana and Ricardo arrived and Juana brought a heaping plate of noodles with fresh beans and peas and shredded chicken meat and a small cloth full of boiled potatoes. When we had all eaten as much as we possibly could (I have learned that, if one is cunning, it is possible not to be constantly overfed in a Quechua village, but there are times when even discreet cunning is unacceptable, and times when it is ineffective!), Ricardo went to the shop to bring a bottle of *trago;* Baltazar said that, by this time last year, they had all been quite drunk, dancing and singing and crying: Hugo had been going to leave the next day to go down to the jungle, to Puerto Maldonado to work.

16. Harvesting early potatoes

Baltazar was telling ghost stories one night, after a day in the *puna*. Teresa had not had to cook a meal to carry that day since Baltazar and Gary were working for someone else, so we had spent a peaceful afternoon watching the chicks in the yard and spinning and late in the afternoon had begun to make a pot of soup to feed Leonarda and Jaime and the men when they returned. We sat outside the kitchen peeling potatoes, the sun broad and full and rich, gilding the west-facing walls. The men and the children came home at dusk and we sat together in the kitchen eating soup and talking comfortably as it grew dark, and Baltazar lit the little homemade kerosene lamp, which cast a smoky, flickering yellow light from the corner, and we said "Buenas noches" to each other, a traditional salute of respect to the night and to acknowledge our presence within it when the lamps or candles are lit. Baltazar was telling us about the old days, the perils of travel before there were trucks, when people were forced to travel in groups to ward off thieves who would attack them in high, quiet, lonely places. And how it is still dangerous to travel after dark, especially alone, for there are mischievous spirits who also travel the night, and in some places—not here in 'Tambo, but on the other side of Cusco, in Ollantaytambo, Chinchero, and especially around Maras—there are *ñakaq*s. Ñakaqs also travel at night, alone. They seem to be pleasant, friendly, handsome people, who fall in beside you smiling, chatting amiably. But soon after you are joined by a *ñakaq*, you will become drowsy and fall asleep, and while you sleep, the *ñakaq* will drain your body of its fat. Awesome changes come over the creature as it thus renews itself: its hair stands on end, its stomach becomes engorged, distended, and its knees swell. Water will repel *ñakaqs*, so if you are thinking fast enough, you can rub yourself with water or crawl into a spring and stay there; the smell of human feces also repels them, though Baltazar discreetly made no suggestion of how one might take advantage of this deterrent. Then the *ñakaq* abandons its victim to certain death. Doctors may diagnose the victim of various ailments and treat them accordingly, but the victim will weaken steadily and, after eight days, will die.

We spent four days in April in Ricardo's potato field on a hillside in Yanchakalla, harvesting potatoes for sale in Cusco: Ricardo, fortunate enough to have a field not immediately required for his family's subsistence, had planted this one especially for sale. And he had been shrewd: most potatoes are grown high in the *puna*, where they mature later in the season. This field in Yanchakalla is much lower in altitude, and if his crop was good—and he had tended it carefully—he would be able to sell it in Cusco before the market was glutted with potatoes, before the price naturally went down. The harvest was carried out just as it is in the *puna*, though the field is only forty-five minutes from 'Tambo: Ricardo and Juana and the youngest boys camped there to guard the heap of potatoes which grew each day, bringing from the village their pots and plates, *chicha*, their chicken, and, in a box, the four new chicks which we had brought them from Cusco. They built a tiny, temporary shelter, a *chosita*, of sod with a thatch of *paja*, a long, tough grass which grows in the *puna* and locally at the top of Apu Seratachan. The potato harvest has the feeling almost of a family holiday, one of the only agricultural tasks which the family performs all together, almost the only days of the entire year which the whole family spends together: Juana and Ricardo and I worked together for all four days, with, variously, Baltazar and Teresa and Gary and Sebastiana; Hugo has been ill. And Leonarda and Sebastiana's little brother Teodoro brought the cattle to graze in adjacent pastures.

The work is hard and satisfying and a hell of a job for someone like me who used to hate to get dirty, even when—perhaps especially when—I was a child of the age at which children seem to delight in dirt of all kinds. Each person worked a ridge from the bottom of the field to the top, though for some reason we left a patch in the middle of the field which was harvested at the end of the last day; our bare feet in the earth warmed by the sun or cool and damp, freshly turned, the fierce winter sun on our backs. Each person has a *kuti* (the short-handled hoe with a narrow blade) and a carrying cloth which he spreads between the rows ahead of him, onto which he tosses the potatoes as they are scrabbled out of the soil. The earth is broken away from the sides of the ridges and a little, carefully, from beneath the plants—potatoes cut by the *kuti* cannot be sold, though they can be used for soups for which raw potatoes are cut into pieces anyway, and they make fine food for the pigs—and the plant with its roots and tubers is pulled out of the soil and shaken. The soil and heavier potatoes fall from the roots, and the broken earth is combed with hands and hoe to discover all of the tubers; children walk over the harvested section of the field, scuffing in the turned earth with their feet to find the potatoes inevitably left behind and delighting in proclaiming each one they find to the person who overlooked it. All of the earth of the field is turned in the search for potatoes, preparing it just as *yapuy* does for the next season's planting; it will not support potatoes again for several years, but other crops, especially barley, can be planted here.

We paused now and then to rest and drink *chicha* and to eat Easter *homenta* which Juana had brought from home, or *mot'e* or fresh corn boiled on the cob or *papa wayk'u,* and, in the afternoon, a meal of greens and fresh beans picked from the adjacent field and always, always, *papa wayk'u*—potatoes we had just dug out of the earth, boiled in a big pot. In the *puna,* potatoes are cooked in a *wathiya* (a small oven constructed of clods of earth in which a hot fire is built): the potatoes are placed in the coals and the earth of the oven is collapsed on top of them, and they are left there to bake. This is very special, a sort of celebration of the harvest, and seems to be everyone's favorite way to eat potatoes, but they are cooked this way only in the *puna,* for if *wathiya* is made in the lower altitudes, where the crop matures sooner, it is believed to bring early frost which can damage the still-developing corn and beans and barley and wheat. We sat in the shade of the bushes at the edge of the field, glad of the cool shade and the rest and the sense of companionship in the work and the glorious autumn days, the rainy season finally past: the mountains looked as if they had been painted sharply in clear, intense colors flat against the deep blue sky. By the end of each day, the sky was absolutely cloudless, a vast expanse of unbroken blue.

The heap of potatoes grew steadily as each worker filled his carrying cloth again and again and slung it onto his back, holding the corners together over his shoulder, and hauled it up to dump his harvest with that of the others in front of the *chosita.* Most of the potatoes were *kumpis,* lumpy with a pale red skin, floury when cooked, though there were a few *papa blancas*—smooth, oval, white-skinned potatoes—and smooth, purple-skinned *maribas,* and a very few tiny, startling *papa lisas,* pink and yellow and bright red. *Lisas* are little tubers about the size and shape of a woman's little finger, with flesh which is slightly sticky and more the consistency of fruit than of potato. Each day there were new blisters on my hands from the handle of the *kuti* and new aches: first my back, then my arms, then the muscles of my legs, though each day's ache was worked out by the next day's labor, until I came home on the last day with no sore muscles at all. The work was so demanding and so much more physically involving than my usual activities that it seemed to make a powerful, bodily impression on me, and I dreamed each night of lumpy, red-skinned tubers half buried in rich, moist, brown earth. After we ate in the afternoons, we worked for an hour or so more and walked home, pleasantly tired, often among herds of sheep and goats which the village children were driving home along the trail at the end of the day in the brief, tropical twilight, the air cool and already damp with night in the shadows of the mountains. People outside the immediate family who helped carried home their last bundle of potatoes from the field as a gift of gratitude: Baltazar, Teresa, and Gary and I brought home altogether almost two full *costales* (the enormous woven grain sacks) full of potatoes. A full *costal,* upright, stands about chest-high. On the last days, Juana and Ricardo and sometimes Teresa sorted the harvest: the largest potatoes would go to the market, smaller ones would be used for cooking and for seed for the next crop. The potatoes from Ricardo's field in the *puna* will be brought home and stored to sustain the family during the year. On the final day, Ricardo made several trips to 'Tambo, once with four horses and a borrowed burro each loaded with a *costal* full of potatoes, later with one horse, and, at the end of that day, three more.

The hours of back-breaking work went surprisingly quickly, and the days blended together, as if the rhythm and the physical absorption created a sort of trance. I remember distinctly only vignettes, like the broken sequences of a home movie: Juana, during one break, holding one of the chicks to her cheek and talking baby talk to it in Quechua, cuddling it, kissing it on the top of its head; Juana and the children standing in front of the *chosita,* shouting and waving their arms to drive away a big strikingly marked black-and-white falcon, who watched from the air for a moment to plunge down and carry off the chicks, Sandor chasing madly across the field barking, not quite sure what he was supposed to do with a creature—unlike a cow or a pig—so smugly out of his reach. One morning, the moment of our first break was determined by Teresa who found a toad among the plants in her row. She was quite upset by it, alarmed because they are supposed to be dangerous, cause illness, and urgently hurried us all out of the field. Baltazar did not kill it—creatures with malevolent powers must be respected—but tossed it out of the field with his *kuti.* And one morning, Baltazar and Ricardo joked about Sebastiana's friend Dominga, who is going to Lima to work, to cook for somebody, saying that she would come back and say to Ricardo, "Achawi, come here and carry my bags!" (Achawi is Ricardo's surname) and, "Why don't you wash, *cholo?*" She would come back wearing pants instead of her skirts, shoes instead of *ojotas*, without her braids; they were joking, but wryly—what a bitter awareness of how people change when they go to the city!

I had some difficulty working with Sebastiana. Women seem often to have the hardest time coping with our presence and tend, when they are in a group of people, to try in various ways to reinforce the solidarity of the bond between themselves against the outsider—a natural, instinctive, and perhaps unconscious response, I suppose, to a possible threat to the security of the known and familiar. Sebastiana, almost every time I spoke, mockingly repeated what I said and laughed at it, even if all I said was "Yes" or "Thank you," and I know, at least, that I say those brief phrases in Quechua well enough that she wasn't simply laughing at my pronunciation, even for the benefit of the others. I began to feel humiliated and hurt, and I brooded about it for hours as I worked, wishing that I could say something to her, that I knew *how* to say what I wanted to say to her, to make her think about our friendship, however offhand it remains, and recognize that it hurts me when she laughs at me. But I realize that most cultures like this one do not train people to think that way, to be as liberal, as tolerant of difference and aberrance as we are. The rigors of traditional, subsistence lifestyles allow almost no alternatives in behavior: individual survival and the survival of the society depend on adherence to certain norms and standards, maintenance of a status quo; and deviance, and the sense of impending chaos that deviance inspires, must be controlled. And a result of that fundamental difference between our two societies—that we don't have to worry about survival and they do—seems to be partly that people here see other people differently than we do: we have the security, as a society and as individuals, to tolerate difference and diversity, and they don't. The sensitivity to other people's feelings that some of us cultivate would be frivolous in this context, maladaptive. It may even be a mechanism which helps to maintain homogeneity to laugh at and ridicule and whisper and gossip as they do about people who do not conform, whether by accident or inability or design—I have seen people be astonishingly cruel at times, not only to us. But I have always been unreasonably sensitive—a luxury of my own cultural heritage—to criticism or disapproval in any form, and so, even though I could rationalize the whole thing, it was trying to me to be treated, suddenly, like an outcast when I was accustomed to a comfortable acceptance, no matter how simple and childlike I may seem to them. Sebastiana also refused to speak to me in Spanish—though when we are alone, we always speak Spanish—even when I appealed to her for clarification or explanation of something said in Quechua by someone who spoke no Spanish. I finally said something to her one day, when I was working near her and Teresa and another woman, and she turned to me and asked me a question in Quechua. I told her, in Quechua, that I didn't understand,

and she repeated the question, in rapid Quechua. The women all laughed at my very apparent incomprehension. I said to her, "Sebastiana, you know I don't understand Quechua well. You can speak Spanish so that I can understand, can't you? I don't like it when you laugh at me." She looked like someone who wanted to laugh but couldn't bring herself to do it; she looked like a child who has been singled out to be responsible for the behavior of its friends, serious, debating inside whether to accept the dubious honor of responsibility or remain safe within the camaraderie of the group: she understood what I meant to say to her. Teresa mimicked me, "She doesn't understand," caught up in the game Sebastiana had started and that phrase being all of my little lecture in Spanish that *she* had understood. However, Sebastiana and I got along well after that.

Last night, after dark, Sebastiana came down to spend the night with Hugo who has been ill. Teresa and Leonarda burst into our room, agitated, demanding that we come out with our flashlight: Sebastiana had seen an *alma* (a soul) in the form of an enormous black bull, as she came down the street to the house. We followed the three of them out of the yard and shone the beam of the flashlight up and down the street. All that its unnatural glare showed in the black Andean night was a donkey, standing there dumb and confused in the street. It was odd for it to be there at that hour, obviously escaped from its tether near someone's house, but it was no big black bull. Sebastiana was talking very rapidly in Quechua and without her usual self-consciousness, still frightened by her vision, but there was now nothing there but the *asnu* and she knew this was not what she had seen, so we returned to the yard. It seemed to me that, on such a dark night especially—the sky was clear and full of stars, but the moon had not yet risen—if you *know* as they do that *almas* and *machula*s (the spirits of the ancestors) and other spirits both indifferent and malevolent roam the night, a dark form such as that of the donkey in a place where there should be nothing but the night's ordinary darkness could easily become such a spirit; inclined to accept the potential validity of others' beliefs, I can easily frighten myself if I am out at night, even only a few steps from my door, if I allow myself to think about the dangers the Quechua perceive of being out alone in the darkness here . . .

One night, Baltazar came home from a day of work in the *puna*— rather drunk: "Me han invitado," he always says ("They invited me"), absolving himself of responsibility for his condition—and came in to talk to us, sitting in his customary place when he visits us, at the end of the bed. A puma had killed a burro near the path to Yanchakalla the day before, and he began telling us about pumas and then about *atoq*s (foxes). He called the puma *machu compadre* (old *compadre*); the people of 'Tambo almost never use the word puma, always saying instead *machu* *compadre* or *hatun compadre* (big *compadre*). The puma, Baltazar told us, is an *hijo de la tierra*, a child of the earth; he lives in caves in the earth and the earth advises him, in the way that *paqos* and *altomisayoqs* are advised, men who in traditional Quechua society are diviners and curers, who consult corn kernels and coca leaves, the *apus* and the earth. Because of this power, we must show the puma only respect and always speak of him with respect. Baltazar told us of a man he knew, a chicken of whose had been stolen by a puma; while he was traveling, away from home, the angry man cursed and threatened to take a gun and hunt down the puma who had taken the fowl. When he returned to his home, he found two of his horses dead, killed by the cat. So when he kills one of our animals, instead of cursing him, we say, "*Machu compadre,* we invite you to this meal. We hope you eat well!"

The puma and the *atoq* are brothers, both children of the earth. But while the puma hunts at night, the fox sleeps at night and hunts, not always successfully, during the day. The puma often invites his brother to share his kill with him when he wakes. The people listen to the cries of the fox in the night as he howls from the peaks of the *apus*; in the spring, in October and November, the fox fasts and keeps vigil, and if his howls in the nights of these months are strong and pierce the night, the people know that the summer will bring much rain and a good harvest, but if his cry is weak, they know it will be a bad year.

Hugo had been ill for almost a week when we left for Cusco on Saturday, so ill that we were afraid that his life was in danger and offered to take him with us to Cusco, to the hospital—but their suspicion and fear of doctors and hospitals is deeper and stronger than our doubts of the effectiveness of folk medicine. Hugo had first felt a pain under his right arm. It persisted, and Teresa discovered a swelling in the pit of his arm. As the days passed, the swelling increased, and he developed a fever, as if some inflammation were spreading through his body; he had no appetite and lost weight and strength from lack of nourishment. He lay under a heap of blankets in the corner of the kitchen, or, when it grew warm outside, in the yard under his blankets, moving occasionally, evidencing his weakness in the required motion, to stay out of the sun.

On Wednesday, Gary took him to the *puesto sanitario* (the health center) in 'Tambo, which is sometimes manned by a young man who seems to have little training and about as much authority as a grade-school nurse; much of the time he is not there and the *puesto* is closed. We had given Hugo the last of our antibiotic capsules and then aspirin until our supply had run out, but it had hardly made a difference in the pain, and Hugo was frightened enough to be willing to walk, in spite of pain and weakness, from the bottom of the village, where we live, to the top, where the *puesto* is. The young *sanitario* gave him a nonprescription antibiotic and something stronger than our aspirin to relieve the pain. Gary bought the medicines for a nominal price: the services of the *sanitario,* such as they are—he has barely enough training, it seems, to make a more perceptive diagnosis than we could—are free, and for medicines there is a charge of only a fraction of their cost in a pharmacy.

But the medicines seemed to have no more effect than ours had, and Hugo's condition yet worsened. On Friday, Teresa went to call on a *curandera*—her own skill as a *curandera* is in treating bones and muscles, not diseases. A woman returned with her and examined the swelling beneath Hugo's arm and a cup full of his urine, saved from the night. She and Teresa discussed the recipe for a herbal poultice, and then she left and Teresa went to gather the medicinal herbs. When she returned, Sebastiana brought a handful of white roses, and Teresa came back with handfuls of both green and flowering plants—*balbas t'ika, willk'u, api kisa, motoy, qhaya qhaya, hawas rapi,* and *p'irqa.* They also brought a handful of dried beans and a chicken egg. Teresa tore the petals from the roses and set Hugo the task of pulling the flowers from the stems of the *balbas t'ika*—only the white flowers were needed for the poultice.

A different woman came to the house while these ingredients were being assembled, an old woman with graying hair, wearing a handwoven cloth about her shoulders, as old women do, instead of a shawl bought in the market. She and Teresa talked about the recipe for the poultice, and I heard them talking about *atoq lisa*s, a long, bright red *papa lisa:* the poultice was supposed to include a fresh *atoq lisa,* but there were none to be had. The old woman also examined Hugo, and then they set about preparing the medicine. The old woman broke the egg into a bowl and beat it with the handle of a spoon until it was a thick white froth, and with Teresa's grinding stone from inside, Sebastiana ground all of the other elements together on a flat slab of stone which has always stood beside the kitchen door. Hugo and Jaime perforated a sheet of white paper using a large needle and Teresa's shawl pin. The old woman mixed the ground herbs into the beaten egg with the fingers of one bony hand and began to apply it to Hugo's back; they had to remind her that it was his right side rather than his left, a correction which she accepted with an old woman's offended dignity, pretending to have known it all along. She smoothed the green paste across Hugo's back, over his right shoulder, on his chest on the right side near the arm, and under the arm, but not on the swelling itself. Teresa pointed this out to her, thinking it was an omission, but the *curandera* shook her head. She tore the paper in half and covered the poultice on Hugo's back with it; around his shoulder, she covered it

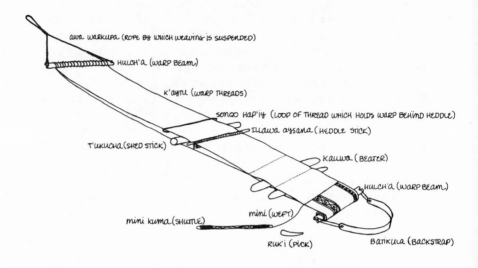

awa warkupa (rope by which weaving is suspended)

hulch'a (warp beam)

k'aytu (warp threads)

sonqo hap'iy (loop of thread which holds warp behind heddle)

illawa aysana (heddle stick)

t'ukucha (shed stick)

kallwa (beater)

hulch'a (warp beam)

mini kuma (shuttle)

mini (weft)

ruk'i (pick)

batikula (backstrap)

with whole large, heart-shaped *api kisa* leaves, and they helped Hugo put his shirt back on. Even if it was not an instantaneous cure, Hugo seemed in much better spirit after she had gone, buoyed by confidence.

The rest of the day was devoted to weaving: Baltazar had begun the new *costal* for the potato harvest and had spent one full day weaving already. On days when he does not work in the fields, he has been making the wooden parts of a loom for me, one by one: two *hulch'a*s (the end beams), two *kallwa*s (beaters) so far of four, two *pallana*s like fine, slender *kallwa*s for picking up the threads in *pallay,* and the *illawa aysana* (heddle). He had been talking to the judge one day about his plans to weave a *costal,* and the judge had offered to sell him the lower leg bone of a *taruka,* a small Andean deer, to make a *ruk'i* (pick), an essential implement in the process of weaving. Baltazar told us that if we gave him the money he would buy it for us—the judge might ask a higher price of us because we are *gringos*—and make one for me instead. *Ruk'i*s are traditionally made of llama bone, and Baltazar's is of wood, which he claims is better than bone. I would have liked to have one of llama bone, wanting all of my tools to be as traditional as possible, but realized that the *taruka* bone was probably as close as I would get since there are no llamas in or near 'Tambo: they have been replaced entirely by sheep and horses and pigs as providers of wool and meat and as beasts of burden. Baltazar went

to the judge and returned with the slender bone, at the end of which remained the delicate cloven hoof and a ring of reddish hair. He cut it to an
asymmetrical point, leaving the hoof end intact, and worked the bone as
smooth as he could with a knife; it will be smoothed and polished by the
wool itself as it is used. As he worked, he scraped the marrow from the
hollow of the bone and saved it. When the little boys appeared, he rubbed
it on their knees, so they would be able to run like deer.

Gary wanted to try his hand at weaving, and Baltazar was eager to
teach him, allowing him to work and advising him as he rested. He was
much less eager to teach me, feeling apparently that as the weaving of
grain sacks is a man's affair in his family, so it should be in ours, and I
finally had to insist that I be given an opportunity to try it. And so we
each sat in the harness for the first time and discovered that what looks
like a pleasant and effortless task is damned hard work. Baltazar, because
of his once-broken leg or because it is simply the way men do it, sits on a
section of eucalyptus log, off the ground, and I suspect that sitting on the
ground as women do might make the work less strenuous: I found myself
having to struggle to keep the stump upright against the pull of the long
warp attached to a roof pole. When Baltazar stopped late in the afternoon to let me try it, Gary bought a bottle of *trago* at Baltazar's suggestion to bless the weaving and the careers of his two apprentices. We drank
as I began my first painful attempt at weaving on a large scale, and any of
what may have looked like facility was attributed to the *trago:* as I
worked, an old, old woman, a friend of Celestina, came into the yard and
made a *t'inkasqa* over the half-woven *costal,* sprinkling a few drops of
trago over it and over me as well, and then don Andrés did. With such
venerable blessings, I felt, I couldn't fail. I also felt the benefit of having
simply watched often enough to have absorbed an amount of almost vis-
ceral understanding of the motions involved in the work. I had told myself that this was a good reason to watch others weave, consoling myself
when I had no opportunity to try it myself, but I had had no idea that it
might actually make some difference. About dusk, I had to stop, my
lower back aching from straining against the pull of the warp. Baltazar
said that it isn't good to weave at night, which makes sense—you can't
see then anyway. I felt satisfied, almost exhilarated, by my first experience
with weaving, in spite of my weary, aching back.

We had agreed with Ricardo and Juana to meet them at the truck stop
in Belén on Sunday afternoon, when they would arrive in Cusco with
their harvest of potatoes to sell, or if the truck was late—we didn't want
to wait like vagrants in Belén all evening—to meet them at the bridge
over the market the next morning. We planned to accompany Ricardo
when he took his potatoes to be weighed, hoping that the presence of two
gringos, and our little electronic calculator, would intimidate the dealer

who bought the potatoes—they often cheat the villagers, and the villagers are well aware of it, though, almost as often, there is nothing they can do about it. We had also planned to take Orlando to the cathedral to christen him, but when Gary and I went to the cathedral to inquire about the procedure, we were told that the ceremony of christening is performed only on the first Sunday of each month: this was the third. We waited at the truck stop until six-thirty, after dark, and still the truck had not arrived, so we went home. We waited on the bridge the next morning for an hour and finally left a message and our address for Ricardo at the Coronels' store, where Teresa had stayed. The proprietor told us that Ricardo and Juana *had* arrived on Sunday, but the truck hadn't reached Cusco until eight or eight-thirty; they hadn't spent the night there at the store though, and he hadn't seen them yet that day.

About midmorning, as I sat on our patio writing, Ricardo's impish face appeared above the low stone wall between me and the stairway below. He was followed by Juana, Sebastiana—who had come to have photographs taken for her *libreta,* a document of identification—and dauntless Orlando. We stood talking in the sun on the patio for a few minutes, and then we asked them in. They, of a more worldly generation, were not as visibly impressed by it as Teresa had been, and they seemed comfortable there. I made coffee and we talked; Juana and Sebastiana discussed the weavings from Potolo and Titicaca which hang on the walls, and Ricardo and Gary and I talked about Ricardo's potato transaction and the thwarted plans for Orlando's christening. Ricardo and Juana had gone to the cathedral early that morning and had been told the same disappointing news but had managed to have Orlando's name placed on a list of names for christening and found out also that the Archbishop of Cusco himself is supposed to come to 'Tambo in August, for the festival of the Virgin of the Assumption, so that, though such reports are not often very reliable, there is a possibility that we might christen Orlando in the church in 'Tambo.

They had returned then to Belén to have the potatoes weighed; Ricardo showed us a tally of weights and prices and we added it up with the calculator and it was correct, and Ricardo knew that it was a good price, so he hadn't, apparently, been cheated. Orlando meanwhile bounced on the beds, inspected every small object he could reach, and explored the patio and would have explored the rest of the *hostal* and perhaps all of Cusco as well had someone not realized he was gone. We went out for lunch, leading them to the Algarrobo, where we had taken Teresa. The restaurant did not intimidate them either: they were clearly much more accustomed to the ways of the city than Teresa was. We ordered *pescado a la Chorrillana* for everyone and two liter bottles of beer. When those two were gone, Ricardo expansively ordered three more, obviously intending to buy them himself to treat everyone—he had reason to feel wealthy: he had exchanged his potatoes, at 95 *soles* per kilo, for almost 74,000 *soles,* about seventy-five dollars, a literally inconceivable fortune in a village like 'Tambo. But Gary, under the facile guise of going to the restroom, went to the cashier and paid the entire bill. Ricardo's genuine surprise was gratifying. We walked with them up to the Plaza San Francisco, where we parted, feeling somehow like old, old friends.

17. Cruz Velakuy

My parents arrived on Wednesday, the twenty-first of April, to stay for a week, during which we did and saw everything they—and we—had the stamina to endure. We settled them in a room at the Hotel Alhambra, a beautifully renovated colonial building full of red carpeting, highly polished wooden and tile floors, colonial paintings and pots of geraniums, in a small side street not far from our apartment—their room overlooked the narrow, cobbled street through a large wooden-framed window with a wrought-iron grating and pots of red geraniums hanging below it—and left them to rest and recover from the trials of their journey, which had been remarkably eventful: there had been mechanical problems, a fight, a bomb threat, and their luggage had almost been left in Panama in the middle of the night.

The next morning, we inaugurated their custom-designed tour of Cusco and environs, starting with the requisite visit to the bank to change money and hours of poking around in shops full of handcrafts. In the succeeding days, we took them to the ruins of Pikillaqta, to the church at Andahuaylillas, to the cathedral and Coricancha, to Sacsahuaman, Qenko, Puka Pukara, and Tambo Machay. I went with them one day to Machu Picchu on the train. Through all of these sites my parents hiked enthusiastically, in spite of the ankle my mother sprained the morning after they arrived, unaccustomed yet to broken and uneven Cusco sidewalks; she wore a Peruvian elastic bandage and carried a straight eucalyptus branch which Gary cut for her to use as a walking stick—unusual but, for her, ironically appropriate souvenirs: how many visitors take home mementos which have the potential to so evoke the experience of a place? One day we took them to 'Tambo: they wanted, were determined, it seemed, to go there (parents' concerned curiosity about the welfare of a wayward child?). We warned them of what it would be like: eight to ten hours of difficult travel there and back and the conditions in 'Tambo—the lack of bathrooms or even the uncomfortable privacy of an outhouse, in 'Tambo or anywhere along the way, the water they couldn't drink, and food, which they would almost certainly be offered, which they might not want to eat. Yet, we set out at seven one morning, Gary driving a slightly cramped Lada Niva, a Russian-made four-wheel-drive vehicle which we rented, on roads which had dried like cast concrete under the winter sun into their great rainy-season ruts, and stopping occasionally to take pictures—an opportunity which Gary, traveling on the truck, has had no more than has my father. We had sent a message with a truck driver the day before that we were coming but caught up with it ourselves when we found the truck broken down along the way—the message had never gotten to 'Tambo.

Nevertheless, we were greeted on the plaza, shyly, by Teresa and then quite proudly by Baltazar, who had heard the car's approach from the house. He was so apparently dumbstruck and excited that he was nearly trembling as he shook my father's hand, and his hat, as it usually is when he is trying to be casual in the midst of some occasion when he is clearly important, was pushed far back on his head. At the house, my father delighted everybody with his Polaroid camera, taking pictures of everyone, recording every conceivable permutation of the group—Baltazar and Teresa; the whole family including grandchildren; Hugo and Sebastiana; Juana and her children; Juana and Sebastiana, with and without the children. He kept a few of them but gave most of them to their subjects. My father directed them in English where to stand, and they spoke to him in Quechua—they got along beautifully. Teresa offered to massage my mother's bruised ankle but, to my mother's relief (though she was touched by the offer, she wasn't sure she wanted anyone to lay hands on her aching ankle), there wasn't time. My parents brought as gifts bread and exotic fruits, for 'Tambo—a bunch of grapes and a watermelon, which we suspected, judging by Baltazar's slightly guarded thanks, that they had never tasted before, though he considers himself very worldly and would never have admitted it. We neglected to mention to them how to eat it, or even that it was a fruit and not a squash, and hoped later that Teresa wouldn't cook it; a watermelon looks a lot like a *lakawiti*. She was terribly embarrassed that she hadn't prepared food for my parents, but she served them boiled fresh corn on the cob and boiled potatoes with *ají*, fortunately simple and familiar foods, except for the *ají;* and my parents tasted—and liked!—the *chicha* she poured for us as we left.

So when they left again for the States, my mother and father took with them, I think, a more real sense of Peru than most tourists do. People who come with the tour groups must often leave with the impression, if they think about it, that Peru is nothing more than the remains, the ruins, of the Inca Empire and the Spanish colony that was superimposed upon it, both exploited by the industry of tourism—the tour agencies, hotels, restaurants, cab drivers, the vendors of handcrafts and antiquities, and the money exchanges. They leave without a notion of the civilizations which preceded the Inca and which live on after them, however more apparently humble a culture they seem. Though they had been there only a few days, the night before they left, my mother said wistfully that she was going to miss Cusco; in the dark street, I smiled to myself. Everyone who comes here misses Cusco when they leave.

My parents left Baltazar a gift which will be remembered by everyone long after the taste of the watermelon, however it was finally eaten, is forgotten, a gift the proportions of which they had no suspicion: they left him a new story to tell, which, I have little doubt, will take its place in Baltazar's repertoire with the story, slightly dated now, about when President Belaúnde landed in a helicopter in the plaza of 'Tambo, when the village was made a district capital, and Baltazar, as one of the town's officials, shook his hand.

Hugo is on his feet and smiling again. On the day we left for Cusco to meet my parents, Baltazar asked Gary for some coca and cigarettes to offer to the *paqo* whose services he was going to enlist to cure his son. The efforts of the *curandera* hadn't succeeded. The *paqo,* a man named Martín Molina who plays the *quena,* came and examined a small bottle of Hugo's urine. He requested from Teresa a guinea pig, which she brought to him, and he rubbed Hugo's body all over with the creature, so it would absorb his illness. He then killed and skinned the *qowi* and examined its carcass: he found, under its right foreleg—the position of its body corresponding to the center of Hugo's pain—a slight swelling filled with a white fluid. He then punctured the swelling under Hugo's arm with a shard of a broken glass bottle and drained the infection. And Hugo, apparently, was cured, though he is still thinner than he was and a little pale. Martín reported that the illness had been caused by Pachatira and *pukyus*—the earth and the springs. Illness is most often attributed to accidental proximity or exposure to such topographic features as caves and springs, from which cold winds are believed to issue, the breath of the spirits of the ancestors; or to the cold night wind; or to the heat of the sun. It seems, in a way, to be quite arbitrary, accidental, rather than the result of or retribution for some error or wrongdoing or omission, and therefore, logically, illness is unavoidable.

May third was Cruz Velakuy, or Santísima Cruz—the day of the Holy Cross, the festival when the great crosses, decorated lavishly once again with their sashes and with fresh flowers fastened all along their trunks and arms, are brought from the mountaintops by the *carguyuq*s of the *ayllu*s to reside in 'Tambo until the day of San Andrés in November. On the eve of Cruz Velakuy, the crosses are carried to the houses of the *carguyuq*s and established in a place of honor; an altar of some sort is built for each one, in the house or the yard—a table covered with a cloth and decorated with more flowers and pictures of saints and Crucifixions, or a bower of flowers in a corner. The *carguyuq*s invite kin and *compadres* and other members of their *ayllu*s to come to honor the crosses, to pray, then to drink, less and less solemnly, and dance all night in the presence of the crosses, as candles burn constantly on the altar. On the following days, the crosses, shorn of decoration, are carried to the church to lean against the front wall for a time, then are brought inside, where they remain until November.

We spent the day of the second baking bread for several of the *carguyuq*s, who often offer their guests pieces of bread and cups of *trago* as wine and the Host is offered to worshippers in a church. In the early evening, we, the four of us, shared a bottle of *trago*, though Baltazar was already rather drunk: the *carguyuq*s each had brought a bottle of *trago* which they shared with him as he worked, to thank the baker for his services. About eight-thirty or nine, we were to go to the house of a young *carguyuq* named Claudio, of Ayllu San Miguel, for whom we had made bread earlier in the day and who had invited us all to come. As we were preparing to go, Mariano Castellanos arrived to relay an invitation from Teresa's brother Julián, which threw our plans into confusion. Teresa felt that, as he is her brother, we should go to Julián's house, but Baltazar felt that we were already committed to go to Claudio's. It was decided, with much difficulty and ill will, that we would visit Claudio and then go to Julián's house. So we walked, by moonlight and supporting Baltazar, up to Claudio's house; Teresa's lips were pressed together in a thin line of impatience.

The cross of Ayllu San Miguel was set up on a table in a small courtyard at the top of the compound belonging to Claudio's family. As we entered, we each took off our hats and knelt before the cross, Gary and I feigning the prayer we didn't, unfortunately, know. We sat with the other guests around the edges of an area bounded by two storehouses, along

whose walls were benches and the altar, and on the open sides logs to sit
on, all of us arrayed around the *taytacha*. We were served *chicha* in great
quantity, huge glasses full, and *trago*. The *trago* was served very formally,
not by Claudio, but by an older man, whom we learned later was the
sacristan (we had never seen him from close enough to recognize him
now), who filled two *copitas*—a typical little, cheap glass one and a fine
one of wood, turned perhaps on a lathe—placing them each time he filled
them on the table-turned-altar beneath the cross, then offering them side
by side on a plate to each guest. Before accepting them, the guest often
removed his hat in honor of the *taytacha*. Soon, the record player, which
had been playing quietly in the background, was turned up, and people
began to dance; Baltazar fell asleep, leaning against my shoulder. A little
later, it was turned off, and each guest was offered the two *copitas* of
trago on a plate with a piece of the bread we had made for Claudio earlier, cut into quarters. I drank my *trago* and took one piece of bread, but
everyone around me urged me to take all four, which I did gladly: I ate
them all hungrily, surreptitiously because I suspected that this might not
be the most respectful way to do it, hoping that it would absorb some of
the *trago*. A prayer was spoken after all had been served, our bare heads
reverently bowed, and then the music began again and a supper was
produced, *mot'e* and a plate of *tarwi* and potatoes to be passed among
us. And people began to dance again, more lively still than before, and we
decided to try to sneak away—we would never be allowed to leave if we
announced our intentions, whatever reasons or excuses we offered—and
after a couple of unsuccessful attempts, escaped. Gary helped Baltazar,
who had awakened somewhat refreshed and willing to begin again,
through the streets at the top of the village to Julián's house, though
Teresa now thought, contrarily, that he was too drunk and that we should
all just go home, in spite of her brother's invitation. She and I went down
to the plaza to buy a bottle of *trago* from Juana for Julián, then climbed
the street toward her brother's house. In a yard at the end of the street
stood a huge and extravagant altar; music, amplified by a loudspeaker,
blared from the yard out over the village—all night and all of the next
day and night. Though the whole yard was brightly lit by a bonfire, I
didn't get a good look at the altar as we hurried by to avoid being seen
and invited in: Teresa by herself probably wouldn't have been, but I, the
gringa, undoubtedly would. We crossed the bridge at the top of the village (dry now; during the rainy season, as much water flows over it as
under it) to Julián's house.

Julián and his family live in a house which we have wondered about, a
big house with a sort of colonnade of whitewashed arches which stands
prominently, proudly, over 'Tambo. The road passes just above it, and an
ancient foot road just along its rear wall below the modern roadway, so

we have passed it often; it always looked deserted. We learned that it was one of four houses built around 'Tambo by the old *hacendado* Coronel for his four sons: Julián had bought it at the time of the Reform, instead of building a house, for a good price. We entered by a large double wooden door into a walled and terraced courtyard, the shallow terraces which might have been gardens now overgrown with short, tough grass, and followed a roughly paved path, also overgrown, to stone steps which led up to the porch behind the whitewashed arches. Crossing this, we entered a long room with smooth, painted walls—not unfinished adobe— empty but for a makeshift bench of planks laid across adobes along one wall and an old, richly carved wooden writing desk left from the house's more prosperous days, the days when it had belonged to the son of a *hacendado*. The *taytacha* stood on the floor in a corner, framed by an arch of withes covered with flowers. One candle burned before it. The guests sat at the far end of the room. The mood of this gathering was different, solemn, almost somnolent, more like the vigil which is the model for this ritual. There were no batteries for the record player, and the *trago,* except for the bottle we brought, seemed to be gone. The men sat on one side, on the bench, and the women, with their jars full of *chicha,* on the floor opposite them, and old don Andrés lay stretched out along the end wall between them, sleeping (Andrés is Teresa and Julián's uncle—"tío ligítimo," Baltazar says). The liveliest moment of the whole night occurred when I sat on poor, dear Andrés: his head lay in the darkness of the corner and I mistook the length of his stretched-out form for a blanket-covered bench or log and, when I was waved to that end of the room to sit, sat, approximately, on his knees. There was a hoarse exclamation from the corner, and I slid quickly off his legs onto the floor. We all laughed, with a faint tremor of hysteria—facing the daunting vigil, what looked to be a long night—and for a while after the laughter died away, one person or another would think of the incident and giggle. We sat drinking the *trago* we'd brought and then sipping *chicha,* all talking quietly. Baltazar fell asleep again and tumbled from the bench, and the men stretched him out on the floor, not to be awakened. Gary and I eventually lay down beside Andrés and fell asleep ourselves. Sometime during the night Teresa left, and when he woke, which must have been about dawn, Baltazar left. We left soon after sunrise, narrowly escaping the enormous glasses of *chicha* we were offered for breakfast, and went home, assuming that that was where Baltazar and Teresa had gone. But when we got there, the houses were still locked and the yard was empty. We made coffee and drank it gratefully and later returned to Julián's house, where we found them, Baltazar sleeping once more now in Andrés' place in the room with the *taytacha*. Teresa sat with another group of guests in the sun in another courtyard beyond and above the first, enclosed by a wall on the west and buildings housing a kitchen, a storeroom, and, behind us facing the after-noon sun, an open room with pink plastered walls and another arched colonnade; we sat on earthen benches along the walls of this room, the sun pouring through the arches and across the floor, filling the room, to eat a meal in the late afternoon. Among the enameled tin plates—all I had ever seen in the village—were a few old, chipped china plates, painted with faded flowers. Here we sat, peacefully if rather aimlessly, until dusk.

Cruz Velakuy was, for the most part, over, except for the blare of the amplified record player from the house above. The crosses were brought to the church and propped against the front wall on either side of the door. One remained to be returned to the church, the *taytacha* of Ayllu Pumatambo, the sash of which we had been accused of stealing. Late Wednesday afternoon, at the end of a day of watching and helping Baltazar stretch the warp of a second grain sack, we heard music—a record player—from below the village; we all went down to the pasture to see. On the road from Pumatambo, a troop of people accompanying the cross had stopped to rest, to drink *chicha* and dance in the path, the cross held upright nearby. We watched them for a while, then went back to the house to wait with a sense of anticipation. As they drew nearer, we went up to the plaza to await their arrival. They came, near dusk, in the twi-light up the path by our house, the *carguyuq* bearing the flower-laden *taytacha*—with its sash—a man playing an enormous Andean harp with its great half-conical sounding box resting upside down against his shoul-der, strapped to his body with a scarf, and a number of drunken people carrying the record player and jars of *chicha*. They paused at the entrance of the street onto the plaza, then proceeded across it and up the street by the bell tower and into the churchyard. They paused again by the door, prayed, and carried the cross into the darkness of the church. I sat with a couple of young women in a window in the broad churchyard wall, my hat respectfully in my lap. The party left the churchyard and went on to the house of the *carguyuq* who would carry the *taytacha,* on the day of San Andrés in November, back to the mountaintop above Pumatambo. And we went home.

18. Potato and barley harvests

The days of the potato harvest have come and gone, and our Walaychu—young Daniel the wanderer—did not come home. The whole
family watched in anticipation as the trucks from Cusco climbed the
mountain road, paused at K'airamayu below the potato fields to dis-
charge passengers, and went on to 'Tambo: none of the passengers was
Daniel. We listened each morning to Radio Tawantinsuyu when the disc
jockey, a Chumbivilcano also nicknamed Walaychu, reads messages, but
there was none from Daniel. Baltazar had received a letter from him
about a month after he left again for Quillabamba and that evening had
reported its contents to us: Daniel had said that he was well and working
for a man whom Baltazar had known well during his own years in La
Convención and that his father shouldn't worry about him. We asked if
Daniel was coming home for the potato harvest as he had said he would,
and Baltazar said, Of course he'll come home, making it sound as though
Walaychu, Walaychitu, had reassured him of this in the letter. But I had
read the letter: it had been brought to Paqopata, a village through which
we passed to the *puna* when we were plowing the potato fields, by a boy
from Quillabamba, who had given it to a boy from 'Tambo, who in turn
had delivered it to Celestina, who knew Baltazar. That morning, as
Teresa and I sat in the yard spinning, Celestina came over with a pitcher
full of *chicha* and told us that she had a letter for Baltazar, then went to
fetch it. Teresa looked at it carefully and said it was from Daniel—her
stubborn Quechua accent transforms the Spanish name into "Ranilcha,"
with the affectionate diminutive "cha" added—and asked me to open

and read it to her. I brought a pen knife from the house and began to slit the envelope open, but she stopped me in a panic, and gestured that I should pry it open so we could seal it again: she didn't want Baltazar to know. I read the letter, which was written in Spanish, then translated as much of it as I could into Quechua, as Teresa and Celestina sat with their dancing spindles. What Daniel had written was: Papa, I don't know when I'll be home. Don't worry about me.

The tenth of May had been decided upon by the community as the first day of the potato harvest at K'airamayu. Baltazar and Hugo and Jaime went up the day before, with two horses laden with straw—*ichu* grass— and the *chakla*s (withes) with which to build our little shelters, Baltazar riding the third horse, and Leonarda driving the cow and bull calves. Gary walked to K'airamayu the next morning; and Teresa and I, laden with one of our backpacks, most of Teresa's pots and plates in a bundle, a large quantity of fresh beans and a watermelon-sized squash, and a basket containing the chicks, rode up with Juana, Eloy, and Orlando on the truck. Most of the passengers on the truck that morning were women carrying their households to K'airamayu. One of them asked me if I couldn't hold her chicken for her, and so I rode to K'airamayu holding in my lap a large and apparently contented red hen. The frameworks of our huts had been constructed against the side of an enormous boulder beside the field, which would shelter us from the wind. Baltazar and Leonarda had slept in the larger one, covered with a sheet of plastic. Hugo had returned to 'Tambo to sleep with Sebastiana; Baltazar joked that Hugo had been so anxious to get back to his sweetheart that he had built the larger hut in a great hurry, making its arch much too high to keep out the wind. When we were finally all gathered there, we covered the domed, open-ended frames made of withes lashed together with tough *ichu* grass, with a loose thatch, standing bundles of the straw upright thickly along the base, then making a thick mat of *ichu* by letting bunches of it slip straw by straw from our hands onto the ground to tangle it, and lifting these mats onto the tops of the frames. We covered both of the little huts, one behind the other, with one length of plastic, tied at the corners through the thatch to the withes. On the floor of each we laid a padding of grass, which Teresa covered with skins and blankets and I with our big rain poncho, Gary's wool poncho, and our sleeping bags. Teresa cooked a soup over a fire in a shelter built of stones and clods of earth in front of their hut. We ate, and then began the harvest.

Though it was twelve-thirty by the time we started, we got a lot of work done by the time the sun sank below the mountains and it grew suddenly cold after the heat of the afternoon. Just the four of us worked that day, beginning in the middle of the field. At dusk, we ate *papa*

MORNING MATE
(JAIME)

wayk'u and *ají* and cheese that Gary and I had brought from Cusco, and as it grew dark we huddled in Baltazar and Teresa's hut and drank hot, sweet coffee to warm ourselves. Then we lay in our own hut, remarkably warm and comfortable though it was so small that our shoulders and heads would not fit inside, listening to Baltazar tell stories, legends about the stars, until we fell asleep.

We worked rather randomly through the rows in the following days, working with Hugo, then with Sebastiana as well, then helping Hugo harvest his own small field above ours on the slope, and finally finishing our own on the last days. Each day, we woke at dawn and lay watching the sunrise and listening to the radio, listening to Walaychu reading messages—his program, broadcast twice daily in Quechua, is the most reliable form of long-distance communication between the villages of the central Andes around Cusco—and playing *huaynos*; one morning we were startled abruptly awake when, in the midst of the stream of Quechua to which we half listened, we heard Walaychu say, in English, "Good morning, ladies and gentlemen" (as if he knew that somewhere, at four-thirty in the morning, within the range of his broadcast, there were a couple of *gringos* listening: as if he knew we were there!). We ate bread and drank instant coffee—they drank *maté*—and then worked for a while until we ate breakfast, soup of fresh potatoes and beans, noodles and squash, and then returned to our work. In the early afternoon, Hugo would build a *wathiya* in the field out of the big clumps of earth, forming a dome in which Teresa built a hot fire. She shoved potatoes into the oven through the opening left in the side, and then pushed in part of the roof of the dome to pour in an armful of beans, still in their pods. She collapsed the entire structure over the vegetables and tubers and left them to bake. A while later, she called us to eat: the potatoes and beans were always perfectly cooked, with a faintly smoky flavor that is utterly distinctive, like nothing we had ever tasted before. We ate them with *ají*, with lettuce or cheese or salads of canned sardines and onions, brushing soot and earth from the potatoes and peeling them, breaking open the pods of the beans and peeling the beans to eat just the soft meat. Now we understood why everyone looks forward to *wathiya*.

We worked until a little after sunset and spent the early evenings mainly trying to keep warm as the cold *puna* night fell until it was time to sleep. Sometimes we had more soup, sometimes just the last of the *wathiya* and coffee, made from ground Quillabamba coffee beans and sweetened with brown sugar. Each day except the last, Hugo returned to 'Tambo with the horses laden with potatoes, nine huge sacks and a little more in all; on the last night, both he and Sebastiana slept in the tiny hut with Baltazar and Teresa and Leonarda—I don't think they managed to sleep very much. During the days, Goyo Coronel and his brother, nephews of the four Coronel brothers, who run a shop off the plaza in 'Tambo and have no land, walked among the fields trading *trago*—for warmth—for potatoes; and men from Nayhua traded oranges and lemons and limes and even sprouted corn, for the women who were working in the fields could not be at home making *chicha*.

The work was easier here in the *puna* than in the fields in Yanchakalla, for in the *puna*, proper ridges can be made, the clods, or *ch'ampa*s, lifted from the earth bound together with the tough roots of *puna* grass. When the potatoes are planted in the ridges, the *ch'ampa*s are simply lifted and the seed potatoes dropped into the space between them and the nearly impenetrable earth beneath them. In this space, where warmth and moisture are conserved, the tubers grow. The process of harvesting is a matter of dismantling the ridges, laying them open by lifting the *ch'ampa*s with the blade of the crooked hoe to reveal the potatoes; this is fairly easy, especially when the ridges are skillfully constructed, less so when they have been carelessly made. I found that I could work much faster than I had in Yanchakalla, where I had always fallen behind the others, once I learned to recognize the edges—or the *esquinas* (corners), as Baltazar said—though I still couldn't quite keep up. But still, after three and a half days, my back and arms were tired, though not sore, my hands blistered, and my right hand achingly bruised from the repercussions of the blows of the blade of my *kuti* against the hard earth.

On the last morning, we finished the last ridges and dismantled the little huts; Baltazar would return to 'Tambo with Leonarda and the cattle and Gary and the horses, loaded now with the *ichu* grass which we would use for starting fires, the withes for building a bin in which to store the potatoes, and the last of the harvest. Teresa and I waited for the truck while they waited for Ricardo to return with the horses they had loaned him. Teresa paid our way home with a cloth full of *papa wayk'u*. In a little green valley at the curve of the road just beyond the last fields lay the white form of a dead horse. On the hillside above the little valley, we watched condors land, ten of them, enormous, gliding one by one through the blue sky to gather there, the dark *kondor auki* and the black-and-white *yuraq kunka* ("white neck"). *Auki* is a title of respect, like the title *apu*, which is reserved for the most powerful of beings; *auki* is the title for beings not quite as grand or powerful as *apu*s. They sat quietly on the hillsides, some spreading and arching their wings in a display of threat or dominance over the others. A few days later, there was nothing left of the white horse in the green of the grass but the empty cage of its ribs.

1 JUNE 1982, CUSCO

Dear Elizabeth, We return to Cusco wind-blown and covered with dust, cheeks burned by the sun and wind, shivering from the sudden winter cold when the sun sinks behind the mountains, more weary from the five-hour truck ride than the time spent in the field, and go straight to the post office—letters! The mail seems to be a little slower here than usual, maybe because of this little war in the Malvinas/ Falklands—though it's on the other side and end of the continent and thousands of miles away, there have been marches and demonstrations, mostly in Lima, against the British, and against the U.S., in support of "our Argentine brothers," so maybe they're "inspecting" the mail from the States more carefully than usual; God knows what they do with the mail. But I got your letter and postcard.

The post card, the one with the neon sign on it, very nearly made me cry. All of those things you meant to remind me of . . . I have reached a point at which I am terribly homesick at times. It's odd, or really I guess not so odd, that there is something equally idiomatic and *true* about Peru that corresponds to each one of those things—Oklahoma, "Your Cheatin' Heart," lilacs in spring, Hank Williams, screen windows, all of it. And each one of these aspects of Peru is absolutely, profoundly *different* from its North American counterpart. There is Radio Tawantinsuyu which plays *huayno*s and *marineras,* the country-and-western of Peru, and the disc jockey from Chumbivilcas nicknamed Walaychu who reads messages for people in the villages from their uncles or brothers-in-law in other villages and whom every *cam-*

pesino in the highlands knows, the way we know our favorite anchor on the evening news. There is sitting on the Plaza de Armas in Cusco on sunny afternoons, and the nun in a white habit carrying an armful of creamy-white calla lilies through the market. Each one as simple and common and colloquial as Oklahoma and screen windows, and each one deeply—as you wrote: astonishingly—foreign to us. It amazes me sometimes that I can live here, taking it finally for granted; thinking of myself walking in the streets of Cusco, turning the corner into Avenida Sol to go to the post office, behaving remarkably as if I belong here, or, more remarkably, walking through the village as if I belong *there*, climbing the street of broken cobblestone to Juana's house to help her cook . . . I guess that it's simply that you *can't* really think about it, the foreignness, or you couldn't just live here. Anthropologists say that the true culture shock that you experience is coming home again. But we've been in Peru nearly a year now, and sometimes I'm so homesick that once I had a dream about a shopping mall in Ohio. (And I've never *been* to a shopping mall in Ohio!) . . .

June. Beautiful winter days; deep, deep blue sky and hot sun, and nights that are brilliantly clear—we watch the moon and the stars now and talk about them; and cold, leaving frost on the thatched roofs and on the grass of the pastures outside the village. I sat in the sun on a hillside one afternoon, watching a pair of brown-and-white barred hawks hunting, sweeping low over the little fields of barley, only inches above the heads of the grain, searching the golden shadows among the stalks for small creatures, prey. Barley is beautiful, more lovely and graceful and more golden when it is ripe and dry than wheat: tightly braided heads of grain with long whiskers that catch the wind. When the sun shines full on a field of barley now, it seems somehow to radiate light, as if returning to the sun the light it has absorbed during its season of growth, no longer needed.

The men have been harvesting the barley for the brewery, working with *ichuna*s (the small sickles). They work the fields in swaths, gathering handfuls of stalks and drawing the curved blades through them, toward themselves, stacking cut grain in small, prone sheaves throughout the field behind them. Gary wears a pair of goatskin chaps to protect the legs of his pants from the myriad varieties of little irritating burrs; Baltazar says that everyone used to wear them when all men wore the woolen *bayeta* pants (wool seems to draw the damned things out of the air, I've discovered), though now only a few men wear them, often old men who also still wear *bayeta* trousers, like don Andrés. The stacks of cut grain are gathered into enormous bundles, drawn tight with a rope, and carried—often by some improbably small boy who looks as if he will surely be crushed by the load—to a clearing nearby. It is sometimes left there to dry a little more, and then it is threshed.

We made *wathiya* in a nearby field the first two days—apparently the critical factor is not where *wathiya* is made, in the *puna* or lower down, but rather when: it is winter now, and all of the crops have matured and the frost, nightly now, will not harm them—and sat for a long time, our family and Asunta and Nicasio and their children, Sebastiana and the two younger boys, Seferino and Teodoro, enjoying the warm afternoons and the picnic feeling of the *wathiya*. While the men were working, I helped Asunta and Teresa make *ch'uño* (the "freeze-dried" potatoes). We had spent a couple of days sorting the potatoes we'd harvested in K'airamayu into categories of size—some, the large ones, for *papa wayk'u*, medium-sized ones for seed, small ones and those cut by the *kuti* for soups and dishes for which they would be cut up anyway—and some for *ch'uño*. Teresa and Asunta each brought to the hill in Yanchakalla two big sacks full of potatoes, which we scattered over the grass all across the hilltop where the men were harvesting. We left them there for two or three nights, where they froze each night under the hard frost and thawed in the hot sun of day, until the flesh of the tubers began to release its moisture and shrink away from the skins. We set aside a small quantity of the potatoes for *moraya*. Then we gathered the rest together into little heaps and danced on them, a performance called *ch'uño saruy* (*saruy* means "to step on"). It looked ridiculous, all of us spread across the hilltop, dancing on little heaps of shriveled potatoes, shifting our weight from one foot to the other, sort of shuffling to keep the potatoes under our feet—not much different from dancing a *huayno* only without the benefit of music. This dancing works the skins loose and presses out some of the moisture. Then we gathered the little shriveled potatoes up again, combing the grass all across the hilltop with our fingers to retrieve every one of them, and took the *ch'uño* home to soak in the basin under the tap and in a big tub for a week or more, then spread them out in the sun in the yard to dry. On the way home, we left the potatoes we had put aside to make *moraya* in the mouth of a spring on the hillside to soak in its icy water; in a few days, they would be bleached white, and one of the boys would return to fetch them home to dry with the *ch'uño*. When the results of all this labor were stored away, the *ch'uño* looked like small clods of dessicated earth, and the *moraya* like lumps of chalk. They looked like anything but *food*. Meanwhile, however, we ate a lot of *ch'uño*.

19. Corn harvest

On June fifth, 'Tambo sent its dancers off on the pilgrimage to Qoyllur Rit'i. In the morning, we passed by the house where they were assembled; they had danced in the plaza the evening before and had probably been drinking most of the night in preparation for their journey. The arrival of the truck in the morning seemed to be a signal—Choro, the driver, was to take the dancers as far as Cusco; from there they would ride in a hired truck to Ocongate to make the rest of the pilgrimage to the snow-capped peaks called Qoyllur Rit'i (the name means "star snow") on foot. When the passengers of the truck had disembarked, Choro drove it out of the plaza, and the dancers entered in two lines led by a man carrying the flag of Peru and one carrying the wooden box which contains the image of San Juan and followed by a small group of musicians playing *quena* and *tambor*. The image of San Juan had been carried throughout the village the week before, calling at each house to request small donations of money to support the pilgrimage; Teresa had gone to hide in one of the storerooms, instructing me to say that she wasn't home. The dancers climbed to the churchyard and stood in two lines extended out into the yard from the door, the image of the saint facing them from the doorway. They knelt and prayed, led by the sacristan, and danced briefly. At the head of each line were five or six men dressed as *majeños* (a word pronounced by the people of 'Tambo as "majines"), costumes like the clothes Chumbivilcanos wear—cowboy-style hats, brilliant red ponchos and long white scarves; a few had stiff plaster masks of *mestizo* faces, with small goatees, moustaches, and a rather cold, cruel glint in the eyes.

Each *majeño* carried a bottle. Behind these dancers was a larger group dressed in the costume of the *ukuku,* long black tunics with rows of fringe—bands of brilliant color—with large triangular scarves tied over their shoulders like shawls, a ruff of fur hanging between their shoulder blades, and each one wearing a knitted mask—a combination of cap and mask, with a face knitted into the front. From the front of each tunic, a variety of objects dangled on the chests of the *ukuku* dancers: miniature ceramic pots, plastic toys, whistles—but each collection included a tiny doll sewn from scraps of cloth and a bell. Each *ukuku* bore a whip, a braided leather thong attached to a wooden handle carved into a spiral. The last dancer was dressed as a *sanitario* (a rural doctor) in a white tunic-coat and white pants, carrying by its handle like a briefcase a white box with a red cross painted on it.

The procession of dancers left the churchyard and crossed the plaza to the door of the town hall, where the two lines stood side by side extended out into the plaza, facing the town hall door. The image of the saint again faced them, and they were addressed by the *alcalde.* Then they performed the entire dance of Qoyllur Rit'i. The musicians, standing by the doorway, altered their melody and rhythm to accompany first the entire group, then the dance of the *ukukus,* then the entire group again. When the *ukukus* dance, the *majeños* step back to leave an arena at the head of the formation. They dance in place, while the *ukukus* in succeeding pairs dash into the space between them, dance together for only a moment, then, their hands joined, begin to whip each other on the calves of their legs with increasing violence: at the site of Qoyllur Rit'i, each dancer is paired with a dancer of another village, and as they are strangers and their faces are hidden by their masks, this battle can, is supposed to in fact, become quite earnest, to the point of drawing blood; the dance is called *yawar mayu* (river of blood). Baltazar, who once made the pilgrimage to Qoyllur Rit'i as an *ukuku,* says that the dancers wear several pairs of pants, one over the other, and bind their legs with heavy cloth to protect themselves from the blows of the whip as well as from the cold of the glacier. The battle of each pair of *ukukus* is disrupted by one who acts as a sort of referee, who blows a whistle and comes between them to force them apart. When each pair of *ukukus* has fought and returned to their lines, they perform a more light-hearted "dance" which consists of whirling in place, ringing their bells, and then running full force at each other, trying to and often succeeding in knocking each other to the ground. Finally the two lines are formed again, and all of the dancers together perform a new step in unison: three thrusts forward with one foot, then three with the other for a distance, turning then to repeat the step back to their original positions. On the final thrust of each foot, they also thrust forward with the corresponding hand their whips or bottles.

Meanwhile, the truck had returned to the plaza, and as the dancers were served *chicha* and *trago* offered them in two *copitas* on a plate by the women of whatever family or *ayllu* bore the *cargo*, the few regular passengers bound for Cusco boarded and the dancers' bundles were brought on. The lines of dancers formed again, more or less, at the foot of the ladder onto the truck, and the group was delivered a rousing speech of encouragement by the mayor. And finally they boarded: the flag, the saint in its box, the musicians who began playing their *quenas* and *tambores* when they had found places, and the dancers, who clambered up to sit atop the wooden sides of the truck. As Choro drove his truck out of the plaza, the dancers cheered like a team going into a contest, the flag snapping in the wind above them.

Beauty does not win them grace. Great flocks of parrots, little *loros,* wheeled in the air above the fields below Qolqeuqru, down the mountainside from 'Tambo toward the river, as green with the sun shining on them as summer leaves driven by a strong wind, filling groves of trees with their chatter which resounded throughout the valley between the mountainsides. But we learned during the days that we camped by the fields to harvest the corn that they are not only as noisy as starlings but also as common, and as unwelcome: they eat the corn. I began to comprehend the fragility of life supported by subsistence agriculture, depending wholly upon your own crops for sustenance each year; in spite of diligence, hard work, and prayer, the crops remain subject to the vagaries of the weather—too much rain, too little, hail—and to disease, insects, and birds. I know now the hope as you hold each ear of corn in your hand, the sinking of the heart when you pull apart the husk to find it ravaged by disease or insects or eaten by birds, and the alternate, instinctually deep satisfaction, a pleasure which must be magnified to joy in the hearts of the family whose harvest it is, to open one that is whole and strong and healthy, which could have come, but for the color—which ranges from almost white through yellow, orange, a deep, rusty red, to purple and a soft blue-violet—from the central Illinois fields of Bear Hybrid Corn.

It is good work, harvesting corn, much less strenuous and dirty than digging potatoes, and too, I suspect that, having grown up in Illinois, I have much more affinity for corn than for potatoes. We camped beside Baltazar's small fields, moving our camp three times, sleeping at night in the open, sheltered by the huge sacks full of the corn we harvested each day and a sheet of plastic to break the wind, under the stars and the full moon, with the Apurimac roaring a half-mile below us; at night, all of us under our covers, Baltazar told us stories about the stars, and when we woke at dawn, we listened, still wrapped in our blankets, to Radio Tawantinsuyu, until Teresa got up to make a fire, stirring us all to action.

Families usually build tiny shelters of corn stalks supported by branches when they harvest corn, and Hugo and Sebastiana did build one, one night, but the horses, tethered too close, ate it. For all their effort, they woke in the morning as exposed as the rest of us except for a bare framework of branches.

A couple of mornings, while Teresa and Sebastiana and I made soup, Gary and Baltazar cut the corn stalks in a portion of a field and stacked them together, and later, while they worked in another field, we simply stood and pulled the ears from their stalks. On other days, we all walked through a field in a phalanx, gathering the ears of corn in carrying cloths tied over our shoulders, and spent hours in the early evening picking the hundreds of persistent burrs from our clothes. One morning I opened an ear of corn—you split the husk above the grain with a pointed stick called a *tipina* (from *tipiy,* which means specifically to remove the husk from an ear of corn), which hangs by a cord from your wrist, and strip the husk away—an ear of corn that was smooth and solid and perfect, so lovely that I didn't want to simply toss it onto the carrying cloth with the others and, standing off by myself in the field, away from everyone or I would have resisted my impulse, I held it to my cheek and against my lips: it was as smooth and cool as if made of gold. *This* is the gold of the Incas!

One night while we were camping, we were all suddenly awakened when the horses startled and Sebastiana's old sheep, which follows her around like a dog and was sleeping near my feet, jumped up, landing with its sharp hooves and all of its weight on my legs. Something had frightened them, and moments later set a dog barking far up the hillside; no animal could have moved so far so fast. We listened carefully. There was nothing. Baltazar said it must have been an *alma,* and as we lay there listening to nothing but our hearts beating and the voice of the Apurimac in the distance, there seemed to be no other explanation.

20. Weaving

Sandor—Sandorcha, as Baltazar has always affectionately called him—has disappeared. He's been gone for a week and a half, since just after the corn harvest, and no one has any idea where he is. Nobody talks about him except the children occasionally, and Gary and I, to each other: we miss him. I guess that in our culture, we have the security and leisure to allow ourselves the luxury of becoming frantic over the disappearance of a pet. Here, people cannot allow disappearance or death, even of their own children, to interrupt the rhythms of their lives: the crops must be planted, tended, harvested, the food cooked and *chicha* made—the living and present must be provided for; there is no time to indulge the human tendency to grieve, and expressions of grief are willfully restricted to the birthdays and anniversaries of departure of those who have left—who may or may not return—and to the inebriation of Todos Santos for the dead. We asked Baltazar one day where Sandorcha was, and he said briefly, "He's gone; we don't know where he went." And one day when we were sitting in the yard with Teresa, Gary, musing, said to her, "I wonder where Sandorcha is." She said, "He's dead," without a pause in her work or a moment of thought. She doesn't know this for certain, but, although I have difficulty admitting it to myself, it is very possible. In fact it is probable. He *may* just have wandered off, a young male dog in search of love and adventure, and show up again one day; or he may have been stolen. At least, if he is dead, he was spared the injustice and eternal indignity of being hit by a car, and perhaps he even died a noble death, felled by a puma. But I hope not; I miss him.

Baltazar gave us a message, revised by Hugo whose name it would bear, to take to the studio of Radio Tawantinsuyu in Cusco to be read over the air by the disk jockey Mario Molina Almanza—Walaychu—to Daniel, or rather to the man he is working for in La Convención. In final transmission it read: "*Atención* Paltaybamba, Señor Miguel Villacorta—from Hugo Quispe. Urgent! Send Daniel Quispe Sullca home immediately; his father is ill." They considered saying "seriously ill" but decided on the introduction "Urgent!" instead. Of course, Baltazar is *not* ill; and since the conception of this ruse as a means to get Daniel home, I have listened carefully to the messages which are read on the air and noted a remarkable proportion which are of the melodramatic nature of "Come home immediately—mother is on her deathbed . . ." I wonder how many of them are ruses like Baltazar's, desperate attempts to retrieve loved ones who have strayed. It must work: even if it is commonly known that such a message might be a trick, how could one *not* go home if it *might* be true that father is seriously ill, mother on her deathbed?

We went to the studio of Radio Tawantinsuyu on Sunday morning, when the station broadcasts a sort of amateur hour, of which the master of ceremonies is Walaychu. Beginning at his usual hour in the morning, five-thirty, anybody can come to the studio with their instruments and they will be allowed to play, their performance broadcast throughout the central highlands. The program lasts until about noon, and, as Sunday is generally a day of rest, almost everyone spends the morning listening to it. Mario Molina Almanza—Walaychu—is a Chumbivilcano from Livitaka, and something of a folk hero. He is, remarkably, the best disc jockey I've heard in Peru—the only one I've heard, at least in the highlands, with any distinctive presence, with any real sense of himself as his audience might hear him. And yet, in spite of his ease and absolutely dependable professionalism, he is the only disc jockey who plays only *huayno*s (others play everything from salsa and cumbias to Menudo to North American and European rock and roll, for which even Orlando expresses distaste) and who speaks to his audience in Quechua. He is real. The people of the villages know where he comes from and that he is one of them, that he knows their life because he has lived it himself. The sign-off for his show, the sort of motto with which he closes each one, is "¡Mikhuy papata!" ("Have some potatoes!"). In person he is urbane and engaging—not a handsome man, especially, but possessed of such command and self-confidence and natural wit that he is somehow attractive. And there is something endearing about the fact that, although he was well, even elegantly, dressed that morning and wore a large ruby and gold ring on his hand, a number of his teeth were missing, never replaced by some city dentist.

We hoped that our message could be read that morning, Sunday, because Hugo assured us that Daniel would be listening to Walaychu that day and that he would be working early Monday morning and till late in the afternoon and might not hear a message read by Walaychu during either of his Monday programs. We asked that it be read at all three times, to be certain, and stayed to hear Walaychu himself read it a few minutes later, as we stood among the small, mostly Quechua audience in the tiny, crowded studio. Now we'll wait and see.

We've been in Peru nearly a year now—we arrived in Lima the twenty-second of June a year ago—away from Hamilton and our life there, our friends and our jobs, and the cat and the comfortable habits of home for almost a year. The approach of that anniversary makes me reflect more often, nostalgically, of home; or maybe it is simply a function of having spent such a long time in such a foreign place. There are moments when all I want to do is go home. There are times when I feel vaguely that this has been a wonderful and fascinating vacation, but now I'm ready to get on with my life—as if this isn't my life. Sometimes, when I find myself thinking nostalgically of home, I realize that the tenor of my thought is more or less how much I will appreciate things, small mundane things, which I never really appreciated before, like Dorothy in *The Wizard of Oz;* as if I might wake up in our bed in Hamilton one morning murmuring, "There's no place like home, there's no place like home . . ." But then there are other moments: early Sunday afternoon after we had left Radio Tawantinsuyu, I walked to the market through the Plaza San Francisco, and in one of the bushes there was a tiny emerald green hummingbird, sitting at the very end of a bare twig. I stood there watching it, and it sat watching me, and then a man, Quechua, and clearly from the *campo,* dressed in patched *bayeta* clothes, a *ch'ullu* and *ojotas,* stopped and stood close beside me to watch it. We were almost the only people in the great sunlit expanse of the plaza, standing there side by side. I looked at him and exclaimed, "¡Picaflor!" and he said, "¡Q'enti!"—Spanish and Quechua for hummingbird—and we smiled at each other. Then he walked away, turning once to wave at me, and the hummingbird flew off— thought they don't really fly away: after no more than a few inches of flight, they seem to simply vanish—and I followed the man at a distance across the plaza toward the market. Moments like that—that funny little bird with his head cocked wryly to one side, eyeing me, the man's smile and wave, and the communion of our mutual fascination—banish nostalgia, make me realize that I ought to concentrate on living every moment I have here fully *here,* fully present.

Late Sunday afternoon, we stretched, between two stakes driven into the earth of the yard in front of our house, the warp of the scarf I have been planning to weave for Gary—on my own loom. I had finally finished re-spinning the yarn for it; four colors: gray for the background, blue and *guinda* (a deep purple-red—the word is Spanish for sour cherry) and rose pink for the two narrow bands of stripes of all three colors along each edge. It is machine-spun yarn, acrylic, bought by the skein in the market, the yarn that many Quechua weavers now use rather than hand-spun and home-dyed sheep's wool for the colored stripes in ponchos and the bands of brilliant *pallay* in carrying cloths, but though it is bought already plied, the yarn is re-spun, twisting the plies tighter to make a harder, tougher yarn for weaving. We sat on the ground outside the door, Baltazar and I lazily tossing the balls of yarn back and forth to each other as we looped it around the stakes, crossing it in the middle between them to make the *sonqo* (the "heart" of the warp), winding it around a thick cord along each stake which would secure the ends of the warp to the end beams of the loom. Gary poured *copitas* of *trago* from a bottle which he had bought—the *multa* (fine) Baltazar had exacted from him for having stepped across the warp at some point: if someone steps across the warp, unless the violator makes amends in some way, it is believed that the weaver will never complete the project.

While we were working, an itinerant salesman came into the yard with an enormous bundle. He said he was from Puno, and the bundle was full of ready-made skirts and petticoats and aprons, pants and flannel shirts and small objects like needles made in China. Teresa and Leonarda and Sebastiana eagerly handled the aprons and petticoats, Leonarda casting pleading looks toward her father, who ignored them. I bought a packet of twenty-five Chinese needles, the last of my good English steel needles having mysteriously disappeared somehow the last time Leonarda borrowed it. This was the only sale he seemed likely to make, so the salesman tied up the huge bundle and made arrangements with Baltazar to stay the night; Baltazar had spent several years as an itinerant salesman in the Vilcanota Valley when he was young and appreciates the hardships of a salesman's life and therefore always gives them lodging when they come to 'Tambo, a practice of which he is proud and likes to talk about, boasting of his compassion and loyalty to his former profession and his somewhat maverick hospitality. We finished the warp and took it off the stakes and wound it up to keep it from tangling, and I put it in the house; and then we sat on the earthen stoop outside the door as the sun set, talking with the salesman and sharing another bottle of *trago* which he had generously offered to buy. He seemed to be interested in Gary and me—I thought it must be something of a surprise to find a couple of *gringos* living and seeming to be at home in some village—and we explained conversationally who and what we are and what we are doing and how long we have been and are going to be in 'Tambo. When the *trago* was gone, the little party began to break up, and I found myself standing alone with the salesman. Speaking quietly and in a confidential manner, he offered to sell me something else, which he hadn't displayed to us earlier. He didn't name what he was offering, apparently expecting that from his circuitous approach and his manner, I, being a *gringa,* would of course understand; but I didn't until I stupidly asked him, "What are you talking about?" and he said simply, without lowering his voice, "Cocaína." I was shocked, perhaps naïvely so: I had never expected to find the stuff here, in the *campo,* in the villages. In Cusco, of course, it is almost common, especially if you are a *gringo,* for people to offer to sell you cocaine, in low voices, right on the street, but *here . . .* It left me dazed. He had violated a boundary that I had wanted to believe existed between the seamy, sordid aspects of modern Cusco and the good, clean traditional life of the *campo;* had dealt a mortal blow to that whole romantic construction, and it upset me deeply. He persisted, to the point of offering me a slip of paper with his address in Puno on it in case I changed my mind, at which point I excused myself curtly to go and fill our kettle with water for the morning; it was almost dark. Later, it made me sad to remember their faces as Teresa and Leonarda and Sebastiana handled with delight the new, full, white-cotton petticoats and calico aprons and my own foolish pleasure in something as simple as a neat packet of shiny new needles. I wondered if they knew, and I wondered what the relationship between the salesman and the people of the village actually was, if it was different from what I had perceived it to be because of the cocaine somehow. I felt hollow with shock and sadness until I slept that night.

21. San Juan, threshing

Celestina and Andrés began celebrating San Juan, the twenty-fourth of June, two days before the saint's day; the preparations which had seemed interminable completed, they sat in the sun in their yard serving festival *chicha* to anyone who visited them and at various times to Baltazar and Teresa and Gary and me—a chance for them to relax and drink casually with their friends and gather themselves for the rigors of the formal celebrations of the eve and day of San Juan, which would test the thoroughness and abundance of their preparations, their generosity and ability as host and hostess. Andrés was one of the two *mayordomos* for the festival of San Juan, a position that bears more prestige than that of a simple *carguyuq*. As *mayordomo*, Andrés had had the privilege of planting and harvesting the community-owned cornfield dedicated to the saint, and from this harvest, Celestina had been making *chicha* for a month, jar upon waist-high jar full, which were stored in their kitchen, the bedroom, and along the walls of their two storage rooms. On Sunday, they had asked me to help them bake bread at the community oven for the festival; they had bought or had ground one hundred and twenty-five pounds—five arrobas—of flour.

The community oven is in a long building high in the village; the Spanish-style adobe oven, like Baltazar's and housed in a shelter like the one Baltazar had built, is attached to a large workroom with a poured cement floor, probably built, I reflected, at the time the other community structures, the town hall and the schools and the *puesto sanitario*, had been built. When I arrived with Celestina, bringing *chicha* and *trago* for the workers—a meal would be brought later—most of the specialized work of the baker had been done: the dough had risen in a long wooden trough along the wall and was ready to be shaped into breads. We spread cloths over a large expanse of floor in one corner and, assisted by an ever-changing complement of women and little girls and one young man, accompanied by the broadcast over the radio of one of Peru's games in the World Cup Soccer tournament, we made hundreds and hundreds of little breads. As they were baked, we scooped them out of the oven and piled them into *costales*. Celestina went in the early afternoon to bring the meal she had prepared that morning and very ceremoniously served the men working at the oven and the women who had helped, and we drank *chicha* and a little *trago* and ate bread hot from the oven. At the end of the day, the huge sacks of bread were loaded onto mules, and Celestina and I each carried home to her house a bundle full of more bread.

On the morning of the eve of San Juan, Andrés came over to Baltazar and Teresa's house where we were eating breakfast and, in the whining voice of supplication which the Quechua assume to ask a favor, asked Baltazar if he could use his table, the one which we now have in our room. Baltazar told him something to the effect that Gary and I were using the table and it would be a great inconvenience to us not to have our table for two days. After Andrés left, having been politely served a bowl of soup as his request was refused and having politely eaten it, and Baltazar had explained the conversation—which we had caught the sense of, though it had been conducted in rapid and complicated Quechua, the formalized language of negotiating favors, but had not been certain enough to interrupt—we were silently annoyed that he had answered on our behalf, denying help we would have been glad to give in spite of inconvenience. Gary went to Andrés after we had finished eating and told him he could borrow the table for as long as he needed it, and then carried the small table over to Andrés' yard.

He placed the table in the narrow end of the yard, at the top of the passage which leads down to Pascuala's house, and laid logs for benches along three sides, so Pascuala and Teodoro had to step over the log and squeeze around the table to get to and from their house, not really much trouble because Pascuala spent most of those two days at Celestina's house helping her, and Teodoro, as children usually do during the preparation and celebration of festivals, roamed about the village playing while the adults' attention was diverted. The table was covered with a new, clean *costal*. People, mostly men, began to gather in the early-to-mid-afternoon and sat around the table drinking *chicha*. At dusk, all of the guests moved inside to Andrés and Celestina's lower storeroom, a large, orderly room with earthen banks at one end to sit on, carefully swept and lit by a kerosene lantern, where I served *qeros* of *chicha* and Celestina served everyone bowls of a simple soup. Then we went back outside, and a band hired by the other *mayordomo* arrived. They played and drank *chicha* with us for a little while, then they led the men and Celestina and a few of the women through the still-moonless darkness, their way lit by two kerosene lanterns, to the door of the church. Before the church door, the men knelt, the slim, white tapers of candles burning in their hands, and prayed. One of the men returned with a lantern to guide the rest of the women, with a jar of *chicha*, our *qeros*, *copitas*, and a bottle of *trago*, up to the plaza. The men had built and lit a bonfire of dry cornstalks which illuminated the far end of the plaza and the wall of the bell tower, and some sat near it in a line below the churchyard and tower, while others stood for warmth around the fire, feeding it. We served *chicha* and the men served the *trago*. The other *mayordomo* and his guests arrived, the men joining Andrés' male guests, the women joining us, and the two groups served each other *chicha* and *trago* for a couple of hours before parting.

We could hear the band the next day, wandering through the streets playing, leading each *mayordomo* and his guests from his own house to the other's and back again. Early in the afternoon, they led Andrés and some of his male guests—all of the women present were in the kitchen, peeling the hundreds of potatoes and cooking mutton for the meal to be served—to the house of the other *mayordomo* to eat and to drink, formally and ceremoniously, from a cup used only during the festival season beginning with San Juan and ending with San Miguel, called a *k'usilluq* ("one with a monkey"). A *k'usilluq* is a large wooden cup painted with intricate designs—the one I saw in red and white and green—which rests on the head and hands of the carved figure of a squatting monkey, who may be adorned with paint and with strands of colored yarn tied around its wrists and waist and ankles. There are only a few of them in the village (if, in fact, there are more than the two that we saw during this festival) in the possession of individuals, perhaps by inheritance—we never learned very much about them, a mystery: nobody seemed to know or be willing to tell us—and whoever needs one in his ceremonial capacity must make some arrangement to borrow one. Andrés and the other *mayordomo* had each acquired one. A *k'usilluq* holds the equivalent of between four and six *copitas* of *trago,* and its contents are downed in one gulp, or perhaps several, but without taking the cup from your lips, at the insistence of the person serving and everyone sitting near the served, as required by ritual. This of course has a certain effect, like drinking a large tumbler full of whiskey all at once, and the prospect of drinking from the *k'usilluq* inspired in the men who left an almost tangible sense of both trepidation and anticipation. A while later, the band led them back, Andrés and his guests, the other *mayordomo* and some of his, accompanied by the sac-

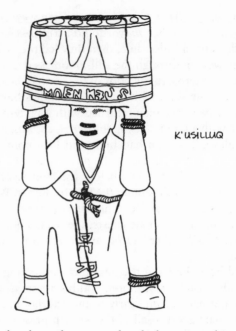

K'USILLUQ

ristan, who appeared to be rather more drunk than most, his voice loud, voluble, continuously audible. They sat at the table, the *mayordomos*, the sacristan, and other more elder men at the head and the other men along its flanks. The women sat across the small yard in a line along the wall of the kitchen, Pascuala near the door with a *chicha* jar, serving *chicha* as fast as she could fill the *qero*s; a young man moved constantly from her side to the table and back again with the *qero*s, urging her to hurry whenever he stood near her. Then, *trago* was served—from the *k'usilluq;* Gary had told me that when the *k'usilluq* appeared at the house of the other *mayordomo*, a hush of intimidation or anticipation had fallen over the guests: the large cup filled with *trago* is indeed, when you are faced with it, a formidable prospect, its effect predictable—almost instantaneous intoxication. But that other *k'usilluq,* the first of the fiesta, having been filled and drained twice by most of the men present, this occasion was somewhat less solemn. All of the men were served by two men, one holding a plate bearing the *k'usilluq* and one pouring *trago*, then all of the women by two women, then all of the men and all of the women a second time. Many women, more intimidated by it perhaps than the men were, tried to share their *trago* with as many people as they could; any time you are served *chicha* or *trago*, you might normally, to be polite, offer a sip before drinking to someone else to honor them, to show respect, saying, "Kuskan" ("Together") or "Tomasunchis" ("Let us drink together"). But now the offer to share was almost a plea, a desperate ploy to diminish the amount of *trago* in the cup, the good manners a pretense. When they received the *k'usilluq*, they offered it to the servers, as one often does, who always refused it and then to other women sitting near them, and the servers always intervened, insisting that each woman drink the whole cup herself, or prevented her from offering it at all. All traces of solemnity among the guests vanished. Then the meal was served. The *costal* on the table was covered with a cloth. Andrés brought a big bundle full of the bread we had baked, and arranged a row of stacks of three breads each down the middle of the table and stacks of two all around the edges. Bowls of soup were placed among the bread. The sacristan managed to make his way through the tangle of legs of the men sitting along one side of the table to the other end, where no one sat. We all took off our hats and he knelt before the table and said a prayer. As Andrés then gave each person three pieces of bread and handed bread to any children who were bold enough to come all the way into the yard, bowls of soup—rich broth from the meat, with potatoes and fat noodles and a chunk of mutton in each bowl—were served, first to the men at the head of the table, and, as bowls were emptied and returned, to the other men and the women. And then we drank again, *chicha* and *trago*, though the *k'usilluq* had vanished and we now drank from ordinary *copitas*. It was fully dark; the little yard lit by the kerosene lantern and filled with people who had become, in a matter of hours, very familiar felt as warm and secure as a house though it was open to the night. Orlando, who naturally had not been at all shy and had been right in the middle of the proceedings most of the day, crawled onto my lap and fell asleep, and I sat there with him for a while, sipping at a cup of *chicha*—if I could manage to keep this cup, and no one noticed that I hadn't yet finished it, I might not be hurried to drain it and inevitably given another full one—and finally lifted him in my arms and took him home.

With the celebration of San Juan, the season of major festivals begins. The threshing is the last agricultural activity of the growing season, and then, for a couple of months, people have less work to do—no time-consuming work in the fields until planting—and a lot of time to celebrate, and so they do. In between festivals, they spend quiet days at home, perhaps weaving, or they do work within the village like making adobes and building new houses and storerooms, rethatching roofs.

The threshing is beautiful to watch, an act somehow infused—by its visual beauty, because it is the last task of the agricultural cycle, because the year's harvest is all gathered now—with joy. The men carry the stalks of grain, which lay drying near the field, in enormous bundles tied with a rope slung around their shoulders to an *era* (threshing ground), a flat, grassy place on one hillside or another outside the village; the threshing grounds are distinct in the landscape now: they, rather than the fields, are golden with the stalks and chaff of the grains against the brown and faded green of the winter land. The stalks of grain are heaped together in a great pile. Horses do the main part of the work: three or four—Baltazar employed his three plus Ricardo's horse, and Ricardo the same team—are tied together side by side, a rope looped around one horse's neck then the next with a short length of rope between them. A man stands to his knees in the midst of the heap of golden grain with the end of the rope in one hand, in his other another short rope which he swings in the air to keep the animals moving, around and around him, their heavy tread loosing the grains from their stems. Other workers circle the heap of stalks and grain, sweeping stray stalks scattered by the horses' trampling back under their hooves with thorny branches cut from bushes near the threshing ground. The stalks are also beaten with thick, heavy staves called *qasona*s, often the haft of a footplow, wielded by the men. When this work is done, the stalks and grain are swept back together and the task of separating the grain from the chaff begins. With forks, like pitchforks with two or three tines made from a forking branch, stripped of bark and scraped smooth with a knife, polished by use, the stalks are tossed into the air, higher if the wind is not strong, and the wind blows away the weightless dry stalks and chaff, the grain falling more directly to the earth. This is called *wayrakuy,* incorporating the word for wind, *wayra.* And this is the most beautiful part, the golden grain and stalks in the air on a bright, sunny day, yellow against the blue sky like sunlight made tangible. The grain finally lies in a heap to be put into *costales,* an arc of chaff, a smudge of gold, on the hillside away from the wind.

Sandorcha has not come back. We must accept now that he never will. I woke up one night and for some reason thought of him, coming into the house in the morning though he knew damned well that he was not supposed to—we started keeping him out at the height of the flea season—tail wagging so enthusiastically that the whole rear half of his body wagged with it, laying his head happily, innocently, irresistably on the edge of the bed which I had not yet gotten out of, just to say good morning—and I couldn't keep tears from coming to my eyes: he was such a fine, handsome dog. Soon after we came here, he had begun to accompany me wherever I went, to the extent that Baltazar had begun referring to him as El Abogado de Señora Julia (Señora Julia's Lawyer) eventually shortened to Abogado. And he was the only dog that I've met in Peru who didn't cringe or flinch or flee with its tail between its legs when a friendly hand was held out to it: for most dogs in the *campo,* the only experience of physical contact with human beings is a boot in the rear or a sharp blow with a stick. Dogs, like all animals, are functional; they bark when strangers or predators come to the house or threaten the live-stock, and they may help in herding. They are not pets, though Sandor had been treated more like one than most are, and his distinct lack of skill and prudence as a shepherd was generally overlooked (he would often catch sight of someone's herd of sheep or goats and, having the general idea that he was supposed to chase these animals, run barking into the middle of them and scatter them, causing some poor child perhaps hours of work to regather the herd). We began one day to try to explain to Bal-tazar about *qowis*, guinea pigs, in the United States, how children keep them in cages and play with them or just watch them and take care of them, that they are never eaten, they would never be eaten, but aban-doned the explanation in the face of Baltazar's expression, one of the dis-interest of total incomprehension. But Sandorcha nevertheless was the closest I've seen to a pet in Peru, and we, at least, had adopted him whole-heartedly as ours. And now he is gone.

Daniel, however, whom we didn't really expect to come home, or didn't allow ourselves to expect it in spite of our message broadcast three times by Radio Tawantinsuyu, *did* come back. He wasn't here when we got back to 'Tambo a couple of days after the broadcast, and we thought, He's not coming back. Someone suggested to Baltazar and Teresa that maybe he hadn't heard the message, which was possible, but not prob-able, and anyway, like his boss, Miguel Villacorta, most of the young men that Daniel worked with came from around 'Tambo, and somebody surely would have heard it and told him. But Baltazar maintained his hope, telling us that Miguel Villacorta always comes to Cusco for the fes-tival of San Juan and Inti Raymi on the twenty-fourth of June, and he would certainly bring Daniel with him: he would come on Monday—San Juan was on Thursday. He didn't come. We listened for the truck each day, and Teresa, as soon as it arrived, went up to the plaza to see if Wa-laychu had come home. On Tuesday, Hugo and Sebastiana went to Cusco to deliver Hugo's barley to the brewery and came back on the day of the festival without Daniel. The celebration ended and on Friday the men went back to work, threshing the wheat on a hillside near the house, just across the *quebrada*. When the truck arrived that morning, it brought Daniel home at last.

Teresa had gone to the plaza when she heard the approaching truck, and Hugo was just on his way back from the threshing ground with the ropes they'd been using to haul the wheat and came into the yard prac-tically shouting, "Walaychu's come back!" I said in disbelief, "He's here?" and Hugo told me, "Go and see!" I ran up the street to the plaza, passing on the way Teresa carrying a big bundle, and met Daniel himself at the top of the street. My natural inclination was to hug him and I had to re-strain myself—it would have been outrageously demonstrative: I've never seen two Quechua people greet each other with any gesture more affectionate than a handshake, and Daniel didn't even get that from the members of his own family—and instead I touched his arm and asked him if there was anything more to carry. There was no great commotion over his return, though the atmosphere around the house was electric with excitement. Watching the scene on a film, you might have thought he'd been gone no more than a couple of days, that no one had worried or wondered about him, his return on this day a certainty. He had brought coca and coffee and cacao beans from the valley and oranges and bananas, so we just sat eating fruit and talking casually for a while; Baltazar and Gary were still at the *era*. I finally went down the path to the pasture to call to them across the *quebrada* that Daniel was back. Gary stayed with the horses while Baltazar returned to the house and stayed for a few minutes, eating bananas. Most of the time he was there, his long-lost son wandered around outside the house, the little boys tagging at his heels, and sat with Andrés and Celestina in their yard drinking *chicha*. Soon, Baltazar and Hugo returned to the threshing, and Daniel went with them, and they worked the rest of the day.

That night, as Walaychu went with Leonarda and Jaime and Orlando to watch the sheep for the night, the rest of us celebrated. We bought *trago*, Hugo even got out the record player, and we danced. Even Hugo and Sebastiana drank *trago* and danced, happiness and an infectious need to celebrate overcoming their youthful inhibitions. And Daniel, the cause and object of our festivities, simply went back to work.

22. San Pedro, weaving

Baltazar had sat me down, the morning after we stretched the warp of my scarf, to show me how to begin the weaving. I'd wanted to start earlier in the day, but Teresa had needed my help to shear the wool from a sheep, a laborious operation executed with a dull kitchen knife; I was required to hold the unhappy creature still—I sat on it. I worked that day at the weaving for as long as I could until I had to stop, hands aching and blistered, back and thighs aching from pulling against the tension of the long warp strung from the roof pole. Baltazar had proposed that I finish the scarf by the festival of San Pedro on the twenty-ninth of June so Gary could wear it then for dancing. That gave me eight days, which seemed like a lot of time—but still, unused to having schedules imposed on my creative efforts, I chafed under the suggested deadline. But I was determined to prove myself, so I accepted it and resolved to finish the weaving by the day of San Pedro. Smug about his ability as a weaver—with reason of course—Baltazar chuckled about the amount of time he predicted it would take me, and I gritted my teeth in silent irritation each time he explained to a curious visitor that he had taught Señora Julia how to weave and that I was making a scarf for Gary to wear for San Pedro, adding, always, that *he* could have finished it in one day. I had heard him boast like this before: it had taken Celestina eight days to complete the *costal* she had woven and had taken Baltazar only two or three to finish each of the two he had made. And he *is* an able weaver, but at the time I had thought, yes, it's easy for a man to boast: he doesn't have to watch children and keep the chickens away from the drying corn and go out and pick beans and gather herbs for supper and peel a few dozen potatoes every day and keep the fire going for the hours it takes to cook breakfast, lunch, and supper; he can simply weave during the days when there is no work to do in the fields and spend entire, peaceful, uninterrupted days weaving until he is finished. Now I thought, Yes, and you aren't a compulsive perfectionist who is doing it for the first time, and that he probably would have had the sense not to have undertaken the project in the midst of all the activity of preparation for and celebration of San Juan and San Pedro—major festivals only days apart—and the distraction of the growing, almost tangible, excitement leading up to them. But I had already, in my heart, accepted the challenge.

The next morning, however, Andrés and Celestina asked me to help them bake the bread for the festival, and by the time I got home, it was already four o'clock, not long before dusk. I got everything out and sat down to weave anyway and worked until it was too dark to see. I wove the next day, the eve of San Juan, until midafternoon, when a thread of the warp and one of the weft broke almost simultaneously. I struggled unsuccessfully to fix them until Gary and Baltazar returned from cutting wheat and then asked Baltazar if he would help me. But he and Gary had not taken much *chicha* with them when they went out for the day, and Baltazar had clearly been thinking of going over to Andrés and Celestina's house—where the celebration was already beginning—when he got home, and he looked at it and began to explain to me that the threads were broken—which I knew—but not how to fix them; he said simply, "No se puede" ("It can't be done"), and strolled over to Andrés and Celestina's yard where some people sat drinking *chicha* and talking and laughing. So what was I supposed to do? I knew the problem was not irremediable, but whatever he meant, the whole thing was infuriating. I struggled with the broken threads for a few minutes more and then thought, To hell with it—I was frustrated and tired anyway—and decided to accept the repeated invitation to come over and drink *chicha*.

After finally succeeding in understanding how to and then fixing the broken threads myself, which in the end took a couple of hours, I wove the next day, the day of San Juan, until I finally felt foolish working so diligently when everybody else was drinking *chicha* and having a good time. Gary had just been led away with Andrés to the house of the other *mayordomo* to drink from the *k'usilluq,* Hugo saying as they left, "They're going to get drunk—they're going to drink from the *k'usilluq,*" with deep respect if not awe in his voice, when someone came over from Celestina's house with a *qero* full of *chicha* for me, and having grown tired of being hard-working and self-righteous—my diligence did not seem to be impressing anyone anyway—I thought again, To hell with it. When I finished the *chicha,* I put away the weaving and took the *qero* back myself and stayed, drinking *chicha* and helping the women peel hundreds of potatoes to feed all of the guests.

When I went out to start weaving on Friday, the day that Walaychu came home—and after the commotion of the festival had ended—I found that Hugo had taken the ropes by which the loom is suspended from the roof pole, and which, like Baltazar, I leave tied there, to use to haul the cut wheat to the *era* for threshing. There were no others. Hugo didn't bring them back until the truck arrived late in the morning, bringing Daniel and all of the joyful excitement of his homecoming, and then, suddenly, the weaving became unimportant, so I helped Sebastiana peel potatoes. When Walaychu went with the others back to the threshing ground, I got the ropes and began but worked for only a while, until Teresa called me to come in and eat, and then, because I had never seen threshing done, decided to help her carry the meal out to the hillside where the men were working. I stayed to watch for a little while and then, although Teresa and Sebastiana stayed there to help and I felt a little guilty about leaving, I went home to weave for a few hours.

On Saturday, I worked on the scarf, almost uninterrupted except by my own weariness and need to rest, for an entire day—and I was certain, perhaps naïvely certain, that even Baltazar couldn't have finished it in one day. I reasoned that the amount of time required to finish a weaving depends not on its general size, but, unless it involves *pallay*, only really its length and the thickness of the fibers that will make up its length, factors more critical I felt then than the experience and the familiarity of the weaver with the motions and the rhythms of the work. So, although the scarf is much narrower than a *costal*, it is as long or nearly as long as a *costal*, and since it had taken Baltazar two or three days to weave a *costal* of thick, hand-spun wool, I concluded with some satisfaction that even he couldn't do a scarf in one day, a conclusion which, even if not informed by the most lucid objectivity, served to keep my will from flagging and me from giving up in frustration.

Sunday, a man and his wife came to Baltazar to make bread. Although this did not necessarily involve me, Baltazar himself asked me to help at several points in the process, and because the man had brought only his wife to help him and I was sitting just outside the *comedor* where they were working, I felt I couldn't refuse and assisted his wife in shaping countless little breads. The next day we made bread for Juana and Ricardo because Ricardo had a *cargo* for the festival of San Pedro—and then I wanted to help and did; and then for another man and his wife, who tacitly requested my assistance by offering me *chicha* and *trago* as they served Baltazar, and again it would have been inexcusably rude to refuse. Tuesday was the day of San Pedro and, nine days after I had begun weaving, the scarf was only three-quarters completed. I went early in the morning to help Juana cook breakfast for the men who were helping Ricardo build the altar, and spent the day there, feeling rather useless, even though it was a holiday, just sitting around drinking *chicha*, waiting with the others for the all-night vigil to begin at dark, but also feeling that my presence was desired and appreciated. So I sat. I decided that I would finish the scarf for Gary's birthday instead.

I had observed with curiosity the reactions of the visitors who had come to the house—and in the midst of all the festival activity, there had been quite a few—to my weaving. Most seemed to be genuinely impressed by the fact that I had learned, and though men didn't usually offer any comment on the quality of my work, women usually praised it, and the praise, I felt, was genuine and made me feel quite proud of my work. The women would look critically at the evenness of the rows, scratch the fabric with a fingernail to test its smoothness, tap it with a finger to see how tight and solid the weave was; and they would exclaim, "¡Qarachay-llaña!" which translates as something like "It's just like skin!" It was a comparison which I heard made over and over, and I concluded that the texture of skin is the standard by which weaving is judged. But whoever looked at it and watched me work for a few minutes, man or woman, each had some advice to offer—"But you should do it like *this*"—and most often insisted on demonstrating that advice for me, taking whatever tool I held at the moment in my hand and showing me how it *should* be done, even if they had just praised what I had accomplished by doing it the wrong way; so any approval, whether actual praise or tacit recognition of the simple achievement of having learned—which they had perhaps suspected that a *gringa* couldn't do—was almost ritually qualified by advice. I continue to learn Quechua.

One day while I was weaving, Juana came into the yard late in the afternoon with Eloy's knitted cap in her hand, followed closely by Eloy, who wanted his hat back. She came to me to show me what was in the cap, which she held upside down by its hem: in the bottom of the blue cap was a tiny and obviously terrified field mouse, which the men working at the threshing ground had discovered and carefully captured and sent home with Eloy in his hat; I had the feeling that four-year-old Eloy was not entirely happy about having a mouse in his hat. Unable to resist animals, I immediately reached into the hat and withdrew the mouse, held it quivering in my cupped hands, attempting to soothe it by stroking it. Juana and Teresa looked at each other significantly, and then Juana began to tell me something which I didn't understand, though I knew she was asking me to do something and that it had to do with the mouse. She made motions of stroking her own head with her hands. Baffled, I looked to Teresa for explanation and held the mouse out to her so that she could do with it whatever it was that Juana wanted me to do. But she recoiled from the tiny creature trembling in my hands and explained to me that Juana's head ached—Juana has been ill in some vague way for a while, and a few days earlier, the *paqo* Martín had come to perform a coca divination to discover what was wrong, a ritual which we had not, unfortunately, been allowed to witness nor been told the results of—and indicated that Juana wanted me to rub her head with the mouse. When I turned back to Juana, she had taken her hat off, confirming Teresa's instructions, so I stroked Juana's hair with the petrified mouse, almost losing it a couple of times as it tried frantically to escape, and then Teresa lifted Juana's sweater from her back, and I stroked her back with the mouse and then her belly above the tight waistband of her skirt and between her breasts. Then she put her hat back on, readjusting her sweater with her other hand, and I gently replaced the mouse into the cap, and she left, followed closely by Eloy, still hatless.

It occurred to me later that what we had done with the mouse was precisely analogous to the cure Martín had performed for Hugo, the *qowi* replaced by the field mouse, and I wondered if this had been Martín's prescription based on the results of his divination and whether they had taken the creature to the *paqo* when they left, for diagnosis of Juana's illness.

We left 'Tambo a day earlier than we had planned—to buy special things in the market for the celebration of Gary's birthday—the morning after the festival of San Pedro, the patron saint of 'Tambo, on the twenty-ninth of June. San Pedro, like Cruz Velakuy, is also celebrated by a *vela*, but this one even less resembles the solemn devotional vigil which I understand the Catholic tradition to prescribe: observing the vigil in this case meant that a bonfire was built before each altar on the plaza, and the celebrants drank and danced in earnest all night around it to the music of a record player or a hired band. Gary helped Ricardo build his altar on the plaza in the morning, one of three constructed of red and white panels and banners on scaffolds of eucalyptus poles, and we spent the day at their house drinking *chicha* and awaiting the arrival of other family and friends who would dance with him at the altar that night: it is important to have as many people at the altar as the *carguyuq* can gather together, a demonstration of the solidarity of kin and *ayllu*. But by the time dusk began to fall, we had learned that the bonfire wouldn't be built until after midnight and, as sorry as we were to let Ricardo down, we were terribly weary and had already had enough to drink and went home to bed when the beginning of the *vela* was still hours away. About one-thirty in the morning, Ricardo came and pounded on our door, but we couldn't face drinking all night and told him, Yes, yes, we'll be there right away, and went back to sleep. I woke at four-thirty and got dressed and went to stand at the edge of the plaza, where I wouldn't be seen, to watch: it was beautiful, the three tall altars lit from below, the clusters of men in ponchos standing around the fires, dramatic silhouettes; groups of people dancing in circles, the women huddled together beside their *chicha* jars in the cold night; and the music—one of the *carguyuqs* had hired a band which played a *quena,* a violin, an accordion and an Andean harp, and a deep-voiced drum, and in the pauses between the scratchy records the other *carguyuqs* played, their gentle, haunting music filled the plaza. At six, Gary and I, not wanting to disappoint Ricardo entirely, joined the people at his altar—and were immediately served about six pairs of *copitas* of *trago* and enormous *qeros* full of *chicha* in the competition of ritual hospitality and generosity, everyone trying to serve us first and the most. As a result, as soon as we had downed two *copitas,* we were faced by two more: twelve within not much more, I judged, than five minutes of our arrival. And we fled as soon as we could, slipping out of the grasp of the many hands which tried to hold us. We sat in the house, drinking coffee—we usually make only one pot of coffee in the morning, but this time we made a second—and trying to collect ourselves, which, after that much *trago* in that little time, proved to be impossible: there seemed to be no means by which to reconnect ourselves with reality, except possibly, we speculated, by getting a good night's sleep, but it was only seven in the morning. After a while, we returned to the altar to help Ricardo to Baltazar and Teresa's house, closer than his own—as the *carguyuq,* he had been the focus of most of the zealous generosity during the night and was, at seven in the morning, barely conscious—and then to bring Baltazar home, who was in a better state than Ricardo was but required some support and some persuasion. We put them both to bed and, since the celebration was supposed to continue all of that day as well, decided vaguely to go to Cusco and went to pack our things, still rather dazed and muddled: we forgot a lot of things we should have taken with us. And then we waited for the truck to take us to Cusco, first in the yard and then in the back of the truck before it left, watching the procession of the second morning; there had been one the day before, but we had been at Ricardo and Juana's house and hadn't seen it. The priest, an ample, balding man from Yaurisque wearing a brown turtleneck sweater and a simple wooden cross hanging from a leather thong under his white tunic, led the images of San Pedro and San Juan on their litters from the church, men in white tunics with censers, boys in white tunics carrying slender banners and standards on long poles, a following of village men and women with bare feet and their hats in their hands. They stopped before each altar to sing a hymn and say a prayer, censers swinging. The truck driver waited respectfully until the procession returned to the cool darkness of the church before he started the engine. Nobody knew we had gone except the children.

23. Gary's birthday, the Fiestas Patrias, Hugo's house

Dear Elizabeth, I am sitting in the Café Ayllu, on the plaza, late in the afternoon: long, golden light on the ornate adobe-colored facade of the Compañía, the church of the Jesuits, and cutting deep shadows in the mountains across the valley. The Ayllu is a coffeehouse, long-established and perhaps the only real coffeehouse in Cusco, even though the coffee is not very good—other places have those elaborate copper cappuccino machines; the Ayllu has only an old stove and a kettle. But people come here, in shifts so regular that they might have been scheduled, and the café is filled in the morning, all morning, with *gringo* tourists and in the late afternoon with Cusqueños, drinking coffee and *café con leche*—Spanish for *café au lait* (why is it that North Americans have never learned to drink coffee with milk?)—and eating pastries, for which the Ayllu is famous, and little sandwiches. Two of the walls are covered by enormous paintings in the sort of socialist commentary style; one portrays Quechua tradition, the moon as a woman watching over womankind, the sun as a man with fiery hair watching over men, and Pachamama, the Mother Earth, embracing the new generations. The other painting, by the same artist, seems to me to contradict this one: it is a heavy-handed invitation to industrialism, a great red figure beckoning with enormous hands the sleeping Indians to a city of smokestacks and cogged wheels. The Ayllu is almost the only establishment in Cusco, it seems, where the music is not either an in-

And one morning, I went up to the plaza with a real purpo[se,]
going to dye some of the wool for my scarf and needed the aci[d of]
[l]emons to fix the dye. There is a regular trade now on the pla[za,]
[two] or three trucks arriving each day, the shops open, women selli[ng]
food and *chicha*—even Leonarda sometimes makes and se[lls]
[i]t fifty *soles* a glass—and sometimes women selling produc[e,]
[a]nd cabbages and lettuce, and sometimes women from Nayhu[a]
[le]mons and limes and oranges. There were no lemons or limes th[at]
I made a discovery, on that day in particular, which came to m[e as a]
[gra]tifying revelation: we are, finally, after almost a year, no longe[r]
[outsiders] in the village society, not even treated with the wariness or exces[sive formal]
[cordi]ality afforded to strangers or outsiders. Looking for my lemons, [walking]
through the middle of the crowd of people around the truck[s, people]
of 'Tambo and of the annexes: people just watching, vendors[, truck]
[ow]ners, passengers arriving and departing. People are accustomed [to see]
[in]g us, *know* us, and I was greeted by women, as women greet other[s, and]
[seen] by the truck driver and his assistant, by the mayor; and I stopped [and]
[tal]ked to Fortunato Castellanos, a young man with whom Gary has [worked]
[as] before, with the governor, with Goyo Coronel, with Juana and [her]
[fami]ly. The relationships are different: the truck drivers and people like [the gov]
[e]rnor, though he is of the village but an official and of a hacienda [family,]
however fallen, see us as like them, more sophisticated and worldly [than]
[th]e villagers; the people of 'Tambo, however different from them we [are]
[may be], see us in a way as belonging to them, to their society, and as gov[erned]
by the customs and rules of that society: we are their children—[and]
[by] now they have trained us to be proper human beings. We've been [accept]
[e]d, accepted by all. I came home without lemons but happy.

[In t]he late afternoon of the eve of the Fiestas Patrias, or Independence [Day]
[—]July twenty-eighth—Hugo and Daniel concentrated all of their [creat]
[iv]e energies upon constructing lanterns for the little boys to carry in [the]
[sc]hool parade that evening. These were complex assemblages of sticks [tied]
[t]ogether to form boxes with any number of sides or hollow star[s]
[shape]s or airplanes or cars, the framework of sticks covered with paper [or plas]
[t]ic cut from plastic bags, like Japanese lanterns. These were affixed [to pol]
[es], and the little boys went with an obvious sense of importance off [to the]
[th]e school. At dusk, we waited on the plaza, Juana and Teresa and I [sit]
[t]ing in the door of Ricardo's shop, Gary and Baltazar standing [near]
[b]y, for the grade-school children to come in a long procession, led by [Lu]
[cre]cia, the director of the schools, and one of the other teachers and [carry]
[i]ng aloft their lanterns, lit in the deepening twilight by candles placed [insid]
[e] them. The children were all terribly solemn, expressions of ab[solute]
[rapt]ed concentration on their faces as they passed by us in their circuit of [the plaza]

[in]sidious Muzak or leftover, early-seventies rock and roll. The proprietor—a rather portly gentleman with iron gray hair that is white at the temples and cut short in something like a North American burr, who always wears a turtleneck sweater and a sport jacket and is slightly cross-eyed—has a collection of classical music, mostly only the best-known composers and works, but classical music still, and a fine stereo in the café. So you can sit here late in the afternoon watching the light on the mountains and listen to Debussy or Ravel's *Bolero* . . .

We live, consume, the days in great gulps: straddling the lifestyles of two different centuries bridged only by a five-hour truck ride, a ride which emerges, perhaps only because of its repetition, as almost the most real part of our lives here. We won't be here in the highlands much longer: only two more mornings of getting up at three-thirty to catch the truck at five, watching the sun rise far down the valley from the back of the truck. We'll move out of 'Tambo at the end of August and return there to stay with the family as guests for the village's major festival, Natividad—the Birth of the Virgin, on the eighth of September: one last truck ride. Teresa cried one night, the day we celebrated Gary's birthday with them, because we are going to leave soon. I cried too. But we begin, of necessity, to talk about buying tickets or renting a car to get to the coast; about when we can see friends, archaeologists and anthropologists who spend as little time in Cusco as we do, before we leave . . .

In the wake of the exuberant celebrations of San Juan and San Pedro, it had looked like our own private "cargo"—for Gary's birthday on the seventh—might be a disaster. We were going to bring fish from the market in Cusco to bake in the oven, but fish is sold in the market only on Tuesday, and Tuesday was the day we returned to 'Tambo—Gary's birthday was on Wednesday—and, leaving the house at a quarter to five in the morning, it was impossible to buy it that day (I might have been able to if I had gotten up even earlier and been very quick, and lucky). I couldn't find the beets which can be used instead of strawberries, now out of season, to sweeten and color *chicha*. When we made bread on the morning of the birthday fiesta, we found that the vendor in the market had sold us flour of barley rather than wheat, and the bread was dark and bitter: only Orlando would eat it, and when he realized that no one else was eating, even he disdained it. The gravest aspect of the situation was that there seemed to be no *trago* left in the whole village. Gary bought the last of the supply from Ricardo's *tienda,* not quite a liter bottle full, the rest having been consumed during San Pedro, and Hugo found some, enough to fill a couple of bottles, early in the morning, and Andrés had a little left which he contributed, but that was all, for a full day's celebration and a lot of people; the only other store in 'Tambo, that of Goyo and Vinicio Coronel, was closed, its proprietors gone to Cusco.

Baltazar sat in our house with us early in the morning, drinking *trago* to inaugurate the celebration. After breakfast, we sat outside and collared don Andrés on his way out of the yard into the street with a bundle on his back and a hoe in his hand. He went back to his house and put away the bundle and the hoe and came and sat with us. Celestina, when I went to fetch her, was stuffing the mouth of a jar full of *chicha*, her gift to Gary, with a corn husk, and I carried it to our house for her. We baked the bread and then half of a mutton we had bought to substitute for the trout and three *qowi*s; these, at least, turned out to be delicious, though we didn't eat them until the next day. (Teresa reasoned that there were too many people to serve adequately, and for the most part they were not in a condition to really appreciate it anyway—so we had the guinea pig for breakfast the next day and the mutton later in a wonderful stew which Teresa made, potatoes and big chunks of meat in a rich spicy sauce.) By midafternoon, we had collected a lot of guests, and we danced in the yard to scratchy *huayno*s played on the record player powered by new strong batteries, Gary wearing the scarf which I had finished weaving the evening before. Don Andrés bestowed upon him a traditional blessing given by an elder on a birthday: they took off their hats and Andrés stood before him and placed his hands on Gary's shoulders and said a sort of prayer, which requested the blessings of San Juan and San Pedro, whose images reside in the church, and the *apu*s. That evening, the *trago*, perhaps fortunately, gone and Gary gone to bed, we sat in the warmth of the kitchen drinking *chicha* and still dancing among the conversations, sometimes maudlin—there must have been enough *trago* after all—which filled the room. I remember dancing with Nicasio, who is normally very shy with me, and not being permitted to sit down to rest, and holding Jaime on my lap. Finally, I too slipped out of the room and went to bed.

Baltazar, the next morning, produced a nearly full bottle of *trago* which he must have hidden somewhere and had flavored with wild anise. The celebration of the *corcova* (the day after one's birthday) is rather a matter of pride, and it was expected that Gary's fiesta would carry on. He served the *trago* to us after breakfast, which Gary had not been able to eat, and its effect decidedly strengthened Gary's resolve to refuse even *chicha* that day: if someone had produced a bottle of rare French champagne, I don't think he would have accepted a taste of it. So Baltazar celebrated the second day of Gary's fiesta on Gary's behalf, drinking *chicha* served by Teresa and Celestina and playing the record player, turned up loud so the neighbors would hear it.

An early morning rain, hardly ever
enough to settle the dry season dust,
scent of rain in a desert.

There really is a lot of work, less vis
quiet days of this lull in the agricultural
ing his new red poncho, and Teresa h
woven border which will be sewn arou
have rethatched the roof; and the men
which they will build a house for Hugo a
the pace of the work of this season is the
less critical timing—it is generally not wo
and harvesting of crops, on which surviva
is individual labor rather than labor re
therefore achieved through *ayni* (the sys
work done at home or within the village,
depend upon arrangements made with oth
sure: on whatever day and at whatever ho
though Gary usually has something to do—
with Baltazar to bring back the dry corn s
the trees for fodder for the horses and ca
sometimes Baltazar make adobes, and I hav
another scarf (this one of alpaca and real
acrylic stuff), and there is always the cook
and does not have to begin so early, and we
all to serve the results of the effort—we have
the simple entertainments which the people
the minimal diversion of watching the truck
ing: sort of like sitting on the front porch on
the traffic go by, a small-town pastime. Men
row of shops; young girls sit in the arched
wall above the plaza on the other side. I stan
hand, among other women with their spindl
San Juan at the end of the row of shops, mos
side of town—me, Asunta and her old mo
Sebastiana, sometimes Casimira from across th
ning and watch people. They gossip and I liste

With the men making adobes, I have too a
of the family, to stroll occasionally up through
how the work is going, a better reason if I thin
Quechua woman, as I have learned to do, but
has never observed the process of making adol
freedom: there have been whole weeks during

the yard
we were
juice of
with two
prepared
chicha
onions
selling l
day, bu
as a gra
pariahs
of form
walked
people
store o
to seein
women
and tal
worked
Ricard
the go
family
than t
remai
erned
they k
adopt

In t
Day—
creati
the so
tied
shap
or pl
to po
to th
squa
near
Lucr
bear
insi
sorb

the plaza; they sang patriotic songs, in the inimitable, undoubtedly universal, style of grade-school children. Every once in a while, inevitably, one of the lanterns caught fire, creating a brief commotion swiftly quelled by the solemnity of the occasion and the children's apparent sense of responsibility and patriotic duty.

In the morning, a platform was set up in front of the town hall and a couple of rows of chairs from the school rooms placed in front of it. There was another parade, this one more formal, though it again included the schoolchildren, a real parade led by the community officials and other important citizens—Baltazar had been asked to march with them and did so very proudly, with the officials at the head of the procession—and accompanied by marches broadcast over the loudspeaker from the town hall; someone at the head of the parade carried the flag of Peru. And then the children, carefully rehearsed and much prompted by their teachers, performed a series of patriotic skits and folk dances and read poems they had composed. It was a performance as charming as any such children's production must be, I suppose, anywhere in the world, and we could feel the children's sense of importance, the radiance of their parents' pride in the little ones on the stage; the whole community's sentimental pride in this young generation.

A kind of tension builds in us: we have only about a month left here. There is an excitement growing in us about going home again, but there is also a gnawing, deep-seated dread of leaving 'Tambo. We will see the festival of Natividad again, with the eyes of acculturated "'Tambinos"— when we witnessed Natividad, 'Tambo's major festival, last year, we knew nobody, understood nothing of the village, and we know now how little we comprehended of what we saw then. Too, it completes a cycle, which seems right somehow, aesthetically and emotionally if nothing else. And it will be a perfect time for the inevitably maudlin reminiscence and nostalgia of a *despedida* (the traditional farewell party). Or maybe everyone will simply be so drunk that we'll be able to get on the truck for the last time and nobody—neither they nor us—will realize what's happening, like when we left after the *vela* for San Pedro. But the nearer the time comes to go, the more impossible it seems that one can simply leave: how can you just *leave*? Leaving here has too much sense of finality: people we've known now for a year, our friendships forged with the powerful bond of having overcome all of the cultural differences, distrust, suspicion, and superstition, are going to be damned hard to leave with little or no assurance of ever seeing them again. Damned hard: nearly impossible. I already want to come back.

Hugo is building his house—Sebastiana's house—on the site, high in the village, of the house Baltazar inherited from his father. We had thought that he and Sebastiana were going to move into the house Gary and I now inhabit—the house which Baltazar and Teresa lived in when they were first married—but one Sunday afternoon when we were sitting with Ricardo in his store, both he and Juana uncharacteristically drinking on a day which was not a holiday or a birthday (Ricardo was building up to asking us to "loan" him twenty-five thousand *soles* so he could buy a horse, and it would have been too obvious even in Quechua society to ply us with *trago* without drinking himself), Ricardo made an insistent point of the fact that this house officially belongs to Juana. By Quechua rules of inheritance, a woman inherits her mother's properties and a man his father's, buildings and lands; Teresa had inherited this house from her mother, and now, officially, it should go to Juana. There has always been some carefully suppressed tension between Ricardo and Baltazar, perhaps nothing more than the tension, normal in any culture, between a man and his father-in-law, and once in a while, they seem to do things just to spite each other. Shortly after this occasion, Hugo began working at the site of Baltazar's long-abandoned house.

They began by knocking down most of what remained of the walls of the house. Baltazar seemed to feel no sentiment such as I reflected that I might feel in the act of demolishing my parents' house, however ruined, a house I had grown up in. But all activity here looks toward the future: one works for one's children, always, and so it was for Hugo; it must, too, be a common practice, and besides, there really wasn't much left of the house. We hadn't even known it existed. A few days later, when they were dismantling the last few rows of adobes, some of which they saved to use again, and were excavating the earth at the base of the walls, Baltazar made jokes about the fragments of broken pots, an old spoon, and whole unbroken bottles they unearthed, imaginatively reconstructing their histories.

The old adobes, except for the whole ones, were broken up with picks and hoes and shovels and soaked down with water brought by means of a borrowed piece of rubber hose from a faucet at a house above; they disintegrated eventually into a mountain of clayey mud. As a binder, fine straw, like *ichu*, is mixed into the mud by a laborious process they call *pisando barro:* the men scatter the straw over the mud and, with their shoes off and their pants legs rolled up above their knees, trample it into the mud with their feet. The children, helping whenever they feel inclined to, have a great time doing this, but for the men who must take the work rather more seriously, it is an exhausting chore, battling the suction and weight of the mud—they come home with aching muscles in their thighs and calves and ankles. After the straw is trampled into it, the mixture rests overnight to dry out a little.

The site where Hugo is building is on two levels; on the upper level, within the walls of the old house, they mix the *barro* for the adobes. They are making the adobes themselves on the lower level, where the house will be built, bringing the mud down in a borrowed wheelbarrow: partially dried, of the consistency of clay, the mud is dumped onto the ground, gathered up with the hands, and packed into a mold, a rectangular wooden box of forty or fifty centimeters in length without top or bottom and with handles at both ends. The surface of the mud in the mold is smoothed with water and the mold is drawn up, leaving a wet brick of adobe mud. Into every tenth adobe, Hugo plants a twig to facilitate counting; he needs five or six hundred to build a simple room, for now, a kitchen without a storeroom above it. They are already planning additions. They allow the adobes to dry for a day or two—the bricks are always impressed with the pawprints of dogs or cats by the time they are dry—and then stack them up to make room for more.

24. Mamacha Asunta

August: already the season of rest begins to end. Watching the comings and goings on the plaza in the morning, I see men going down Calle San Juan which leads into the path to the fields on the *pampa* below the village, driving pairs of bulls and horses bearing skin bags full of *chicha*, carrying on their shoulders the long wooden plows used to plant corn. Corn planting is one of those tasks for which the *chakrayoq* must provide plenty of *chicha* and *trago* for those who help him, and everybody is usually quite drunk by the time they return to the village; one night, well after dark and before the moon rose over the crest of Aqchakar—I don't know how they managed to negotiate the path by only the light of the stars—we heard a group of people come up the path, the women singing in the high-pitched, wailing style of Quechua women, the men hooting and making animal noises. And yesterday, don Andrés planted his field. I helped Celestina cook for them: a meal of potatoes and macaroni, a salad of slivered onions and carrot and *ch'ini challwa* (the little dried fish), which Celestina toasts in a ceramic pot rather than frying them as Teresa does, and rice, little cakes of *quinua,* and mutton *charki*—a special, ceremonial meal. And so the cycle begins again.

It strikes me now what we have done: lived here, in an environment and culture so foreign, a life so different from our own, long enough to have memories of the same time last year and to be able to look forward. To know—not with a fraction of the depth of instinct that these people have, of course, of this life, their own life, but to know—what comes next: that you plant corn now and then potatoes; that the rains will begin soon. And the cycle of festivals—Natividad, San Miguel, San Andrés, Todos Santos, Navidad, Carnaval . . . To *know* what it means to plant and to celebrate, to know what they will think about and who they will cry for when they are drinking together on the day of Todos Santos, how it will be when they camp in the *puna* to harvest the potatoes, the stories they will tell. And I feel a longing to be here then, not to miss it, and sometimes it seems all wrong that we should leave now: we would do it all so much better the next time. They would be so proud of us.

Our house has become a veritable commercial center. Leonarda makes *chicha* in the evenings to sell on the plaza the next day—she even got herself a little *chicha* jar from one of the vendors on the plaza. Baltazar has a couple of times made bread to sell, and they sell by handfuls the arroba of coca which Daniel brought back from Quillabamba, so almost every morning one man or another comes to buy a handful or two of coca, and almost every day a couple of children are sent to ask for a few pieces of bread.

It is also the season for traders, and Baltazar has been lodging a succession of them in the *comedor* over the last six weeks or so, the most recent a man and an old woman and a very shy little girl. The man was the same trader who had been here the day we arrived in 'Tambo for the first time, from the province of Espinar. They had come together this time, though the relationship between them was never clear to us, and were from the town of Yauri or somewhere near there, and were trading *bayeta* and wool and *llipta* for corn and wheat and beans, crops that cannot be grown at the altitude at which they live. Always carrying bundles, they left the house and returned separately many times each day, going from house to house throughout the village for nearly a week. By the time they left, they had filled four or five *costales* with grain. The old woman was small and heavy-set but wiry, graying hair under a small round bowler hat, dressed all in *bayeta*—a skirt of finely woven black fabric with skirts of coarser, undyed *bayeta* underneath, a jacket of black-and-white herringbone-weave *bayeta,* collarless and buttoned to the throat, with embroidered panels down the front. She spoke not a word of Spanish, and I understood little of her Quechua; Leonarda, evincing the attitude typical of 'Tambinos—like that of some Northeasterner in the States toward, say, the English spoken in Arkansas—said she didn't speak Quechua right. Though she knew I didn't understand her most of the time, she stopped and spoke to me kindly each day; it must be difficult, even impossible, for someone who has spoken only her own language all of her life and never had reason to even think of learning another, and never encountered anyone who *didn't* speak that language, to comprehend that someone might simply not understand—difficult to grasp what the phenomenon of language really is—the same difficulty, I suppose, which prompts tourists in a Spanish-speaking country to speak loudly and slowly to clerks and waiters in English or German when they seem not to understand what was said the first time, as if they might simply be hard of hearing. I sincerely appreciated her efforts, disregarding as they did my difference from everyone else she encountered in the village, and desperately tried to understand what she said, straining to recognize phrases or words or even rudimentary sounds that meant something to me, and was gratified when once in a while I was able to make an intelligent response. (On the other hand, I didn't hear the little girl speak a word for days until I surprised her, by coming up behind her one morning and greeting her, into saying, "Buenos días," and giving me an utterly charming smile; I didn't hear her say another word after that but she always smiled at me.) Teresa allowed the woman to use her fireplace when she wasn't cooking; they gathered their own firewood and cooked their own soups and potatoes, though sometimes Teresa also offered them food she had cooked for us. They left just before the festival of the Virgin of the Assumption.

We finished, at long last, my *bayeta* skirt, just in time for me to wear it for the festival. The actual process of making the skirt, from dying the fabric to sewing on the waistband and ties, takes astonishingly little time; the aspect of the process of making *my* skirt was persuading Teresa to finally begin it, the critical elements the persistence and insistence of my nagging. She had helped me buy all of the materials in March, and at that time they were excited about making me a proper skirt to wear. I brought the things we had bought to 'Tambo and thought that we would make it right away, but there seemed, somehow, never to be any time. Perhaps I was impatient—the men were just plowing the potato fields, and the whole of the harvest was still ahead of us—but it seemed to me that there were many days when there would have been plenty of time. After a couple of months of bringing up the subject of the skirt periodically and being put off for one reason or another, I gave the dye to Teresa and paid her five thousand *soles* for the five varas of *bayeta* I would buy from her, thinking that the transaction might inspire in her a sense of responsibility. Nothing happened. A while later—weeks later—we discovered one day that Baltazar and Teresa were temporarily keeping their flock of sheep which Vicentina and Honorato usually keep for them at Cruzq'asa—and that they had marked the whole herd for identification with daubs of *rosado* dye—my *rosado* dye! Our reaction to the liberty they had taken with something I had entrusted to Teresa (and something that could not be replaced without returning to Cusco) impressed Baltazar and Teresa enough that they agreed that we would begin the skirt the next week. Still nothing happened. I finally acquired a persuasive and undeniable argument for making the skirt immediately when my denim skirt, worn constantly and scrubbed diligently by Señora Tupayachi in Cusco for nearly a year, began to disintegrate into irreparable tatters. Teresa then told me resignedly that I again needed lemons for the acidic mordant to fix the dye, and so, after I had attempted a few times to buy them myself, Juana offered to get me some lemons from a woman she knows who sometimes comes from Nayhua to sell them from house to house, and I gave her one hundred *soles* to buy them with. I had to remind her for a couple of days, and finally she brought me some lemons. Then Baltazar explained to me that there wasn't enough firewood to boil the tremendous pot of water we would need for the dye as well as for the regular cooking, and the boys didn't have time to go and gather it.

After practically bribing Hugo and Daniel to go with Gary for the firewood, we finally seemed to have everything we needed—my denim skirt was by this time unwearable, and I had only another very thin one which my mother had sent me to wear—and we sat down one day when nobody was doing anything at all and cut five varas of *bayeta* from the length and washed it. The next morning, I cut the nearly fifty lemons and squeezed them with my hands into a bucket of water, which took hours and made my hands ache. Teresa and I strained the lemon water through a cloth and added more water to it in a big pot, which we put on top of the fireplace to boil. In the end, we actually used about three sticks of firewood. Teresa added the powdered dye and, when the water was boiling, the cloth and a handful of raw wool. She allowed the cloth to steep in the dye for fifteen or twenty minutes, stirring it with a stick and lifting the cloth occasionally to check the color. It turned out a rich rose red instead of the bright pink we had expected, and it was beautiful! We spread it out over the fence in the afternoon sun to dry, a brilliant red banner. When the raw wool dried, Leonarda and I spun it and plied it into a coarse thread with which Teresa sewed together the four panels we cut from the length of *bayeta*.

This much accomplished, the skirt now had to be taken to the man, Agustino the flute player, who has a treadle sewing machine and cuts and faces the scalloped hems of the skirts and, on the machine, does the decorative stitching around the hem. Baltazar and Teresa agreed that Teresa should take the skirt to him, partly because I don't know where he lives but also because he might be liable to charge me more as a *gringa* than he would charge her. She delayed this for a couple of days, which I understood and forgave her because she would have to go all the way up to Wayninpampa to deliver it, and I was so grateful to have coaxed the project to that stage that I hadn't the heart to press her. She did at last go one morning and when she returned, she reported that there wasn't enough thread. I was annoyed: surely she had had some idea how much thread would be needed—how many skirts had she sewn for herself, for Juana and Leonarda?—and to get more, Gary and I would have to make a trip to Cusco. She said she would ask someone to bring it from Cusco that day, and then didn't, nor did she the next. Baltazar suggested that this was because there hadn't been anyone she knew going to Cusco, and I peevishly pointed out that she hadn't even left the house to *see* who was going to Cusco. Finally, in a fit of irritation, we decided to go to Cusco and get it ourselves and left abruptly. We sent it to 'Tambo a couple of days later with Goyo Coronel, getting up at four in the morning to go to the truck stop hoping to find someone we could trust to deliver it, if only the driver or his assistant who could give it to Ricardo or Juana at their shop without going out of their way.

A few days after we returned to 'Tambo, Leonarda told me—though I still don't understand exactly how she found out—that the sewing was done, the skirt was ready, and she said she would go and get it for me. Several days passed. I suggested that Gary and I could go and get it, but they said no, Leonarda would go. One day I asked if someone couldn't possibly go and retrieve it, since they were reluctant for me to go myself, and Baltazar said that Teresa and the boys were busy and Leonarda had to go to school. I said it was Saturday and there was no school, and he said something like, "Oh." So Leonarda was found and I gave her money and she went on the truck to Wayninpampa. She came back without the skirt, saying that nobody had been home, but returned in the afternoon on foot and came home with my skirt.

I was a little surprised to find, after all of the trouble about the thread, that the border had been sewn with *celeste* (sky blue) after all, instead of the deep red that I had bought and had gone all the way back to Cusco to buy more of. I had chosen it of course to go with the *rosado,* a paler color than the rose red that had resulted, and even that—*rosado* and *guinda*— wasn't a combination that a native 'Tambina would have chosen: not enough contrast. What had happened apparently was that Agustino had begun to sew the patterns in *guinda* and, after appraising it critically, had judged the combination to be ugly and refused to continue. I was honestly forced to respect that: an artist must maintain his standards. After a period of disappointment—I had bought in a shop in Cusco an antique woven band to sew on at the waist of the skirt, a band which would have gone nicely with the *rosado* or even the red with the *guinda* stitching but looked truly awful with the blue—during which Teresa and Leonarda tried gently but sincerely and with the insistence of conviction to persuade me of how ugly it would have been (and the Quechua do not mince words: that is the word they used—*millay,* ugly), I accepted the rather drastic alteration of my color scheme. It *is* pretty anyway: leaves and double spirals and stylized butterflies in deep sky blue on rose red—much truer of the Quechua aesthetic than my final choice had been. Teresa told me the names of the patterns, and Baltazar later contradicted almost all of them: the leaves which Teresa called *mallki* (tree), Baltazar said were coca leaves; the spirals Teresa said were called *kuti,* but Baltazar said, No, no, no, and gave them some other name which I don't remember. They agreed only on the butterflies, which can hardly be anything else.

Teresa sat down to finish the skirt immediately, as eager now as I was. With the rest of the thread Leonarda and I had spun, she gathered the waist with two rows of stitches—she measured the gathered waist with her hand: the span of the hand is supposed to equal one quarter of the span of the waist, and even if it is less than a quarter, women pull the ties of their skirts so tight that they fit anyway—and sewed on the waistband, another woven band which I had bought from a little girl in Chinchero one day and which had some blue in it; finally she sewed on at each end of the waistband a narrow woven band to tie it with. I put it on as soon as she finished her work and felt in the atmosphere a sort of consensus of pride and satisfaction; I wished we had gotten it done sooner. The women— there were other people at the house that day for whom Baltazar was baking bread—all laughed and exclaimed over it, how pretty it was, and asked me to give it or loan it to them; Baltazar proclaimed me a true daughter of 'Tambo. Celestina, when she spotted me, rushed into the yard, seized me by both hands and swung me around, saying that *now* I had a proper skirt to dance in, *now* we would dance! All new clothes, from skirts to ponchos to scarves, are made for dancing . . . Its weight and fullness are wonderfully luxurious and luxuriously protective, and, I have discovered, it *is* fun to dance in, inside the heavy, rich swing of bright fabric. And I do wish, ruefully, that I'd had it to wear months ago.

The next morning for the fiesta of the Virgin of the Assumption, I put on my new red skirt, delighting in its luxury and brilliance compared to my drab, old, patched denim one and at the same time steeling myself against the attention it was sure to draw to me, however well intentioned and gentle that attention, I knew, would be: I hadn't yet been out of the yard in it, and I am shy anyway and it had taken me months to learn to freely accept the attention I receive simply by being a blond-haired, blue-eyed *gringa* in a Quechua village without drawing attention to myself by wearing this flag of a skirt. But that attention was, of course, not always good-hearted; this, I expected, would be, and it was. When I ventured out of the yard and up to the plaza, women laughed and came over to admire the stitching, asking me again to loan it to them or give it to them for the fiesta and men joked with me about marrying them; or else it seemed to simply be accepted that I finally had a proper skirt to wear, and no notice was taken at all.

The *vela* had been the night before. There were two bands in town, hired by the *mayordomos* of Ayllus Qoipa and Yanchakalla, one the usual motley assortment of local musicians but the other a band from Santiago in Cusco, a well-practiced *conjunto* with a harp and accordion and flute and a big drum on which was painted "Orquesta Los Jóvenes, Santiago, Cusco." One of the bands was playing early in the morning in a yard below the plaza on the other side of Calle San Juan, near Asunta's house. We went up to the plaza with Baltazar who, equipped with a broom of branches and an old woven-plastic *q'epina* (part of the fabric of a grain sack from the brewery) was supposed to sweep the *chuta* of Aylla Nayhua, his duty as the *segunda:* each *ayllu* is responsible for one section of the plaza—its *chuta*—which runs from the shops to the wall of the church-yard, for cleaning it for important festivals, especially when there are processions of saints or when the priest is coming. Gary wanted to photo-graph the execution of this responsibility as an illustration of a principle of both spatial and social organization and had his camera ready, all of the settings adjusted. Baltazar first found someone to talk to and stood by the wall of the shops in the sun chatting for a while. Then he went over to help the group of men building the one altar that was erected—though two *ayllus* had *cargos*, only one for some reason built an altar—and who were firing their efforts with plenty of *chicha* and *trago*. We waited. Fi-nally Baltazar disappeared into Ricardo's shop, and we abandoned our hope of recording for posterity the event of don Baltazar Quispe Herrera of 'Tambo sweeping the *chuta* of Ayllu Nayhua on the occasion of the festival of the Virgin of the Assumption, and followed him into the shop. He never did sweep his *chuta*. We sat in the shop with Ricardo for a while, Baltazar offering *trago* to whoever came in, and, when the altar had been completed, stood outside the shop with our hats in our hands to watch the procession. Baltazar had set out to celebrate the holiday, even though it was not his *ayllu*'s festival, and after the procession, he retired to the house to continue his private celebration, coaxing Gary to buy *trago*. That was not difficult: Baltazar is always happy to talk when he has a little *trago*, and Gary has a lot of things, and very little time, yet to ask him.

That evening, Nicasio, very drunk, came to invite us to his and Asunta's house, where they were celebrating Asunta's birthday. Teresa, who usu-ally tries desperately to avoid drinking, seemed for a change to be in the mood for it, maybe because it was in honor of Asunta. We all ended up getting very drunk. Teresa bought more than one bottle of *trago* and served it herself insistently, almost aggressively—once she gets started, Teresa goes at celebration with a vengeance, though she always pays for it dearly the next day. Finally, under the cathartic influence of *chicha* and *trago* and overwhelmed by sentiment inspired by our impending departure, I started crying and couldn't stop. I was deeply touched when Nicasio, a very shy man who is always very formal with me, uninhibited now by the *trago,* came to me saying "Ama waqaychu, ama waqaychu" ("Don't cry, don't cry"), and put a hand on my shoulder and with his other hand very gently wiped the tears from my cheeks: this was a celebration, I shouldn't cry. It only made things worse. We finally crept home and went to bed; by that time, no one seemed to notice.

As fascinating as it had been to be involved in Andrés' *mayordomo*ship and Ricardo's *cargo,* it was nice the next day not to be associated intimately with the formal celebration of the festival of Mamacha Asunta. In the morning, instead of being obliged to peel potatoes and drink more *trago,* I was free to watch the entire procession: I hadn't in all of this time seen one from the time it left the church until it returned. When the bells of the *campana* began to ring, I went up to the plaza and squatted in front of the shop with Juana, with little Orlando on my lap. This part of course was familiar: the priest and the sacristan and boys in white tunics, the men and women carrying long staffs with ornamental silver heads or banners, the image of the Virgin borne on her litter, and the crowd of people, bareheaded and solemn, who followed her progress; the prayer, the hymn. As the procession climbed the street to return to the church, I crossed the plaza, holding Orlando by the hand, and we climbed up to the churchyard to sit along the side and watch, along with a lot of other women and young people and children. One thing I had been curious about was the simple logistics of turning the saint around before it reenters the church: it is always carried in backwards, so that it faces the people who have followed it faithfully. The men bearing the image stopped just before the steps of the church and turned the litter carefully in place, then transferred the poles of the litter with equal care to their opposite shoulders, so that they faced once again the door of the church ready to enter it, the Virgin facing out. This time, though, they did not proceed into the church but put the litter down on a dais in front of the church and the Virgin, one hand raised, watched over the election of next year's *mayordomos.* The discussion went on for a long time, with a lot of teasing, banter, and laughter; the bands stood on either side of the doorway, the local musicians patiently, the young men from Cusco growing increasingly bored with the provincial ritual. I had almost decided to leave myself, uncertain of how long this would go on, when it was over. The men lifted the litter and the Virgin bowed three times to her followers, the men in front, facing the gathering, crouching slightly and with obvious effort under the weight of the litter while the men at the back remained erect, and then, the litter-bearers turning carefully once more under their burden, she retreated coolly into the church. And as she vanished into the stone and adobe darkness, both bands began to play at once, two different songs at full volume.

I managed at last to be the recipient of Teresa's ministrations as a *curandera*. Something bit me, some insect or spider with a mildly venomous bite, on the back of my upper left arm. This not being a part of my body that I have frequent opportunity to see, nor cause to look at, especially in 'Tambo where, like everyone else, we seldom change our clothes and I normally take off only my skirt and petticoat to sleep, I didn't notice it for several days, perhaps a week. When I finally looked at the wound in a mirror, I discovered that it was quite swollen and red. I let it go for several days more, thinking that it would heal itself naturally, but it soon grew very painful, and I inspected it again: it had swollen further and was now an angry red, infected either because of my neglect or the poison of the bite itself. Gary insisted that I show it to Baltazar, who might know what had bitten me. Baltazar called to Teresa to come; she looked concerned, almost alarmed, and her response as a *curandera* was immediate. She left our house, where we were sitting in the doorway for light, and Baltazar said reassuringly, "She knows what to do." She returned a minute later with a cactus spine and a chunk of peeled cactus flesh. As she worked, Baltazar explained that the bite had become infected and hot because of all the *trago* we'd been drinking, because *trago* is considered to be *hot*, and almost all common ailments are believed to be caused by heat and cold or combinations of hot and cold elements, like a combination of *trago* and sun. He advised me not to drink any *trago* that day, which was fine with me, glad to have an authoritative excuse, not negotiable in the face of adamant hospitality, to refuse. Teresa pricked the infected area with the cactus spine and gently pressed the skin around the wound to drain it. Then she cut thin slices from the flesh of the cactus, sprinkled them with white sugar, and covered the wound with them: they were sticky and cold, startlingly cold, and she explained that they would draw the heat out of the wound. She wrapped my arm with one of Gary's handkerchiefs, tied in place with bits of yarn, and told me not to sleep on it that night.

We unwrapped it the next morning. The cactus and sugar had dried on my skin and we moistened it and peeled it gingerly away. It did look a little better, though it still hurt, and I assured them both that it felt better. Teresa pierced the wound again, but from this point on my treatment was rather more mundane and predictable: sulfa powder we had brought from the pharmacy in Cusco and Band-Aids.

25. The brewery

We walked one day, with Goyo Coronel as our guide, out to Hacienda Quinuara and beyond. We had gotten to know Goyo little by little since about November, when he had returned to 'Tambo from Cusco where he had been studying at the university. We had met him on the truck one day: I was sitting on one of the benches across the front of the truck, just in front of Gary, and heard Gary talking to someone. The conversation gradually attracted my wandering attention because it was not the usual one about whether potatoes and corn are grown in the United States, about whether or not the States are *pura pampa* (all flat; No, there are mountains in the United States too, but not like these) and how everything there is done by machine (*pura máquina*). They were talking about anthropology and astronomy and ethnoastronomy, the local knowledge of the stars and their movements and the uses of that knowledge, which had been Gary's primary interest in his doctoral research in Misminay. I grew curious and turned to see who Gary was talking to and saw that it was a young man with curling hair, a little moustache and goatee, and fine, sharp features; in a khaki-colored shirt and new blue jeans, their cuffs tucked into a pair of high-topped, laced black work boots, he was better dressed than most people of the village. He and his brother, Vinicio, subsequently opened a *tienda* in 'Tambo, off the plaza on the street that runs across the village above the church, and we have gone there occasionally to buy *trago* or batteries for the flashlight or kerosene for the stove. Sometimes we have gone there just to talk: talking to Goyo for a few minutes, with his education and his more sophisticated interests, offers a brief respite from the intense effort that life in 'Tambo can be, without enduring the trip to Cusco. Once in a while we have met him at festival celebrations; he is related somehow, distantly, to Teresa, so we sometimes end up in the same places. Goyo had grown up at his uncles' hacienda, Quinuara, about an hours' walk from 'Tambo, had grown up with the lore of that region of 'Tambo's lands and history, and we had solicited his guidance for our trek there.

We had been fascinated by the hacienda house, curious to see it from close by, since the first time we had seen it from the saddle of Qeruru across the *quebrada:* the cluster of large buildings, adobe with tiled or thatched roofs, with a few eucalyptus and cedar trees around it—trees brought to the New World by the Spanish and characteristic of the grounds and gardens of haciendas—and the great swath of grassland below the house, as smooth and green from a distance as the lawn of a park. Fascinated too in a way by the Coronels themselves, the two of the four brothers, Goyo's uncles, whom we see fairly often in 'Tambo, both extraordinary characters in the setting of the village: portly, dignified Julián, who is always referred to as Julián Coronel, imperious, almost haughty, dressed in a suit coat and knitted vest and laced, leather shoes; and Antonio, whom we'd first met not long after we came to 'Tambo, who is called simply Coronel or El Coronel (the Colonel), so that for a long time we had thought it a title of rank rather than a name—a lively and energetic man, much slenderer than Julián, who wears tennis shoes and a baseball cap over his gray hair and whom Goyo calls the Crazy One. Gary had also become increasingly interested, as he read the old documents in the archives in Cusco and listened to the stories told by the people of 'Tambo about the history of the *ayllu*s, in the lands that lay in that direction: one of the mountains is said to be the origin place of Ayllu Quinuara, and one document from the 1500s mentions "el pueblo viejo" (the old town) of Quinuara, which no longer exists. And out beyond the hacienda are the impressive ruins of an Inca city called Mauk'allaqta, and Pumaorqo, an outcrop like a massive natural tower carved at the top in quirky Inca style into inexplicable seats and basins and platforms and, at the point where you climb onto the top of the outcrop, the curled figures of two sleeping pumas, little bigger than housecats, back to back, both of their heads broken off in early Spanish efforts at the extirpation of idolatries. Between Quinuara and Mauk'allaqta is a rock believed by the people of 'Tambo to be where the Inca Ayar Auka, one of the four brothers Ayar, the original Incas, knelt to hurl stones with his sling across the Apurimac, breaking a gap in the formidable ridge of the mountains of the Otra Banda and creating a series of lakes where the stones bounced beyond it. For his unruliness, his brothers forced him back into the cave of Tambo T'oqo from whence they had come and sealed him inside it with a rock and left him while they journeyed on to the valley of Cusco to found the city.

We went to Goyo's shop early in the morning and waited as he sold *trago* and rice to a couple of women and finally managed to shut the doors before any more customers came. We climbed through the upper streets of 'Tambo to the road, followed it to where the path to the hacienda and the villages of Toqtohuaylla and Pacheqti and Mollebamba branches off, and followed the path around the broad base of Apu Aphitu in the early sun. The path wound into the valley of a little river and trailed along it, running after a while below the hacienda. We crossed the stream and climbed toward the house and sat on the hillside just below it, talking to an old man named Pancho, who had green eyes and spoke only Quechua; he had grown up there and had always worked for Julián, herding his sheep. With Goyo acting as an interpreter to be sure he got the names right, Gary drew with Pancho's help a rough map of the mountains and valleys, springs and lakes and streams, to compare to the accounts in the documents; we recognized many of the names from the ones we had read and from the stories and legends. Then Pancho followed his flock of sheep and goats which had wandered, grazing absently, down the hillside toward the stream, and we went on up the hill. Above the house we stopped, and Goyo pointed out where there had been a mill and an oven, now gone. And then we climbed and walked along the crest of the ridge toward Inkaqonqorina, where Ayar Auka had knelt.

We passed through a cluster of houses, the cooperative community of Toqtohuaylla which works lands which had belonged to the hacienda before the Agrarian Reform. Everyone there knew Goyo; an old couple called to him and we sat outside their house while the old woman served us *chicha* in the traditional manner—one person served at a time, draining the cup, the cup then filled again and offered to the next. Gary and I, as special, unusual, guests, were served first and Gary, the man, before me—then Goyo, then her husband and, at our insistence, herself. Thirsty, we drank gratefully. In Goyo's manner toward them, theirs toward him, I thought I sensed vestiges of the relationship which must have existed between the hacienda families and the indigenous population whose land they had usurped and labor they exploited in a virtually feudal state for hundreds of years, until the Reform gave the lands back to the Quechua in the late 1960s; vestiges which lingered in spite of the drastic and rightful alteration of the relationship brought about by the Reform: the simple, practical, human affection of people who have known each other all of their lives—whatever their formal relationship—which underlay the uneven balance of unjust power and authority and wealth on one side and respectful, obligatory deference to authority on the other. That old relationship no longer exists, legally or practically, yet beneath the familiarity, there is an easy, accustomed, self-assurance of authority in Goyo's manner with them, a suggestion of deference in theirs toward him. We were invited to come back later.

On the top of the ridge beyond Toqtohuaylla is a small lake, Phuyu-qocha (Cloud Lake), its existence startling at that altitude, its shallow water reflecting the cloudless blue of the sky, its center crowded with tall green reeds growing up out of the water. A few horses stood drowsily in water up to their bellies, munching on reeds. Gary and I, walking with our eyes cast down most of the time, driven by the archaeologist-anthropologist's obsessive instinct to look at the ground, nearly didn't see it. Before long, our guide too was scanning the earth before his feet for pot sherds, searching the grassy hillsides for hillocks which might hide the foundations of walls, ridges which might have been agricultural terraces.

Inkaqonqorina is a large boulder of pale gray stone, weathered smooth, which stands on the top of the ridge above the Molle Molle, which runs into the Apurimac just beyond a curve out of sight. In the side of the rock away from the rivers is a deeply worn depression where some giant might have braced his knee to hurl boulders across the river at the mountains on the other side. We could see the gap in the wall of mountain and specu-lated about the story. It is not doubted: here is the rock and there the deep fissure in the opposite ridge, and people traveling to Cusco from Chum-bivilcas have told you of the lakes beyond the ridge, and why they are there. (On the other side of 'Tambo, on the way to Cusco, there is a rock in which can be seen the footprints of the llamas the brothers drove; the rocks at that time were soft, they say, and held such impressions.)

We walked on, farther along and down the side of the ridge, until we could see the rivers and, in the other direction, into the valley where Mauk'allaqta is, and stopped to take photographs, to sit in the sun to rest and drink the bottled soft drinks Goyo had brought from his store and gaze into the valleys. Gary said something about the slope below us which, unlike any of the land we had walked through, was barren and badly eroded, and Goyo told us a story his grandfather had told him about *ukuku*s, the Andean spectacled bears, represented in the tradi-tional dances by the men in their heavily fringed tunics of black or dark brown and strange knitted masks, about the times when *ukuku*s used to come up the river valleys and climb the mountains looking for food, frightening the people who had never seen such animals who walked sometimes like animals and sometimes upright like men, and came into the villages to kill their pigs. After the last *ukuku* disappeared, driven away down that slope of the ridge toward the river, nothing grew there any more, and the rains began to wash away the soil. That was when his grandfather was a boy: Goyo's grandfather had seen the *ukuku* himself and had seen the land change. I looked at the mountains and the rivers, the vast, overwhelming beauty and scale of the Andes under a flawlessly blue sky on a warm late winter day, stunningly beautiful and powerful, and thought again, How can you leave this place?—a place and a life at once terribly mundane and yet magical, a place where a simple story be-comes, truly, a legend, and the legends are etched into the land itself—feeling absurdly sentimental again, even without *trago,* because we would leave 'Tambo for Cusco the next day to return only once more for only a few days before we would leave the highlands for the coast and, finally, Peru for the States.

At last, we turned back: it was getting late, the sun west of us, and it would take us hours to get home even if we didn't stop at all. Going back through Toqtohuaylla, though, we were hailed from a different house by the old woman who had offered us *chicha* that morning. A young couple had put the roof on their new house and everyone who had helped was celebrating—the roofing of a house is a joyous occasion—and clearly had been for a while. They called to us and we hesitated—we were thirsty and the thought of *chicha* was tempting—but we knew it would be hard to get away, so we waved back and kept walking until a man came over to us to insist that we come. It would have been a little impolite then to refuse absolutely, and we *were* thirsty and had nothing left to drink and it was still perhaps a couple of hours to 'Tambo, so we succumbed and followed him to the newly thatched house. We drank *chicha* and as little *trago* as we could get away with and danced a couple of *huayno*s accompanied by scratchy records played on an unreliable record player and finally slipped away, our hosts trailing after us, determined that we couldn't leave yet. It took us till dusk to get to 'Tambo, through the shadowed valley of the little river and the changing light of the late afternoon.

We traveled to Cusco the next day with Baltazar and Daniel. Teresa would come the following day. Baltazar directed the loading of his seven sacks full of barley onto the truck in the plaza, the grain he had con-tracted to grow and sell to the brewery in Cusco and one that Daniel was bringing on behalf of Sebastiana, to whom Nicasio had given it to sell for money to buy things for the household that she and Hugo would estab-lish. We would go to the brewery the next morning, all of us, where the quality and quantity of the grain would be examined, tested, and Baltazar would be paid for his crop according to the contract. Baltazar and we were hoping that our presence would gain him an advantage in time, if not also in profit: not many *campesinos* come to the brewery with a doc-tor of anthropology from the United States, one who had also entertained one of the chief *ingenieros* in his house besides. We had the man's busi-ness card: Raúl La Torre López, and Baltazar would ask for him.

Baltazar had been to Cusco only twice since we'd come to 'Tambo, once when we had come the very first time and found no one there but Daniel—he had gone to sell barley that time too—and in January when he had gone to search for Daniel, the runaway. He seemed as excited as a child, though he tried to conceal it; Daniel was as nonchalant as only a fifteen-year-old can be, the seasoned traveler. We sat together just behind the cab of the truck, on top of an enormous stack of *costales:* many people each day now are bringing barley to the brewery. Baltazar talked most of the way to Yaurisque, pointing out and naming places, rocks, mountains, telling us stories about them. He was quiet for a while after we stopped at Yaurisque, watching the mountains with almost as much reverence as we did—we, with the painful knowledge that we would make the trip from 'Tambo to Cusco only once more, trying to see everything, to engrave it in our minds. As we neared Cusco, he told us the story of when his father had brought him to Cusco when he was a child, on foot, his father carrying him some of the time on his shoulders, pointing out to us the path which descends to the city from the *puna,* still used by the people of Oqopata, the village high above the end of the Ccachona valley.

We reached the city at dusk, and the truck stopped down in the market, below the Puente Belén. Baltazar and the other men who had brought barley made arrangements with the driver: the truck would be parked there for the night, with a guard to watch the grain, and be driven to the brewery first thing in the morning. We climbed the stairs up to Avenida Grau in the gathering dusk, Gary and I carrying our packs, Baltazar their bundle wrapped in his new red poncho, and Daniel the red plastic jug of *chicha* that Teresa had sent along with us. On the street, Gary hailed a taxi and we put all of our baggage into the trunk; as I watched them fit our backpacks in beside the poncho and the jug of *chicha,* I thought how odd it was, as I had felt each time that our family from 'Tambo had come to Cusco, the juxtaposition of two lives—the two that Gary and I live— which were normally for us separate, and the slipping of those boundaries which seem to exist only for us. I realized how differently I felt about it now than I had before, more accustomed to the oddity of the experience, the slight disorientation; and knowing how natural it was for them, however infrequent their visits to the city are, I now began to see what coming to Cusco meant to them, how the city fits into their lives, and I was proud to be there with Baltazar and Daniel. And we were going to show them some of our life in Cusco, what little there was of it, the nearest they would come to knowing anything of our life in the United States: they, and Teresa when she came, were going to stay a couple of nights at our house rather than at the house of Baltazar's sister as they usually do—they would really be our guests, as we have been theirs for almost a year.

Although we were certain that he had seldom been in a taxi, in any vehicle other than trucks and the ancient, crowded city buses of Cusco, Baltazar, being Baltazar, behaved as coolly as if he rode in taxis every day, chatting with the driver easily in Quechua; we envied the instantaneous relationship, perfectly natural, the *belonging* which, even here in the city, we could never achieve. Cab drivers always, always, ask us if we have just been to Machu Picchu, as if we were any tourists. When we got to our house, we dropped our baggage and settled, tired, into chairs and on the beds. I served *chicha* from the jug, pleased to be serving *chicha* in my own house, even though the *chicha* was not mine. We discussed where to have dinner. Gary and I had thought of two alternatives, one a *pollo a la brasa* place—a restaurant which serves chicken roasted on spits over a fire—which, although it is on the corner of the Plaza de Armas, is a more typically Cusqueño place, in atmosphere more like the *picanterías* where Baltazar would, we assumed, have been more accustomed to eating, and not heavily patronized by *gringo* tourists; we thought they would feel more comfortable there. The other was a pizzeria which had become our favorite restaurant, where we customarily eat the night we arrive in Cusco when we come. We couldn't resist considering it. But it is on Calle Procuradores, the center of Cusco for young *gringo* tourists, and only occasionally are any of its patrons even Peruvians, much less *campesinos*. We explained these possibilities to Baltazar, trying subtly to imply that he might not feel comfortable among all of the *gringos,* but Baltazar was undaunted: we had described pizza to him before, in the course of some improbable conversation, fantasizing about making it in his oven in 'Tambo—it would have been possible but we'd never gotten around to it—and he wanted to try it. So we went to the pizzeria. In the dimly lit restaurant, we suggested a table under the stairway at the back of the small room, which is where we usually sit because it is quieter, thinking that we would be less conspicuous there, afraid that people might stare at us. But Baltazar and Daniel chose the table in the middle of the room, in front of the door, and there we sat. We ordered pizza for all of us. The conversation was one we might have had sitting in Teresa's kitchen in 'Tambo. When we finished, we took Baltazar back to the kitchen—we were welcomed by the people who operate the restaurant and have come to know us: few *gringos* are in town long enough to return—to show him the big wood-burning oven. He inspected it and, in his inimitable style, pronounced his judgment: it was built of brick. Adobe is better.

On the way home we bought bread for breakfast. In our room once again, the exhaustion of the trip overtook us. I poured *chicha* and we finished what was left in the jug. We made plans for the next day, set the alarm clock, and went to sleep.

We had bread and coffee for breakfast, taking turns with our two coffee cups, and I wished, a little embarrassed at the poverty of my hospitality, that I could have given them something more substantial to eat: Teresa would have done better than that, even though bread, especially bread made from white flour as it usually is in Cusco, is a treat. We took a taxi to the brewery. We were there much too early: the truck wasn't there, nor was the *ingeniero*. We waited in the street across from the gates of the brewery grounds, clean and meticulously kept, until almost nine. Then the *ingeniero*, Raúl, arrived and Baltazar talked with him outside the gate; he waved at Gary and me from across the street, and we were glad that he remembered us. He went in and Baltazar joined us in search of a café and another cup of coffee. As we waited outside the café for Gary to pay our bill, the truck, Pedro Pedrito, drove by us on its way to the brewery, the driver recognizing and waving at us, sounding the horn; I hadn't expected the sensation of belonging, of really being a part of all of this and not separate, our hard-won acceptance in 'Tambo following this extension of its life to Cusco—and it was deeply gratifying.

We followed Pedro Pedrito into the brewery, where we found it parked in a line of four or five other trucks, talked briefly to the driver, and then went to find Raúl. He greeted us cordially, as if we were old friends, and he assured us that he would oversee the handling of Baltazar's grain himself. When it was our turn, we should ask for him again. We returned to where Pedro Pedrito was parked and waited as the trucks ahead of ours were guided one by one deeper into the brewery grounds. Outside the office where the barley was inspected were stacked hundreds of enormous sacks of grain and many, many people waited, *campesinos* whose homes we could guess by their clothes. We wondered again at the juxtaposition of cultures, how these people, many in traditional *bayeta* clothing, wearing *ch'ullu*s and *monteras,* saw this great factory, the sparkling buildings and carefully tended flower gardens—these people whose life is the land, the crop—and wondered at what point Quechua society can no longer absorb the innovations of modern Peruvian culture as it has since the conquest. There doesn't seem to be such a point.

Gary and Daniel and a couple of factory employees unloaded our eight *costales* and, having asked again for Raúl, we were attended to immediately. It seemed a little unfair that we were ushered through the procedure ahead of others who had waited much longer than we had, but Gary and I felt that, if Baltazar's preferred treatment had anything to do with our presence there, it was the least we could do for him in return for all he has done for us.

The *costales* were stacked in front of the little laboratory. With a metal instrument, they were pierced and some barley allowed to spill from each one into a plastic basin, which was labeled with Baltazar's name and the origin of the grain, village and province. Raúl took Gary and me into the laboratory and introduced us to the men who were working there, asking them to explain the process of the examination to us. They first observed its color and condition, explaining how one can tell whether the crop received too much or too little rain, had perhaps been harvested too soon or not dried properly. A machine sorted it into grades by the size of the grains, and the proportion of each grade was measured by weight. The quality of individual grains, also by weight, was determined by simply putting ten grains into a glass of water; the more grains too heavy to float, the better the quality. The humidity of the grain was tested, and the weight of a certain volume—it was a meticulous process which I suspected would seem absurdly unnecessary to the people waiting outside with their crop, who would know, for their own purposes, whether the grain was good or not by its look and feel in their hands alone, as these city-bred and carefully trained *ingenieros* could not.

The result of all of these tests was a number, a percentage like a student's grade on an examination: Baltazar's was much better than average; not the best we'd seen tested, but only a couple of points below that one. The result—the "grade"—determined the price he would receive for each kilo of barley, less the cost of the seed provided by the brewery, an average proportion which must be calculated somehow into the price. They transferred the grain from his *costales* to other sacks, and he had only to wait for a check, which could be cashed at another office on the grounds of the brewery. Some people, Baltazar told us proudly, would have to wait until the following day: Raúl had said that Baltazar would receive his check before noon. We thanked Raúl sincerely and invited him to come to 'Tambo for the celebration of Natividad, honestly grateful for his attention. Gary and I went home, leaving Baltazar and Daniel to wait for their checks. They would go and wait at the Coronels' store for Teresa to arrive and bring her to our house in the afternoon.

It grew to be dusk, and we worried. The truck might easily have been unusually late, but we worried that if Baltazar had had to wait that long for Teresa at the Coronels' *bodega*, where mostly they sell *trago*, in quantity, and with a good deal of money and because of it a cause to celebrate, he equally easily might not be able to find our house again through the complicated route from Belempampa to Calle Sapphi. Gary went to look for them. He met them actually not far from our house, on their way, and Baltazar was not in the condition we had feared he might be, though Teresa was nevertheless a little embarrassed; well, he *had* had reason to celebrate, and a man with the means to be generous must necessarily demonstrate his willingness to share . . . She soon relaxed once we had settled in our room. Gary went out and brought back *pollo a la brasa* and fried potatoes from the restaurant we had considered the night before, and Teresa produced *papa wayk'u* and *uchukuta* she'd brought from 'Tambo, and *chicha*. We spread everything out on Teresa's carrying cloth and sat on the floor to eat. Then we talked and drank *chicha* for hours. Daniel fell asleep on one of the beds, and we woke him gently and made a pallet for him on the floor, so Baltazar and Teresa could sleep on the bed, and finally, once again weary, we all slept.

In the morning, we went down to the market with them. We bought a gift for Daniel, a soccer ball, something which we knew he badly wanted and which would be for him a source of esteem among the young men of 'Tambo. Under Baltazar's supervision, we bought materials for the last parts of my backstrap loom which Baltazar had nearly completed; standing in the doorway of a shop where we bought some wire and rope, he manufactured a harness to anchor the loom at the opposite end from me as I wove. I promised Teresa that I would bring, when we returned to 'Tambo for Natividad, onions and *ají* and tomatoes, things I usually bring her when we come from Cusco, and, for the festival, peanuts and lettuce and olives and eggs, to make *papas a la Huancaína*. And then we left them to do their annual shopping, to buy new pots and tools and clothing for the children. We would see them only once again; when the thought of it drew too near our hearts, we willfully drove it away.

26. Sonqo

It felt strange, riding in a truck away from Cusco but in the wrong direction, north and east instead of south, climbing and climbing, and across high, desolate land. The land felt very foreign, almost forbidding, under the broad August afternoon sun, cold and pale like a winter sun. It felt like the wrong direction. The people south of Cusco have a name, *chuchur*, for the people who live out here, on the verge, in Andean terms, of the long descent from the mountains into the jungle, and consider them "savages": they grow only potatoes, don't drink *chicha* because they have no corn, and they still wear old-fashioned clothing—women wear dark *bayeta* skirts with only red woven borders, and *monteras*, and in some places, men still wear *monteras* as well and even *unku*s, tunics like the Incas wore, though not in the village where we were going. The majority of the people, men and women, speak only Quechua.

Before we had left the States, a friend had given us letters and photographs to deliver to the family she had lived with and *compadres* and friends in the village where she had done her fieldwork, several hours by truck from Cusco and a couple more on foot, near Qolqepata. We had kept them in Cusco for more than a year, guiltily admitting to her in our letters that no, we still hadn't gone to the village: it was difficult to decide to stay away from 'Tambo long enough to catch up with our correspondence, buy gifts to take with us to the village, go there—at least a three-day trip—and then shop again for our return to 'Tambo, another day. But now we had to go. We had reservations to fly to Lima on the fourteenth of September and wanted to spend as much time before that as we could in 'Tambo, for the preparations and the main part of the celebration of Natividad, and we understood now how important it was to our friend to let her *compadres* in the village know that she thought of them and to know that they were all right. So I'd gone to the market and bought bread and onions and *ají* and sugar and cans of tuna and sardines to give, and we went one morning to the truckstop beside the Huanchac market. We had asked several people on each of a couple of occasions what time the trucks left for Qolqepata and had been told, each person certain, hours ranging from eight-thirty in the morning to eleven. To be sure—we couldn't afford to lose a day by missing the truck—we got there at eight and climbed on and waited. For four hours. The truck left at noon; we got as far as San Gerónimo, about five minutes out of Cusco, and the driver stopped for lunch.

We sat in a café with the driver's young assistant as he ate his lunch and we drank coffee. He was a boy from Sonqo, maybe fifteen or sixteen, and had just started working for the driver on the truck, but he was dissatisfied: he talked about going to Mexico to study theater—to Mexico to study theater!—exotic ambitions for a Quechua boy, especially, I thought, a "savage." How did he know about Mexico? How did he know about *theater*? He remembered our friend, though he must have been quite young when she was there. He had a wonderful Quechua name: Luis Llaulli Nina. *Llaulli* is the name of a purple-red flower and also of its color; *nina* means fire.

The route was along the main paved road to Urcos, along the Cusco Valley, then off and up into the mountains, along the Urubamba River and away, above it. We got off the truck in late afternoon before it reached Qolqepata, where a seldom-used road branches off, and followed that road to the village. I had worn, for warmth against the cold winter nights in the *puna*, my brilliant rose red *bayeta* skirt and felt distinctly conspicuous walking through that land where women wear dignified black skirts. I know well that red and pink and orange skirts, like the skirts worn in 'Tambo, are visible from a long way off in the Andean landscape, especially in winter, and wished, in spite of the cold, for my thin, faded blue denim skirt; I wondered what, aside from the presence of a stranger, I might be advertising to them. We got to the village a little before dusk and found the house of our friend's *compadres*. Luisa installed us on a heap of sheepskins just across the room from the door of their small house—they cook and sleep in one room—from which we hardly moved until the next morning. She made sweet maté for us and immediately began cooking a soup; she brought a sheep's head and put it on top of the fireplace in the corner. Alcides came home after dark, and soon after him came several other men, also *compadres* of our friend, the news of our arrival having already spread through the small population of the village. We ate *papa wayk'u* and *uchukuta* made from the *ají* we had brought and a simple soup of meat broth and potatoes, and Gary bought a bottle of *trago* from the store of one of the visitors, a man named Crisólogo. We had letters and photographs for some of the men. We all admired the pictures, and I read a couple of the letters aloud for those who requested it. The letters were in Quechua, and since Quechua is essentially still a spoken language with as yet only a relatively new and ambiguous orthography, and the schools teach only Spanish, I supposed that even if they could read, they might have had difficulty with the letters; it occurred to me later that such personal communication might actually be much more natural and intimate transmitted orally, even if by a messenger—the Inca developed no system of writing, and the Quechua experience of the written word since the conquest has been in large part legal documents, which often did them more harm than good, and I could comprehend, even if I fabricated it, a distrust of written language. I read the letters fairly well and was privately proud of myself; in fact, aided by *trago* and necessity, I spoke only Quechua the whole time we were in the village—in 'Tambo, I often fall back on Spanish, which I have discovered that even women understand quite a bit of, even if they don't speak it, when communication is critical. After a while, the other guests went home and we all slept, Gary and I on the skins across from the door from which we hadn't moved since we arrived.

We greeted the next day with bread that Gary and I had brought and maté and *papa wayk'u* and soup, and *trago*. Several of the men who had been there the night before returned, including Crisólogo, with a bottle in his hand. Alcides had to go that day and work, planting *maway papa*s (early potatoes), and as soon as he left, we were claimed by Crisólogo, who lives next door. He took us to his house and his wife, Josefa, fed us a second breakfast—more *papa wayk'u*, more soup—and Crisólogo served us all beer from his store and then *trago*. We spent most of the day with them; we had to force him, a good Quechua host, to allow us to pay for anything, even though I suspect he must nearly have depleted his store's supplies of beer and *trago*. We felt oddly at home with them: Crisólogo told us that he was from Chumbivilcas—*our* side of Cusco!— from Livitaka; he even said that Walaychu, *the* Walaychu of Radio Tawantinsuyu, was his uncle. He looked and talked like a Chumbivilcano, and we talked sentimentally about the Apurimac. He gave Gary a braided leather lasso which he had made: Chumbivilcas is known for this leatherwork, and Baltazar is proud of knowing the technique because his family, his grandparents, were from Chumbivilcas, and no one else in 'Tambo knows how to do it. We felt comfortable with them, even if slightly overwhelmed.

We managed to escape for a while from their abundant hospitality about midmorning to deliver the rest of the letters and photographs, escorted by Alcides and Luisa's son Bonifacio, who must be five or six. With his help we found all of the houses, though one family wasn't at home and we had to stumble back there in the afternoon to give them their letter. We returned with Bonifacio to Alcides' house, but now Luisa was gone as well, so we sat for a little while in the quiet house, collecting ourselves, and then went back to Crisólogo and Josefa who were waiting for us. We drank and danced *huayno*s the rest of the afternoon, in their yard under the sun, our activities observed by a couple of patient llamas who stood quietly in a corral beside the house and withheld comment. Crisólogo dictated a letter in Quechua to our friend, his *comadre,* and I wrote it as faithfully as I could, never having taken dictation before even in English, much less in Quechua, much less under the influence of *trago*. Finally, all of us rather delirious from the *trago*—Gary and I had begun to understand how the lack of *chicha* might be considered a sign of uncivilization: there was simply nothing else for them to offer to us to demonstrate their hospitality, nothing that would simply quench thirst and not make you eventually crazy—Gary and I slipped away, back to Alcides' house, to sleep until Luisa and Alcides came home. In the evening, we ate *papa wayk'u* and soup and talked quietly with Alcides and Luisa and a few men who came again to visit.

We left early the next morning before breakfast. We had decided to walk back most of the way instead of catching the truck in Qolqepata. A friend we had met in Cusco, a German anthropologist, is doing fieldwork in a village called Amaru, above P'isaq, more or less between where we were and Cusco, and we had decided to walk to Amaru to meet him and walk down to P'isaq where we would find a ride to Cusco and he to Calca. It didn't look far on the map, but even a topographic map doesn't give a clear impression of *vertical* distance, nor any impression at all of the kilometers of detour you will walk because people you meet in the fields and ask for directions don't actually *know* how to get there from where they are but will never fail to give you directions anyway. (They'll say, Oh, it's just on the other side of that mountain, or, It's just next to this other place—and they'll tell you how to get to the other place, which you discover is about as far from where you are going as where you were when you asked for directions.) We thought it would take us about four hours to walk to Amaru. We left at six-thirty in the morning and finally arrived at Qellu Qellu at one-thirty in the afternoon. Amaru is a climb of an hour and a half directly above Qellu Qellu, straight up the mountain; we could see Amaru, but lacked the energy and will even to begin the climb. So we waited for Richard to come down and walked with him the three more hours—downhill, thank God—to P'isaq. We figured we walked at least thirty kilometers that day.

27. Natividad again

Baltazar was in the middle of a succession of long days of baking bread for the festival, beginning early in the morning before breakfast and working until sunset or beyond into night, as he had been a year ago when we had first come to 'Tambo. We knew now that the people for whom he was baking bread were the *carguyuqs*. He told us that he had made bread for Nicasio, the mayor, who had the *cargo*—a major one—for the bullfight, for bringing the bulls and bullfighters to 'Tambo to perform on the day of Natividad, and also the responsibility for one of the altars. Baltazar had made bread for him also several weeks ago, when Nicasio had gone to Yaurisque and Huanoquite to ask for the loan of the bulls, to seek the cooperation of the men who would fight them: a formal petition traditionally accompanied by gifts of bread and *chicha* and *trago*. We marveled at the differences in our experience of the celebration of Natividad last year, as newcomers, outsiders, when we had known none of the people involved, nothing of the mechanics of the preparations and celebration, and this year. This time we were *inside*.

It was Sunday; the festival would begin on Wednesday. We savored the rituals of our arrival in 'Tambo, the little boys, Jaime, Eloy, Orlando, appearing as if by some sort of magic as soon as we opened the door of our house, expecting pieces of bread which we always bought for them in Yaurisque; one of the phrases Orlando speaks most clearly is "T'antata qoy" ("Give me bread"). We made them wait while we unpacked and then gave them their bread. No more appreciative than three little vultures, they promptly ran out of the house, making as much gleeful noise

as possible to make sure that every child in the village would know that
they had bread, and we looked at each other, Gary and I, smiling and
shaking our heads fondly as they careened past our windows and into the
street. I took off my jeans and put on my red *bayeta* skirt—I am still too
self-conscious to wear it in Cusco in places where I am known, even in
the pre-dawn darkness of four-thirty in the morning, and unwilling at
that hour to subject myself to the commotion of attention I would be sure
to receive in the truck; and I had had to abandon my denim skirt and so
once more had worn jeans to travel from Cusco to 'Tambo. Into my
carrying cloth I heaped the things I'd brought for Teresa: the biggest,
most handsome onions I'd been able to find in the market, garlic and
cumin, a dozen piquant tree tomatoes, two big handfuls of dried yellow
ají—and peanuts, shiny black olives, lettuces, and eight eggs which I'd
carried carefully, carefully from Cusco in a basket. I walked into her
empty kitchen and laid the bundle and the basket on the floor and left,
knowing she would be very pleased and wanting her not to have to thank
me. Then I brought her some things from our room in Cusco which we
wouldn't take with us when we left: glass glasses, actually jelly jars,
which she called *qespi qeros* (crystal *qeros*), and a wooden cutting board
which we had inherited from friends, which would be for a Quechua
household a ridiculous luxury, unnecessary and not even dreamed of, yet
useful and something which other women would admire, even envy.

When Leonarda came home with the cattle, I called to her to come and
gave her the doll I had bought for her. Teresa followed her to our house
and crouched with her in the doorway as Leonarda speechlessly admired
it: she'd asked for it but clearly hadn't allowed herself to believe I would
actually bring it. Teresa was almost as excited about the doll as her
daughter was, and I could see her longing to hold it, explore it, but she
didn't ask Leonarda to give it to her. Leonarda put it carefully back into
its box and put it away, up in the storeroom. Later in the afternoon, she
made a petticoat for the doll out of scraps of white cloth and started knitting a little bonnet for it. The next morning she bundled it up in Teresa's
red carrying cloth and slung the doll onto her back, like a mother with
her baby, before she went out with the cattle.

By the time we woke the next morning, Baltazar was already at work,
bread dough rising in the wooden trough he had built for it in the *comedor*
and the spicy scent of eucalyptus smoke in the air from the fire in the
oven. Gary and I had planned on this day, before formal public preparations for the festival began, to take a last walk around 'Tambo to take
photographs in black and white. Our wantonness in wandering apparently aimlessly around the village was camouflaged by the camera: people
greeted us openly, warmly; we were wistful. The last time. Tomorrow we
knew we would be engulfed, like the rest of the village, by the festival.

When we returned to the house, I helped Teresa cook: *yuyu hawcha,* which we hadn't made since April or May. *Yuyu,* its leaves young and tender, was growing again in the fields, affirmation of a cycle completed.

On Tuesday, the altars were built in the plaza below the wall of the churchyard. There were three this time instead of two: one erected by the *segundas* of the *ayllu*s of the upper moiety, Hanansayaq, to which Ayllu Nayhua belongs, one built by those of the lower moiety, Hurinsayaq, and one by the *mayordomo* of the Virgen Natividad. The altar of Hanansayaq was the responsibility of the president, Julio Wallpa, and that of Hurinsayaq the *cargo* of Nicasio, the mayor. Baltazar, as the *segunda* of Ayllu Nayhua, set out with Gary early in the morning. I watched for a while from the top of Calle San Juan. Gary came back to the house before long for money: he had been appointed "captain" of the project, which meant mainly that he was expected to supply *trago* for the men working. The organization of the effort, fueled at cross purposes by *trago,* soon broke down, and I was amazed to find the altar completed the next morning. Baltazar and Gary came home late in the morning to rest.

The evening before we'd last left for Cusco, a young man, Jesús (I had met him once before, on the day when Gary presented his papers before the angry assembly in the fields; Jesús had not participated but had sat with us, the women, watching from a distance, and Gary had talked to him all the way home), had come to ask Gary and me formally to be the sponsors, the *padrino* and *madrina,* of the soccer team, and we had agreed. Faced with our departure, I think we were anxious to establish as many ties, whatever form they took, with the people of 'Tambo as we could. In Cusco, I had gone out one day and bought the team a new ball—of leather, in panels of blue and white—even though I know little about soccer and less about its equipment. Now, Jesús came to our house with Daniel and Angélico Araujo to receive the new ball and to invite us to watch the tournament—three polite young men who thanked us with a ceremonious formality which was proper and necessary, but which seemed to us just then almost absurd, knowing that in the gesture of their invitation to sponsor the team and our response to it lay the foundation of a simple human relationship for Gary with the young men of the village, whom he had hardly gotten to know at all and which now would not have time to be realized. I couldn't tell what they thought of my choice of a ball.

Baltazar returned a while later to the construction of the altar, and soon after he left, Teresa followed him up to the plaza, a *chicha* jar on her back—we had frantically searched the yard and houses for a piece of rope to carry it with, rope not employed in holding together the framework of the altar, and I had finally found some—to serve *chicha* to the *segundas* of Hanansayaq. Gary and I waited, then went up to stand at the

top of Calle San Juan to watch; Hugo strolled over to us from somewhere
and we stood there together. The altar was nearly completed, and the
men were standing before it admiring their work and drinking *chicha*
served by their wives: we could imagine the tension of competition, felt
more strongly by the women than by the men, as each woman, with the
others' regard for her husband depending to a large extent upon her,
sought to be the most generous. A few men drifted away, and Baltazar
caught sight of us and came across the plaza. He sent Hugo to fetch
Sebastiana, who appeared, alone, with a key. She opened the door of the
room which had been Ricardo and Juana's store. About a month ago,
Ricardo had moved his shop from this room, which belongs to Baltazar,
to the one at the opposite end of the row, which is much bigger, enough
so that they can have a bed at one end, screened by a curtain—if they had
had to sleep in the other shop occasionally, they'd had to sleep on the
floor under the table—and Juana has a little kitchen at the other end, to
the left of the door behind an adobe wall. And Hugo, with money from
the barley which Daniel had taken to the brewery for Sebastiana, had
gone to Cusco to make the initial purchases of stock for a new enterprise:
his own store.

Gary and I were to be the *padrino* and *madrina* of the store as well,
and so we held a small private ceremony of inauguration. Hugo and
Sebastiana had stocked it meagerly, just starting out, with candy and
cigarettes and matches and sugar and, most important because of the festival, *trago*, which Baltazar had helped Hugo to flavor subtly with wild
anise. Sebastiana filled us a bottle with *trago* from a large glass jug and
went to retrieve Hugo. And so we inaugurated the new shop, Hugo and
Sebastiana a little embarrassed at Baltazar's insistence on the formality of
the ceremony, each of us allowing a few drops from our first *copita* of
trago to fall on the floor on each side of the door and in the middle of the
small room which, except for a shelf along one wall, was empty; they
would move the table from our house into the shop after we left. We
finished the bottle of *trago*, the three of us, Hugo and Sebastiana pru-
dently refusing to drink any, and another half bottle which Baltazar
bought and watched through the door the group of women—most of the
men had disappeared—now serving each other, sitting together to one
side of the altar. And then Gary and I went home and Baltazar returned
to the altar.

They came home about sunset. Teresa was singing, something I've only
heard her do when she's drunk—which she was. It had clearly not been
only *chicha* the women had been serving to each other; Baltazar, for a
change, had to guide her into her own house, supporting her to keep her
upright and more or less on her feet. Gary and I followed them into
Teresa's kitchen and helped Baltazar settle her onto the bank along the

wall where he usually sits. She started crying when she saw me, weeping inconsolably because I was leaving, babbling through her sobs about all the help I had given her and the things I had brought her from Cusco. I sat beside her with my arm around her shoulders, telling her futilely, Don't cry, don't cry; we couldn't comfort her. Gary bought a bottle of *trago* and he and Baltazar and I drank a little, and we tried to get Teresa to drink, thinking it might finally calm her, hoping that she might even sleep for a while. But whenever we gave it to her, she sat with the *copita* untouched in her hand while she cried. She did sleep after a while— Baltazar laid the sheepskins on the floor where he usually sleeps and covered her with a blanket—and woke hardly more sober but at least not crying now. And we spent the evening drinking together, the four of us. This, unplanned, was our real *despedida:* we had spent a day, before we had left 'Tambo the last time, drinking *chicha* and *trago,* and that was supposed to have been our *despedida,* but it simply hadn't felt like one, a lovely sunny day, all of the family around and a guest now and then, and the day of our departure still, then, weeks away. But it was very real now, and we talked about it; at moments we spoke of it with an absurdly simple and lucid practicality, as if it were not we who were leaving but someone else. At times, we cried. When we left this time, it would be for a long, long time. Before we parted on that night, Teresa gave me a black *bayeta* skirt, with a simple border of pink fabric and a single line of pale blue stitching, an old skirt in an old style, which she sometimes wore under her other skirts and which I had admired since the first time I saw it—as a memento. I wore it until we left 'Tambo. And Baltazar gave to Gary a pair of fine dark *bayeta* trousers; they had been his father's.

We woke the next morning, the day of Natividad, feeling like children on Christmas morning. When we went up to the plaza, men directed by the *segundas* of the *ayllu*s were building the ring for the bullfight. As rails for the fence, they used the old *arma*s (braces) of the roof of the town hall, which were replaced when the new roof had been put on it and had been lying in a heap in the plaza for months; the children had played on them as if they had been a jungle gym in a schoolyard. With heavy iron bars, the men drove holes deep into the hard-packed earth of the plaza in front of the town hall and in these planted tall posts to which they lashed the triangular frames of the *arma*s with ropes. We watched for a while, and Gary occasionally helped at Baltazar's bidding. The plaza was full of people, the atmosphere charged with exuberant excitement. In front of their shops, Ricardo and Toribio Delgado, who owns the one in the middle which had never been open the whole time we'd been in 'Tambo, had built *ramadas,* each a framework of thin poles supporting a roof of leafy eucalyptus branches, sheltering tables under them from the sun.

Men sat at the tables drinking beer and soft drinks. The schoolteachers had established a third *ramada* beside Toribio's, where they sold *qowi* and *lechón;* along with a few other people who might have money, we were given a typewritten invitation, in an envelope, to sponsor this enterprise as well, and for a possibly extravagant donation of two thousand *soles* were later served a "free" lunch of *qowi asado* and *papa wayk'u.* All around the edges of the plaza except where the altars stood were vendors from Cusco selling food—*anticuchos* and fried fish and soup and *chicha,* or vegetables and fruit, or candy (lollipops!)—and a variety of clothes and small merchandise—pins and needles and shawl pins and barrettes and toys and more toys. Whenever they caught up with us, Jaime and Eloy and Orlando pleaded with us to buy them little plastic trucks or whistles: when one request failed, they tried asking for something else. By the end of the day, each one had a new toy truck to augment his collection of makeshift toys: matchboxes and tins and bits of string. And there were people arriving from Cusco and Yaurisque and Huanoquite—three trucks now stood in the plaza and three more arrived later—and from the annexes and other villages on foot. And every child in the village and at least half of the dogs, and an occasional flock of sheep and goats.

About midmorning, we started up to the playing field near the school where the soccer tournament was to be held, to watch—officially, as sponsors of the team—the first game. As we crossed the plaza, we could see on the road near the crest of Aqchakar the procession, men on horseback carrying banners and staffs, men on foot bearing litters, bringing the images of the saints from the villages north of 'Tambo—like a vision of medieval Europe, the horses and men and banners and litters silhouetted against the pale sky. On the hillside across the Misk'iunu, at the *era* where we had threshed the wheat and where they had been last year, was a group of people, sitting in two lines, one up hill from the other, serving each other *chicha.* We thought maybe we should go there, since we really hadn't learned much about this aspect of the celebration of Natividad last year, and Baltazar had been invited this time too—though he never went—but we felt somehow, knew somehow, that it didn't concern us: they weren't our people. We waited at the field for teams to arrive on the trucks—the tournament seemed to be more formal this year than it had the last, and teams from Yaurisque and even Cusco had been invited to play—and in the meantime ate *lechón* and *papa wayk'u* which the team had cooked that morning in Baltazar's oven, to sell to spectators. They served it to us ceremoniously, as patrons of the team, when we got there and we ate rather self-consciously, the only ones eating. Some teams were still not there when they finally decided to begin—maybe the truck had broken down—and the captains of the teams which were present drew numbers to determine the order of play: 'Tambo and Yaurisque first. Our team, Los Hermanos Ayares (The Brothers Ayar) won.

When we returned to the plaza, the bullfight was just about to begin. We went to have our free lunch at the insistence of the schoolteachers, giving a lot of it, slyly, to children who were hanging around looking hungry, and found places among the crowd along the fence of the bullring; we leaned through the rails of the *armas* to watch, shrieking and scattering with the others whenever one of the confused animals charged our end of the ring seeking escape. The contest was not very impressive, the bullfighters inexperienced and generally not such flamboyant performers as the *toreros* had been last year, only one dressed for the part in something that resembled a suit of lights—Nicasio, the *carguyuq*, a little drunk, had his picture taken with him at some point in the middle of the contest and was nearly gored by a bull who was still in the ring—and the animals wanting nothing more than to be left in peace. The climax of the event came when one of the bulls charged the fence at our end of the *cancha* and found a way through it to escape down the hill, running headlong between the houses below the plaza, pursued by a lot of men. The day had grown cloudy, windy and cold, a thin, icy rain driven through the air, and we retired to Hugo and Sebastiana's shop where, with Baltazar and Teresa and some *compadres* of theirs from other villages, we drank *trago* and *chicha* until late in the afternoon.

There was a dance that evening in the town hall, for which we had been persuaded to buy tickets, and another organized by the industrious schoolteachers, with a live band playing *huaynos* and *marineras* on accordion and harp and guitars in the churchyard, people dancing around a bonfire which illuminated magically the adobe facade of the church. We wandered from one to the other, becoming separated in the fire-lit crowds or the dark plaza populated by shadows and finding each other again—a remarkable night, what seemed the entire population of the village out in the dark streets, in the plaza, in the churchyard, at an hour when those places are normally utterly, solemnly, fearfully empty and silent.

We went up to Goyo's shop the next morning to give him some things which we wouldn't take with us and wouldn't really be of any use to Baltazar and Teresa, and on the way down again, we were trapped by the people who had been celebrating the *vela* at the altar of Hanansayaq all night, at the foot of the street at the end of the churchyard below the bell tower. We were welcomed by Julio Wallpa, president and *carguyuq*, more drunk and less dignified than I have ever seen him, who reproached us for not having been there and then disappeared; he must have gone home to bed. As at San Pedro, we were served as much *chicha* and *trago* as people could force us to accept. I danced for a while: as soon as one dance ended, I was claimed by another partner for the next, and there was almost an argument at one point over who was going to dance with me—I might have been flattered if they hadn't simply been drinking all night— until I pleaded exhaustion and thirst and found a place next to Teresa among the women, safe. Teresa was, again, very drunk and began— again—to cry when she saw me, and soon all of the women around her were crying, including me, because I was leaving. But people had begun to drift away, the *carguyuq* himself having set the example, and we soon found it relatively easy to extricate ourselves. We went home and made a second pot of coffee.

We remained at home that day, drinking in our yard, or else in Andrés and Celestina's, with Baltazar, who had been wisely at home asleep that morning, and don Andrés and Celestina and, in the afternoon, an old woman called doña Vicentina, who was Andrés' sister and Teresa's aunt— an old, old woman with white hair and exactly one tooth, who wears an old woman's clothes, dark *bayeta* skirt and hand-woven shawl and no shoes—and Mariano Castellanos and Andrés and Celestina's son Alejandro and one of Baltazar's *compadres* from another village. We had been talking, whenever we saw him, with Ricardo about christening Orlando; the priest had come to 'Tambo for Natividad, to celebrate mass each day and to lead the processions of the saints. Gary and I wanted very much to sponsor the ceremony of christening: it would make little Orlando our *ahijado,* our godson, and Ricardo and Juana our *compadre* and *comadre.* Ricardo had hesitated in speaking to the priest until it was too late, but Baltazar had a solution: he said there was an old way which did not require the presence of the priest and which, we suspected, he may simply have invented. The witness of the priest would only serve to make it ecclesiastically official, for Orlando's name would be written in the church records with ours, but this "old" way would suffice to bless Orlando and establish the bond of godson and godparents between us, he said.

In the late afternoon, Ricardo told us to come, and with Baltazar, we went up to the shop to collect Orlando from Juana. We bought a candle and the three of us, Gary and Baltazar and I, took Orlando to the church and asked the attendant to let us in. We sat Orlando on a step in the dim church beneath the image of the Virgen Natividad, to one side of the altar, and placed the burning candle before him. The child must have been utterly bewildered but was quiet and still; I don't think he had ever been in the church before. Gary and I knelt and prayed before the Virgin, holding our hats in our hands, and then rose. Leaving the candle burning before the image, we gathered up Orlando again, Gary bearing him as far as the door, gave the attendant a small tip, and went out into the blaze of afternoon sun. Beyond the door, Baltazar indicated that I should carry Orlando, and I took him, still quiet, in my arms. I carried him down the steep descent from the churchyard and halfway across the plaza before he started squirming, re-transformed into the dear little hellraiser that he is, and I put him down and we both ran the rest of the way across the plaza, laughing.

We ended up that night dancing in the *comedor*. My last dance was with don Andrés: the last dance in 'Tambo, dear old don Andrés. Everybody was too drunk to really notice when Gary and I slipped out of the room.

And then there is the inconceivable sorrow of leaving, simply leaving for the last time of all the times we've come and gone. Leaving these people—Baltazar, Teresa, the kids, old Andrés, and Celestina—whom we've struggled, among ourselves and within ourselves, to know and to understand and, finally, to love. And because it is a love not naturally born, like the love of one's family and people who normally in our lives become friends and lovers and husbands and wives, but *made,* hard-won against obstacles we could not have imagined, and because this sort of severance too is such an unnatural sort of phenomenon, unexpected somehow, or disbelieved even though we all knew all along the day would come, the parting was not something any of us were emotionally prepared to deal with: nothing in all of the experiences of our separate lives could have taught us how to face this.

Gary and I woke early that morning, wishing as soon as we were fully awake that it was still the day before because even just yesterday hadn't been the last day, and today was. Mechanically, we followed our morning routines of making coffee, heating water for washing, feeling the effects of the festival: three—or four?—days of unaccustomed and dizzying activity, a good part of each day spent drinking and, of course, drunk on *chicha* and *trago* and even beer, so that much of those last days in 'Tambo had been passed in the state of uncertain emotional equilibrium of drunkenness, especially of that drunkenness caused by the potent combination of *chicha* and *trago*. Most of the time we had tried hard, all of us, not to let ourselves think or really look at each others' faces because we knew that if we did, we would cry. But we did cry, of course, Baltazar and Teresa and Gary and I, Andrés and Celestina—only the kids didn't, exaggeratedly embarrassed, when they were present, by our displays of emotion, though I think they didn't realize, really, what was happening; mostly they weren't around—so much so that I wouldn't have believed there were any tears left for that last morning. Even people, the *compadres* of Baltazar and Teresa who had come from other villages for the festival, whom we had only just met, cried because we were leaving. The Quechua are not a people who make goodbyes easy.

Baltazar came in and we gave him a cup of coffee; he sat behind the table where Gary had always sat to write. Teresa came in about seven, with a pitcher full of *chicha* and a plate of fried potatoes and onions and lots of *ají*—a festival breakfast, good for a morning when you've had too much *trago* the night before. Then Juana came in with a bottle of *trago* from the shop, and Hugo and Sebastiana with Hugo's radio-cassette player so we could record a message, one final memento. And Daniel, and Leonarda with the doll I had given her; it was a baby doll with, as she had wanted, eyes that open and close and long blond braids; she had named it after me. The whole family. It was good to drink that morning, and even Juana, who knows more tricks to get out of drinking *trago* than anyone I've met, willingly drank with us—and Sebastiana, who is usually offered but not really expected to drink *trago*. We recorded a message, Baltazar speaking first in his most formal Quechua—except that he started crying in the middle: his voice broke and it took him a minute to recover it— recalling all we had been through, and Gary and I, struggling too with voices and words, thanking them for their hospitality and generosity and patience, promising that we would come back. I gave away all of our household, trying to apportion things as appropriately as I could so no one's feelings would be hurt: the pot and kettle and cups and spoons to Sebastiana and Hugo who have none yet; to Teresa the blue plastic washing basin, my shawl, the lock from the door, and my mirror, which she had coveted ingenuously since the day I had brought it to 'Tambo; the extra coffee and sugar and bread to Juana. Then we heard the sound of an engine and Gary and I carelessly crammed what was left into our packs and we all trailed up to the plaza, Baltazar carrying the rest—very little— of the bottle of *trago*, Teresa the refilled pitcher.

The driver said he was just warming up the engine, not leaving for an hour or so, so we put our packs on the truck and stood by the wall of the shops drinking—*chicha*, another bottle of *trago*—lost in the daze of the early morning alcohol, the complexity of our emotions, and the festival activity in the plaza, full of vendors and visitors. We stood at the end of the row of whitewashed shops, at the top of Calle San Juan where we had lived, in front of the one which had been Ricardo's and would now be Hugo's. People came to talk to us, to say goodbye, and Baltazar and Teresa gave us glasses of *chicha* and *copitas* of *trago* to offer to them: it was our place to serve them now, not theirs—they had come to see *us*. Women asked me tearfully why I was leaving, and I couldn't answer them—there was no answer: I didn't *know* why—but, with tears in my own eyes, told them only that I would come back someday. "Kutimusaq, Mamay, kutimusaq" ("I will come back, My Mother, I will come back").

With Baltazar at our side, we stood there absurdly like dignitaries holding audience, talking to a bewildering succession of people, everybody we had ever known in 'Tambo, it seemed, and one irritatingly persistent

young man who had come—from Quillabamba?—for the festival, to
play on one of the soccer teams, who didn't realize, stubbornly refused
to realize, that we did not want, at that moment, to explain ourselves to
some stranger. And then the driver started the truck again. We hugged
Baltazar and Teresa, trying to be brave, not to cry any more, and I hugged
Hugo, who, like any shy eighteen-year-old kid, blushed deeply at being
hugged in public by a woman, and told Daniel—not hugging him because I had just learned what his reaction would be and didn't want
to embarrass him as well—"Adios, we'll see you . . ." And we walked
away numbly toward the truck; *trago* and disbelief caused a sensation of
watching ourselves from a distance, of disconnection from what we were
doing—the emotional distance the mind puts between itself and something which it cannot accept. And those people, ourselves, climbed the
ladder and found seats on the bench just behind the cab and waited for
the truck to leave.

By the time the truck finally started moving toward Cusco, the morning
was a blur of images seen through *trago* and tears: all of us in the house,
the big silver box of the cassette recorder on the table; Baltazar standing
proudly in the sun on the plaza with his hat pushed back and the bottle in
his hand, the father of strange children who were going far away; Teresa
crouching in her orange skirt against the whitewashed wall of the shop,
beside her pitcher of *chicha;* Hugo's blush and awkward sad smile as I
hugged him; Daniel's nonchalance, so deliberate that it could only have
been feigned, as he sat at the top of Calle San Juan with his back to the
truck we were about to get on. And then all over again: while we were
waiting for the other passengers to board, Gary had gotten off the truck
and I waited alone, not knowing where he had gone, and he came back
and told me to come with him; the mayor had told the driver to wait and
in Ricardo's store he and the governor were buying everyone beer in our
honor. Another series of images: the young mayor, Nicasio, swaying a
little, handing me beer in a glass, making a speech for another tape, a
memento for the community this time, in the half-lit interior of the store,
explaining on my behalf when I couldn't speak my part of the message,
with an understanding for which I felt an overwhelming gratitude, that
the feelings were there but the words just wouldn't come; and saying
goodbye again, to Juana and Ricardo too this time, Ricardo in his sky
blue sweater which I had watched Juana make, Teresa and Baltazar as we
stumbled over their feet to the door, shaking hands in the dazzling sun
with the mayor and the governor and his wife who kept saying, "Qué
pena, qué pena," and standing at the foot of the ladder at the back of the
truck while Gary inscribed our address in the States with a blue ball-point
pen on the inside of Angélico Araujo's forearm; and waving one last time

to Hugo, still standing against that whitewashed wall, as the truck pulled out of the plaza.

I felt my skin grow taut as the wind dried my cheeks. There was no one on the truck we knew. We sat up on top of the cab and tried to concentrate on the mountains: the jagged peaks of the Otra Banda, the familiar *apu*s of 'Tambo, the lands we had worked for a year and wouldn't see again for a long time; fighting now against the effects of the *trago* we had welcomed, we finally just left it to the wind and sun to clear our minds. No one spoke to us, all the way to Cusco. They had all been there when we got on the truck—and maybe they had some sense of what had happened. We left. In the end, you just leave.

Epilogue: 1988

B ut, of course, you don't just leave. Such an experience, so intensely lived, so deeply felt, has repercussions and ramifications throughout your life; it touches you, alters you, and, at the very least, becomes, like any other experience, an integral part of the background from which you face the world. 'Tambo has become a part of the mental-emotional land-scape of my life—a landscape of *homes,* places where I have lived and which I have come to know intimately, where I have known people whom I loved, though details of the memory of my life in those places has often become blurred to the point where they are indiscernible.

We took 'Tambo with us when we left, wore the experience like layers of skin, which we shed gradually as we readjusted to our life in the States, losing first, immediately, the simple customs of our life in Peru, adjust-ments we had made which, in the course of a year and a half, had become habits. We felt, at first, overwhelmed by the comforts and the array of technology which prevailed in even the simplest households—we found ourselves, on the day of our return to the States, in Gary's mother's house, lying that evening on soft wall-to-wall carpeting in front of a color tele-vision in the easy comfort of central heating, the supper dishes in the dishwasher—overwhelmed too by the vast profusion of goods available in any supermarket or shopping mall. And, even months later, we felt awkward in social situations, still striving to break ourselves of the habit of greeting people with a hug and a kiss on the cheek. People don't do that when they meet each other in the grocery store in a small town in central New York. And so we gradually adjusted ourselves to our own, "real" lives, though it felt sometimes like driving at highway speed on a busy interstate an old Volkswagen more accustomed to puttering around town.

We realized, after a while, that, realistically, fieldwork is a vital aspect of Gary's career, it's his profession, and that if we wanted or needed to go back to 'Tambo, there would be a way to do so. And we did return, a couple of times, once for a month and a half during the summer and once for just a week or so when Gary had attended a conference in Bogotá, Colombia; and Gary had been back to Peru once with a group of students from the university, a few of whom went with him to visit the community. And then we went back, in June of 1987, to stay for another year, so that Gary could investigate the relationships between the annex villages and 'Tambo itself. We naïvely imagined, because it was all that we knew, living essentially the same life we had lived in 'Tambo before, with only one critical difference: we returned to 'Tambo this time with a child of our own, our son, Jason, a year and one month old, the effect of whose presence on our life there we could not foresee. But things were different. The lives of almost every member of our family in 'Tambo had changed as significantly as had our own with the birth of Jason. When we arrived, Juana was pregnant with her seventh child, Esteban, who was born in August, before we had really gotten ourselves settled again in 'Tambo. Hugo and Sebastiana, who had had a daughter, Lourdes, had two more children, one which had died at the age of more than one year, and René, who was about eight months old. And Daniel was living with a woman named Nicolasa, in Baltazar and Teresa's house, and had by her a son, Cosme, who was half a year older than Jason. And even Leonarda was living with a man named Mario, in his mother's house, and she too— who had not even reached puberty when I had last really known her— was pregnant; their son, Elmer (at the suggestion of Mario's brother who was visiting from Lima at the time of his birth, they first named the child Marco Polo, which we thought was wonderful—he was Marco Polo Quispe Quispe, because both Leonarda's and Mario's surnames are Quispe—but within a couple of weeks, Leonarda decided that she didn't like the name, and they changed it to Elmer) was born in September, just at the end of the celebration of Natividad. Leonarda, whom I had last known as a rather bratty child, was a marvellous mother: she was relaxed and content with her child—she delighted in him and was happier than any mother I had ever known, there or at home. Leonarda had become a woman.

And too, during the years that had passed, we had solidified our relationships with the family and, through them, with the village simply by coming back to visit them whenever we could and also by baptizing or cutting the hair of a lot of children, including all of Baltazar and

Teresa's grandchildren born since we had left 'Tambo in 1982—Juana and Ricardo's twin daughters, Nancy and Elisa, and their son Hernán and Hugo and Sebastiana's daughter Lourdes, whom we baptized in the church in 'Tambo when the priest was there for the festival of the Virgin of the Assumption one August. When we came back to 'Tambo this time, we had—for a couple of *gringos*—a small but respectable network of *compadres* as well as a deep sense of familiarity bred of the relative frequency of our comings and goings.

And then there was Jason: we would finally, we thought, be perceived as normal human beings. And that was true: Jason, who adapted beautifully to life in the village—there were children and animals and dirt to play in everywhere, and people who doted on him—was a passport with a diplomatic visa to women's life in 'Tambo. My meagre vocabulary in Quechua almost immediately expanded to include words from which to conduct whole mothers' conversations about the age of one's baby, its habits, the number of teeth it has. People everywhere, in 'Tambo and in Cusco, were enchanted by him; with his very fair skin and honey-blond hair and round, perpetually rosy cheeks, he must have looked to them literally like a living doll. In Cusco, girls who worked in the shops took him right out of my arms to hug him; they learned his name—which was pronounced, usually, "Yason"—and rushed to the doors of their shops when we passed to beg him to come to them. In 'Tambo, and often in Cusco as well, Quechua people called him Atoqcha in Quechua, or Zorrito in Spanish, or a combination of the words, Zorrucha. It means little fox and is what people often teasingly call children with light coloring, like that of the blondish Andean fox; the name is often accompanied by the epithet Wallpa Suwa—chicken thief. And soon after we had come back to 'Tambo, we reversed the established pattern of favors and asked Baltazar and Teresa to cut Jason's hair, which had never been cut, a ritual ceremony they seemed to feel honored to perform; and so they became Jason's godparents and, finally, truly our *compadres*. And because Baltazar and Teresa took their ritual parenthood very seriously, and Jason seemed to know instinctively that they were people beloved by us and so welcomed them wholeheartedly into his pantheon of adults, a genuine bond developed between them, to the delight of us all. Theirs were the first names he learned, other than Mama and Papa and the name of Gary's field assistant, Jean-Jacques; and when they visited us in Cusco, he brought them his toys and sat on their laps, things he did with nobody but us, except sometimes Jean-Jacques.

The world of 'Tambo, as had my own world at home in the States, looked much different to me through the eyes of a mother.

It was, in the end, a difficult year. We had hepatitis, which kept me, and with me Jason, out of the field for many months, though Gary recovered more quickly. We faced again the rumors and suspicion of our motives, which this time resulted in a vote in an assembly to expel us from the village soon after we got there; Gary managed to clear us of the accusations of excavating for gold and continued his research unhindered, but a more troubling and persistent sense of ill-will among certain sectors of the community than we had ever felt before in 'Tambo lingered long after the event. And while we were there, Juana became increasingly ill, displaying symptoms which seemed impossibly unrelated and which we could not fit together into an amateur diagnosis. Ricardo arranged for several *paqo*s (healers) to come to their house to perform ritual diagnoses and cures, all of which failed. Finally, we took her to a doctor in Cusco who diagnosed a progressive disease, incurable even here in the States, with our state-of-the-art medical technology. I asked him to write down the specifics of the diagnosis for me before we left his office; the last thing he wrote on the slip of paper from his prescription pad was, "Pronóstico: no bueno." Not good, and he underlined it. He spoke to her in Quechua, and I don't know how much he explained to her, but to me he explained everything, including that Juana would probably not live more than a few years longer. We went to a pharmacy immediately and bought the medicines he had prescribed to relieve the symptoms and slow the progress of the disease, and Juana took them faithfully, for a while. But they were seeking a cure, and Ricardo hired three more curers, one a famous *paqo* from a village near Chinchero, north of Cusco; and finally we paid for a visit to a spiritualist—the last resort—who diagnosed witchcraft, and Ricardo undertook the proceedings of an accusation of witchcraft against another shop owner in 'Tambo, whom he suspected of jealousy of the success of his and Juana's shop, the most prosperous in the village. Meanwhile, Juana grew steadily worse; she was only thirty-two and becoming an old woman before our eyes, stooped and drawn. When we came back to the States, we left for her a year's supply of the medicines the doctor had prescribed, and exhortations to take them, and Jean-Jacques' address in Cusco—he would be there for at least another year, pursuing his own doctoral research—and instructions that, if they needed help, they should go to him.

Also during that year, don Andrés died. In the time we had been away from the village, Andrés had finally grown old, and since we had been back, he never left the patio of his and Celestina's house: he sat all day in the sun, in the morning in front of their storehouse, in the afternoon outside the kitchen. He no longer worked his fields or even gathered wood for the fire. And, on the Tuesday after Easter, he died. It was an event we had always recognized the possibility of and always dreaded, but, in the end, we were grateful to have been there when it happened. We spent a week in the rituals of mourning with Celestina and accompanied the procession of mourners to the cemetery to inter his body; he was buried in a new pair of *bayeta* trousers Gary and I had given him for his last birthday in November. I couldn't always be at Celestina's house with the other women cooking and drinking and crying, because of Jason. I felt bad about this, but there was nothing I could do: the other women had mothers and sisters and cousins and *comadres* with whom they could leave their children. I had, at least, *comadres,* but none of them were prepared for the task of caring for a little *gringo* boy for most of a week. When I could be there, I tried to convey to Celestina my sorrow for her, though I was forced to communicate with her in my odd foreign gestures—hugs and kisses on her forehead or her ancient cheeks, as soft and lax as old heavy silk. She accepted these gestures, alien as they were to her, offensively demonstrative as they may have been to others, sweetly: she knew me, and she understood. And when we left, we gave her a new black *bayeta* skirt for mourning: her only dark skirt was tattered, falling literally to pieces. In Cusco, I bought silver rings for her and for Juana and gave them to them before we left, thinking of Andrés buried in that new pair of *bayeta* trousers, thinking that I might never see either of those women again.

But also during that year, we fortified even further our relationships with Baltazar and Teresa and their family: we sponsored Hugo and Sebastiana's wedding in the church of Belén in Cusco, our subsequent festivities in 'Tambo, accompanied by a band we had hired, merging with the concurrent celebration of Natividad; and we baptized René and Esteban and Elmer, and we cut Cosme's hair. And we created new ties: we cut the hair of Julio Wallpa's son, Juan Carlos, and the son, Percy, of a man we had never known before, Benito Baldeiglesias, and baptized the son of a couple in the annex village Qoipa, with whom Gary lived for a while, Alfonso Villegas and his wife, Marina.

And now we are here, living our normal, North American lives once again. The transition between the field and home was not as difficult this time as it was the first, mostly because of Jason, we think—we concentrated so exclusively on making it as smooth and easy as possible for him that we thought remarkably little about how it was for us—but also, in part, because our life in 'Tambo has been incorporated, with the passage of time and our returns to the village, into our conceptions of ourselves and our lives. Those lives, mine and Gary's and Jason's as well, though he's still too young to know it, have roots now not only here, in the familiar soils of the United States, but in 'Tambo too. And now we share with those people not only our memories of the idyll that their life was for us in the good times but also the knowledge of the sorrows and hardships of their true lives, as real and more difficult than our own. Our experiences in 'Tambo have been as much emotional as intellectual, and perhaps this was the essence of the difficulty of leaving 'Tambo that first time: we all, as human beings, want reassurance that those about whom we care very deeply also care deeply about us, and though Gary and I were fairly certain of this when we left the village, we knew there would be no reassurance—there would be no letters, no phone calls. We could only believe it and try to sustain that belief. But now, we have woven a web which binds us inextricably together, though its fibers are stretched taut over the miles, a web of ritual kinship, of *compadrazgo*. Normally, a child's godparents are people to whom the parents can turn for help in times of need, their own or their child's, and at first we warned our friends in 'Tambo that we wouldn't be there, probably, when they needed us; they wanted the ceremony, the baptism or haircutting, anyway. Now we know that for all of us, our becoming the godparents of those children, Baltazar and Teresa becoming Jason's godparents, simply formalized the bonds that existed between us anyway, making us all family, making those bonds real, in a way which gives us all that reassurance. We are the godparents of those children, we and nobody else, even if we should never now return to 'Tambo; and the only godparents our son, Jason, has on this earth are Baltazar Quispe and Teresa Sullca.

Glossary

abogado (SP): lawyer

abstinencia (SP): abstinence

abuelita (SP): "little grandmother"

acequia (SP): irrigation ditch

ahijado/a (SP): godson/goddaughter

ají (SP): a hot pepper

akllay (Q): to select, choose

alcaldín (SP): "little mayor"; a role in traditional dance

allinllanchu (Q): a greeting: "How are you?"

alma (SP): soul

altomisayoq (Q FROM SP, POSSIBLY *ALTO*, HIGH, AND *MISA*, MASS, OR
  MESA, TABLE): powerful diviner

ama (Q): emphatic imperative form of No

añañau (Q): "How lovely!"

anticucho (SP): meat chunks, usually beef heart, grilled on skewers

api kisa (Q): native variety of nettle with large, heart-shaped leaves,
  probably *Urtica magellanica poir*

apu (Q): powerful sacred entity represented by the most imposing and
  mighty natural features, usually mountains

arma (Q FROM SP *ARMADURA*): an armature or framework

arroz con leche (SP): rice pudding

asado (SP): roasted

asnu (Q FROM SP): burro

asta (SP): horn, as of a cow; in 'Tambo, also a vessel for drinking *chicha*

atoq (Q): fox

atoq lisa (Q): wild variety of edible tuber (see also *papa lisa*)

atoqcha (Q): "little fox"

auki or awki (Q): supernatural being related to the ancestors who mediates between the living and the dead; spirit of the high mountains

avenida (SP): avenue

ayllu (Q): in 'Tambo, a named patrilineal social group within the community which holds land in common and bears the responsibility to perform its share of communal labor projects and to organize the public celebration of particular community festivals; there are ten *ayllu*s in 'Tambo, and each of the two moieties of 'Tambo, Hanansayaq and Hurinsayaq, is comprised of five *ayllu*s

ayni (Q): system of reciprocal labor

ayuno (SP): a fast

balbas t'ika (Q FROM SP *MALVA*, MALLOW, AND Q *T'IKA*, FLOWER): a variety of mallow, *Malva* sp. or *Malvastrum* sp.

bandera (SP): banner, flag

barro (SP): clay, mud

bayeta (SP): baize, hand-woven wool cloth

baylun or maylun (Q FROM ENG.): nylon

bodega (SP): wine cellar; in Peru, a shop which sells alcohol

caballito (SP): little horse

caballo (SP): horse

calle (SP): street

campana (SP): bell; in 'Tambo, the bell tower of the church

campanilla (SP): diminutive of *campana*

campesino/a (SP): farmer, peasant; in Peru, people of native villages, especially the Quechua

campo (SP): country, realm outside the cities

caña (SP): cane alcohol

cancha (Q): corral

cargo (SP AND Q): the responsibility for carrying out religious or community duties, such as mounting the public celebration of a saint's day festival

carguyuq (Q): one who bears the responsibility for carrying out a religious or other community duty (see also *cargo*)

celeste (SP): sky blue

chachakuma (Q): a native tree of the Saxifrage family

chakitaqlla (Q): footplow

chakla (Q): withe

chakra (Q): field for cultivation

chakrayoq (Q): owner of a field

ch'ampa (Q): chunk of sod

ch'ampay (Q): to break up sod into *ch'ampa*s

charki (Q): jerky (dried meat)

chicha (Q): corn beer

chicha frutillada (Q): sweetened *chicha* flavored with strawberries

chichería (Q): restaurant which serves *chicha*

chikchi(Q): hail

chimallaku (Q): small or light hail

ch'ini challwa (Q): a tiny freshwater fish, usually dried

chinkay (Q): to become lost, disappear

cholo (SP): "half-breed"; derogatory term used for people of mixed blood or for natives who have adopted the dress and manners of Western society

chosita (SP FROM *CHOZA*, HUT): "little hut"

chuchur (Q): "savage," derogatory term apparently local to 'Tambo, used for supposedly "uncivilized" people of other regions of Peru, especially the jungle

ch'ullo (Q): traditional knit wool hat with ear flaps

ch'uño (Q): potatoes preserved through a process of freezing and drying

ch'uño saruy (Q): the act of squeezing water out of *ch'uño* in the process of making it by stepping on it

chuta (Q FROM *CHUTAY*, TO PULL, STRETCH OUT, EXTEND): a share of the work of various community projects, such as digging irrigation canals or repairing the road to Cusco, which is delegated to individual *ayllu*s of 'Tambo; these shares may be measured by area, so that a particular *ayllu* may be responsible for a particular stretch of road, or by time, so that each *ayllu* may be responsible for working one day in its turn in some construction project

cocaína (SP): cocaine

colegio (SP): in Peru, a high school

comadre (SP): relationship of spiritual kinship; in Peru, a woman who is the godmother of one's child

comedor (SP): dining room

cómo está (SP): "How are you?"

compadrazgo (SP): relationship of godparents to the parents of a child

compadre (SP): relationship of spiritual kinship; in Peru, a man who is the godfather of one's child *concejo* (SP): town hall

conjunto (SP): a band, musical ensemble

copita (SP): small cup; in Peru, a shot glass

corcova (SP): hump, hunch; extension of a celebration for several days; in Peru, the second day of the celebration of one's birthday

costal (SP): sack, bag; in Peru, a sack for transporting or storing grain or potatoes

Cruz Velakuy (SP AND Q): "to do vigil for the cross"; the festival of Santísima Cruz, or Holy Cross, May 3

cura (SP): priest

curandero/a (SP): healer

denuncia (SP): denouncement, accusation

despedida (SP): farewell; in Peru, a farewell party

día santo (SP): saint's day, name day (birthday)

Domingo de Ramos (SP): Palm Sunday

don (SP): title of respect for a senior man; in 'Tambo, usually reserved for men who have completed several *cargos*

era (SP): threshing floor, threshing ground

esquina (SP): corner

estancia (SP): ranch house or ranch

faena (SP): task; in Peru, a work party

gringo/a (SP): in Peru, foreigner

gripe (SP): a cold or flu

Guardia Civil (SP): Civil Guard, the Peruvian national police

guinda (SP): sour cherry; the color of sour cherry

hacendado (SP): owner of a hacienda; landowner

hallmay (Q): to hoe

hallmiyoq (Q): first hoeing of a field

hampi (Q): medicine

Hanansayaq (Q): "of the upper part"; in 'Tambo, one of the two moeities

hatun (Q): big

hatun compadre (Q AND SP): "big compadre"; puma

hawas rapi (Q): leaves of a bean plant (*Faba* sp.)

hijo (SP): son

homenta (Q FROM SP *HUMINTA* OR *HUMITA*): tamal made from ground fresh corn rather than dried corn

honda (SP): woven sling, slingshot

horno (SP): oven

hostal (SP): hostel

huayno (Q): a traditional popular song and dance

hulch'a (Q): warp beam of a back-strap loom (see illustration p. 162)

Hurinsayaq (Q): "of the lower part"; in 'Tambo, one of the two moieties

ichu (Q): a variety of high-altitude grass

ichuna (Q): a small sickle

illawa aysana (Q): heddle stick of a back-strap loom (see illustration p. 162)

ingeniero (SP): engineer; in Peru, anyone practicing a technical trade

Inti Raymi (Q): the Inca festival of the sun

kallwa (Q): beater used with a back-strap loom (see illustration p. 162)

kantu (Q): native variety of flowering shrub

kashwar (Q): the traditional dance of Carnaval among the Quechua

khiki (Q): boil, blister; familiarly, mule or horse

kiska (Q): thorn

kondor (Q): condor

kondor auki (Q): type of condor

kumpay (Q): to knock down

kumpi (Q): variety of potato, lumpy with reddish skin

kunka (Q): neck, throat

k'usilluq (Q): "one with a monkey"; in 'Tambo, a ceremonial drinking vessel

kuska (Q): together

kuskan (Q): half

kuskan tiy (Q): "to sit together"; a particular arrangement in which men sit while resting or taking meals when working in the fields; the men sit in an arc, all facing downhill, each man between the legs of the man behind him

kuti (Q): short hoe with crooked handle and narrow blade; the handle of the hoe; something that turns back upon itself

kutimusaq (Q): "I will return"

lakawiti (Q): variety of squash

lampa (Q): small hoe with broad, spade-like blade

lauta (Q): cane flute

lechón (SP): suckling pig; roast pig

legítimo/a (SP): legitimate

libreta (SP): in Peru, a document of identification

llaulli (Q): variety of wild flower

llaulli puka (Q): violet-red, the color of the *llaulli* flower

llipta (Q): dried or moist paste, usually made from the ash of grain, with which coca is chewed

lliqlla (Q): a carrying cloth

loro (SP): parrot

macha (SP): mussel

machu (Q): old

machu compadre (Q AND SP): "old compadre"; puma

machula (Q): elderly person, grandfather; ancestor

madrina (SP): godmother

maíz (SP): corn

majeño (SP): a role in traditional dance; vendors of cane alcohol from Majes in Arequipa who plied their wares in the central highlands in the nineteenth and early twentieth centuries

majines (Q): Quechua adaptation of *majeño*

mal aire (SP): "bad air"; evil spirits

mallki (Q): tree

mallki kumpay (Q): "tree, to knock down"; tree erected in the plaza at the time of Carnaval, which the townspeople dance around and attempt to cut down with an axe; the couple who succeed in cutting down the tree win the *cargo* to erect the tree in the coming year

mallki mithay (Q): "tree, to cut" (see *mallki kumpay*)

malva (SP): mallow

mamay (Q FROM SP): "my mother"

manan mamitayoq (Q): "one without a mother"; an orphan

máquina (SP): machine

maran (Q): grinding stone, mortar

mariba (SP?): a purple potato

marinera (SP): a popular dance

marka (Q): upper-story storehouse

maway or *mawiy* (Q): to give birth prematurely

maway papa (Q): early potato

mayordomo (SP): majordomo; in Peru, the bearer of a major *cargo*

mayu (Q): river

mensajero (SP): messenger

merienda (SP): afternoon snack or tea; among the Quechua, the meal served in the afternoon

mesa (SP): table, altar

mestizo (SP): person of mixed blood

millay (Q): ugly

mithay (Q): to cut, split, or shatter

montera (SP): traditional Quechua hat, a flat or slightly peaked frame covered with fringed *bayeta;* in 'Tambo, no longer worn except as part of a costume *moraya* (Q): variety of dried potato

mot'e (Q): boiled dried corn; hominy

motoy or *mutuy* (Q): native shrub with yellow flowers, probably *Cassia elegans* or *Cassia florifera*

multa (SP): a fine

ñakaq (Q): supernatural being somewhat similar to a vampire

Natividad (SP): Nativity; the festival of the Virgin of the Nativity

negocio (SP): business; transaction

nina (Q): fire

ñuqchu (Q): native wildflower with scarlet blossoms

odre (Q): large bag made of goat or cow hide for carrying *chicha*

ojota (Q): sandal made of tire rubber commonly worn by the Quechua

padrino (SP): godfather

paja (SP): straw

pallana (Q): slender, flat wooden wand used for picking up threads when weaving patterns

pallay (Q): to pick up; the act of weaving patterns made by picking up individual threads of the warp

pampa (Q): flat; a flat place

panetón (SP): traditional Spanish Christmas bread baked in a tall, round loaf

papa (Q): father, also used as a term of address; potato

papa blanca (Q AND SP): light-skinned variety of potato

papa lisa (Q): variety of *ulluku,* an edible tuber

papa wayk'u (Q): boiled potato; boiling is the most common way to prepare potatoes

paqo (Q): curer, healer

paradero (SP): stopping place; bus or truck stop

parientes (SP): relatives

pasayki (Q): "Come in"

pena (SP): sorrow, suffering

pescado (SP): fish (once caught)

phaqcha (Q): waterfall

picaflor (SP): hummingbird

picantería (SP): café or restaurant

piki (Q): flea

p'irqa (Q): native herbaceous plant with bluish or white flowers, probably *Bidens Pilosa*

pisando barro (SP): the process of mixing straw into mud with the feet in the production of adobe *policía* (SP): police

pronóstico (SP): prognosis

provincia (SP): province; in 'Tambo, the provincial capital

pueblo (SP): small town, village; people

puesto (SP): post, station

puesto sanitario (SP): health center

pukyu (Q): spring

puna (Q): very high land, similar to tundra

puna yapuy (Q): to turn fallow land in the *puna* in preparation for planting potatoes

pura (SP): pure

purun (Q): fallow land

purun yapuy (Q): to turn fallow land (not in the *puna*) in preparation for planting potatoes, wheat, or barley

qarachayllaña (Q): "just like skin"

qasona (Q): heavy stave for threshing

q'enti (Q): hummingbird

q'epi (Q): bundle carried on one's back

q'epina (Q): cloth for carrying a bundle

qero (Q): large drinking vessel usually carved of wood

qespi (Q): crystal

qhaya qhaya (Q): native herb, probably the common nightshade, *Solanum Nigrum* L.

qonchu (Q): dregs of a jar of *chicha;* impure, thick, dirty

qowi (Q): guinea pig

qoy (Q): to give

qoya (Q): woman of high status

quebrada (SP): gorge, ravine

quena (Q): a wooden flute

quinua (SP): high-altitude grain

raki (Q): large ceramic jar for *chicha*

rapachu (Q): man who performs the task of turning over clods of earth when a field is plowed using *chakitaqllas*, or footplows

rapay (Q): to turn the clods of earth cut by footplows

relleno (SP): filled

rocoto (Q): a variety of pepper

rosado (SP): rose-colored, pink

ruk'i (Q): pick used to pack the threads of the weft in weaving, traditionally made from a leg bone of the llama

salud (SP): health

sanitario (SP): sanitary; among the Quechua, the doctor who runs a rural health center

sankhu (Q): traditional dish made of ground wheat

Santísima Cruz (SP): Holy Cross; the festival of the Holy Cross, May 3

saqra (Q): devil, demon

saruy (Q): to step on

segunda (SP): second; in 'Tambo, the title of the position of headman of the *ayllu*, equivalent to the title *mandón* used in other parts of Peru

Semana Santa (SP): Holy Week

señor (SP): mister, sir

Señor de los Temblores (SP): Lord of the Earthquakes

señora (SP): lady, woman; Mrs.

serpentina (SP): paper streamer, festoon

servir (SP): to serve

sirvinakuy (Q FROM SP): period of service, a young woman to her potential mother-in-law and a young man to his potential father-in-law, prior to marriage

sol (SP): Peruvian unit of money prior to 1987

soldado (SP): soldier

sonqo (Q): "heart" of the warp in weaving

suegro (SP): father-in-law

sunsu (Q FROM SP *ZONZO*): SLOW-WITTED

suwa (Q): thief

tambo (Q): resting place, inn

tambor (SP): a drum

t'ankar (Q): a native wildflower; verbena

t'anta (Q): bread

taruka (Q): deer

tarwi (Q): species of lupine which produces an edible bean

tayta (Q): father

taytacha (Q): image of a saint or of Christ, or a cross

taytay (Q): "my father"

temblor (SP): earthquake

tenedor (SP): fork

tiay (Q FROM SP *TÍA*, AUNT): "my aunt"; a common address of young people to their elders, along with "my uncle," *tioy*

tienda (SP): a store

tierra (SP): earth

t'ika (Q): flower

t'impu (Q): traditional Carnaval dish of boiled mutton, cabbage, and fresh and dried potatoes

t'impuy (Q): to boil

t'inkasqa (Q): the act of blessing an object or event by a small libation of *chicha* or *trago*

tío (SP): uncle

tipina (Q): short, sharpened stick used to remove the husk from an ear of corn during harvest

tipiy (Q): to remove the husk from an ear of corn

tiyay (Q): to sit

tomasunchis (Q): "Let us drink together"

torero (SP): a bullfighter

trago (SP): a sip or gulp; in Peru, a strong, alcoholic drink

tunaw (Q): grinding stone, pestle

uchukuta (Q): a hot pepper sauce

ukuku (Q): Andean spectacled bear

unku (Q): traditional tunic made of two pieces of cloth sewn together

vara (SP): a staff; traditional unit of measure, about a meter and a half

vela (SP): vigil, watch; a candle

viejo (SP): old; an old person

wachu (Q): in 'Tambo, ridge formed by digging a furrow

wakatay (Q): native herb used in cooking

wallpa (Q): chicken

wallpa suwa (Q): chicken thief

waqay (Q): to cry

waqaychu (Q): negative imperative form of *waqay*

waraka (Q): a sling, slingshot

waranway (Q): native tree of the Acacia family

wathiya (Q): oven made in the field of clods of earth; food, such as potatoes or beans, baked in a *wathiya*

watu (Q): woven strap or cord

wawita (Q AND SP): "little baby"

waylaka (Q): woman who is negligent of her duties; a role in a Carnaval dance

wayra (Q): wind

wayrakuy (Q): the act of separating the chaff from the grain by tossing it into the air; the wind blows away the chaff while the heavier grain falls more directly to the ground

willk'u (Q): a native vine with heart-shaped leaves and red flowers which grows seasonally in corn fields, possibly *Piptadenia colubrina wiñapu* (Q): sprouted grain, ground to make *chicha*

yanachay (Q): "little dark one"; a term of affection

yapa (Q): "something extra"

yapuy (Q): to turn the earth in preparation for planting

yawar (Q): blood

yawar mayu (Q): "river of blood"; a traditional dance

yuraq (Q): white

yuraq kunka (Q): "white neck"; a type of condor

yuyu (Q): native plant which grows in corn fields, the leaves of which are cooked and eaten as greens, possibly a variety of *Centropogon presl*

yuyu hawcha (Q): traditional dish of greens (*yuyu*) cooked with potatoes

zapallo (SP): variety of green pumpkin

zonzo (SP): dim-witted, slow

zorrito (SP): "little fox"

zorrucha (SP AND Q): "little fox"